MOTHERS OF HEROES
AND MARTYRS

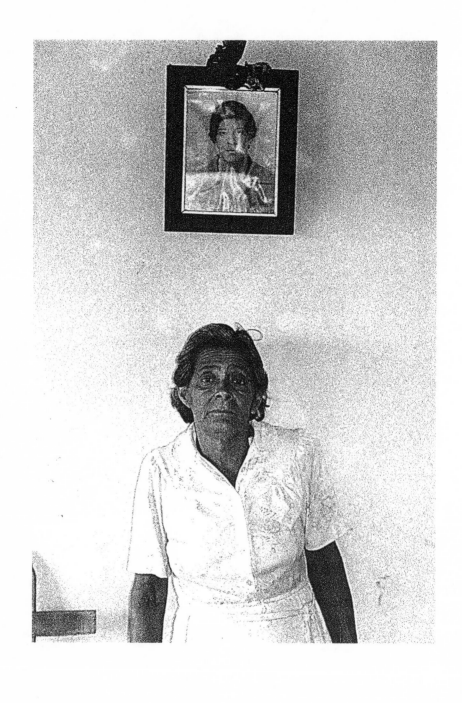

MOTHERS OF HEROES AND MARTYRS

Gender Identity Politics in Nicaragua, 1979–1999

Lorraine Bayard de Volo

THE JOHNS HOPKINS UNIVERSITY PRESS
Baltimore & London

The Johns Hopkins University Press

2715 North Charles Street

Baltimore, Maryland 21218-4363

www.press.jhu.edu

Library of Congress Cataloging-in-Publication Data

Bayard de Volo, Lorraine 1966–

Mothers of heroes and martyrs : gender identity politics in Nicaragua,

1979–1999 / Lorraine Bayard de Volo.

p.   cm.

Includes bibliographical references and index.

ISBN 0-8018-6764-9

1. Comité de Madres de Héroes y Mártires. Matagalpa.   2. Nicaragua—Politics
and government—1937–1979.   3. Nicaragua—Politics and government—1979–1990.
4. Nicaragua—Politics and government—1990-   .   5. Women and war—
Nicaragua—History—20th century.   6. Women in politics—
Nicaragua—History—20th century.   I. Title.

F1527 .V66   2001

323.3'4'09728509048—dc21

2001000239

A catalog record for this book is available from the British Library.

Doña Melida, a Mother of the Heroes and Martyrs of Matagalpa, stands beneath
a photograph of her son. The photograph marks the spot in her house where
Somoza's *Guardia* shot him as a Sandinista supporter.

To my mother, Louise

CONTENTS

6

Testing the Limits of Maternal Identity: Regime Change and
Expanded Membership, 1990–1994

7

Voice, Agency, and Identity: Counting the Mixed Blessings
of Revolution and Maternal Identity Politics

Conclusion

PREFACE

Research Methods

My first contact with the Committee of Mothers of Heroes and Martyrs of Matagalpa was through Esperanza Cruz de Cabrera,[1] the organization's coordinator, whom I met when she was on a U.S. speaking tour funded by an international nongovernmental organization (NGO). She agreed to an interview in which she outlined the history, goals, and accomplishments of the group. She took a straightforward, professional approach in the interview. But as I tagged along with her and her host throughout the evening, she asked more personal questions and began to speak in more emotional terms. In our discussions on the revolution, the war, and the death of her eldest son, her professional demeanor gave way and she spoke as a mother who had both suffered deeply and grown a great deal over the course of a revolution.

She not only reinforced my notion that participant observation would be key to my research, but she also demonstrated to me the deeply emotional tone of this organization. Again and again in my work with the Mothers I would be shown that to learn about them required a willingness to be emotionally engaged, to be fussed over, to be hugged and kissed. I introduced myself to each as a "student" and a "researcher," yet they as often as not positioned me as a sort of unofficial daughter-figure. My recorded interviews contain references to me as *"mi hijita"* (diminutive for "my daughter") as often as "Lorena" (my first name in Spanish). My pseudo-filial position entailed their ability and even obligation as mothers/Mothers to both teach me and take some responsibility for my welfare. This relationship was collectively clarified when my own mother visited me "in the field." Seated in a large circle, members introduced themselves and reassured my mother that although she was my "real" mother, they were my "Nicaraguan *mamas*," and thus she could rest assured that I was well looked-after. As a dutiful daughter, I cared about these Mothers and valued the ways they cared for me. On these terms, they took it upon themselves, one at a time and collectively, to teach me—a "young" gringa uninitiated in motherhood, poverty, and war—about the life of a Mother of a Hero and Martyr.

This study draws upon one year of field research in Nicaragua using several methods of data collection, supplemented with secondary sources and archival research in the United States. In 1992–93, I conducted fifty-five open-ended, loosely constructed interviews with the most active members of the Mothers of Heroes and Martyrs of Matagalpa, Nicaragua. More than twenty-five interviews were also conducted with people who had worked closely with the Mothers of Heroes and Martyrs or the anti-Sandinista mothers' group M22, and with members of the Mothers of Heroes and Martyrs of Estelí and the Mothers of the Resistance who joined the Mothers of Matagalpa. Respondents among the Mothers of Matagalpa were chosen based upon my own participant observations of the organization's activities, through which I compiled a list of the most active participants—*barrio responsables*, committee leaders, and those who most regularly attended committee activities. This list was confirmed by committee leaders, who added several more names. Other respondents also suggested members to interview and introduced me to potential respondents whom I did not know well.

Interviews were usually conducted within the interviewee's home, as it was often the most convenient location for them. Some interviews were conducted in the Mothers of Matagalpa's offices, a café, or the interviewee's place of work. All interviews of the Mothers were tape-recorded and transcribed. Each interview began with demographic questions pertaining to the respondents' socioeconomic position (age, marital status, sources of income, housing situation, number of children, and number of dependents). These questions were a means not only to gather important background information, but also to ease into the interview. At the end of these questions, I asked the respondent if I could begin tape-recording the interview. All the

Mothers interviewed gave their permission. A common list of open-ended questions was asked of each respondent, but they were asked in no particular order, allowing the conversation to flow more naturally from one topic to the next. Opportunity was given for the respondents to discuss other topics, emphasize other issues, and ask their own questions.

Toward the end of the interview, respondents were asked if there was anything else they wanted to add to or expand upon. This last question provided valuable insights into the themes that members of the organization thought were the most important concerning their lives and their organization. It also allowed them to go back and clarify certain points that they felt had not been expressed clearly or emphasized enough the first time. I conducted a second interview with roughly one-third of the interviewees in order to clarify certain issues or because the first interview had been subject to distractions and interruptions. Follow-up interviews of roughly one-quarter of the original interviewees were conducted in 1998 and 1999.

I analyzed over fifteen years of Nicaraguan newspapers (*La Prensa*, January 1978 to April 1993; and *Barricada*, August 1979 to April 1995) at the Matagalpa public library in Nicaragua and at several libraries in the United States.[2] Photocopies were made or notes taken of all items in which Nicaraguan women were a dominant subject, excluding items in which gender was not a primary issue.[3] The newspaper analysis involved not only articles on women but also letters to the editor, photos and photo captions, poems, cartoons, advertisements, interviews, and editorials. Content analysis was conducted on the items in these two newspapers, with a focus on representations of women. Historical data concerning dates, names, and events surrounding Nicaraguan women's issues (for example, laws, protests, government agencies and programs, and ideological debates) and women's organizations were also collected from the two newspapers. To supplement this, the content of U.S. newspapers and Nicaraguan magazines, journals, political pamphlets, songs, poems, campaign propaganda, and political speeches was also analyzed. Unless otherwise noted, all translations are my own.

Through Freedom of Information Act requests, I received from the U.S. State Department and the National Endowment for Democracy documents regarding anti-Sandinista mothers' groups. These documents not only yielded previously unpublished details on the makeup and activities of these groups, but they also offered rare glimpses into the important behind-the-scenes role the United States played in Nicaragua's gender identity politics.

Demographic data on the members of the Committee of Mothers of Heroes and Martyrs of Matagalpa were collected from the committee membership files on over three hundred members. Each file contained information on the member's name and address, the occupation of the member and member's spouse, the number of children, details on fallen children, and the member's pension and marital status. This information was compared to the demographic information from the fifty-five interviews I conducted.

Key to my analysis was my participant observation with the Mothers of Matagalpa between May 1992 and March 1993, as well as one month each in 1994, 1998, and 1999. I attended the biweekly membership meetings, classes, workshops, and celebrations, where I was introduced to members and had lengthy informal conversations. Also, I attended subcommittee meetings and classes and even traveled to other cities with members for meetings, committee errands, celebrations, and workshops. For much of my fieldwork, I lived in the house of Esperanza Cruz de Cabrera, the coordinator of the Mothers' Committee. There, I had long informal talks with those closely involved in the committee and experienced the mundane tasks, discussions, crises, and debates that arose. The inclusion of participant observation as a research method went hand in hand with meeting and gaining the trust of members, which greatly facilitated and strengthened the interview process. Notes, photographs, and videos were also taken to document observations.

In many ways, the women I interviewed cannot be considered typical: they had experiences uncommon to most poor Latin American women. At least five of those I interviewed could assemble and shoot an AK-47 and had stood guard over their neighborhoods during the height of the war. Quite a few were urban insurrectionists or Sandinista collaborators during the 1970s. One Mother had been imprisoned and tortured for months by Somoza's Guardia; another joined the guerrillas after twenty family members had been massacred in her small village. Several displayed scars incurred from the brutality of the Somoza regime. Most had prepared the destroyed body of a son or daughter for burial.

Though many were from the city of Matagalpa, over a third had moved there recently from the depths of the countryside. These women perhaps could write their name, a gift from the Sandinista literacy brigade in the early 1980s, but were often functionally illiterate. Even so, they were the experts on their own organization, a fact that I stressed to many Mothers who wanted to be interviewed but were hesitant to assume that they had anything important to say to a supposedly educated North American.[4] In so many words, I asked them to be my teachers and to let me be their student.

I refer to the Mothers here by their first names, preceded by *Doña*—the expected title of respect that I used in speaking with them. To refer to them simply as Dominga or Rosa just does not seem right. I use their real first names. Each understood that I was planning to use the interviews to write a book about them, and none understood why they might want to exercise the option of using a pseudonym. During the contra war, almost all gave testimonials to visiting delegations and journalists on the violence that touched them and their families.[5] The point of such testimonials was to put human faces and names on those who otherwise faded too easily from public memory. In my interviews with the Mothers, which covered both tragedies and triumphs, they expected their names to be attached to their words.[6]

AMNLAE (Association of Nicaraguan Women, Luisa Amanda Espinosa) has received considerable scholarly attention, both within Nicaragua and internationally. Before the 1990 elections, however, research rarely examined the gendered dimensions of Sandinista popular discourse, nor did it rigorously explore the implications of AMNLAE's lack of autonomy from the FSLN (Sandinista National Liberation Front). Since the Sandinista loss of the 1990 elections, however, criticism of the FSLN's gender policies has been more forthcoming.[7] Much of the information on AMNLAE that follows comes from such research, in addition to the Nicaraguan press and original platforms, pronouncements, and interviews from AMNLAE and its predecessor, AMPRONAC (Association of Nicaraguan Women Confronting the Nation's Problems).

Nicaraguan maternal movements, in contrast, have received almost no scholarly attention. I pieced together their history from a variety of sources. AMPRONAC and AMNLAE documents in AMNLAE's library in Managua and Mothers of Heroes and Martyrs documents from the files of the Mothers of Matagalpa office provided valuable historical information. These organizations released several short histories of women's political participation, which I supplemented with letters, testimonies, press releases, and strategy papers. These yielded information on the organizations' goals, relationships with other organizations, and varied modes of framing activism. Interviews conducted by scholars, international activists, and myself also illuminate how and why certain organizations were formed, and their levels of autonomy, goals, and priorities.[8]

My primary sources for the history of Nicaragua's maternal mobilizations and gendered hegemonic struggle were the pro-Sandinista newspaper *Barricada* and the anti-Somoza (pre-triumph) and anti-Sandinista (post-triumph) *La Prensa*. Both *Barricada* and *La Prensa* were openly political newspapers. From its inception in 1979, *Barricada*, the "Official Organ of the Sandinista Front," took on a mobilizing role to disseminate the FSLN's ideological line.[9] Similarly, as Nicaragua's perennial opposition paper (until 1990) headed by Violeta Chamorro, *La Prensa* supported first the anti-Somoza insurrection, then the counterrevolution. As the anti-Sandinista newspaper, it opposed Sandinista economic policies, mass-mobilization campaigns, and the draft.[10] Accordingly, in the 1980s these two newspapers represented an important ongoing battle on the ideological front of the contra war. Such struggles were also played out through political publications, popular slogans, political advertisements, T-shirts, billboards, posters, artwork, songs, poems, graffiti, plays, and speeches.

I searched the pages of *La Prensa* and *Barricada* for information on women's political activities, organizations, and individual and collective contributions to the revolution and contra war. The political involvement of individual women was noted, yet my main focus was on texts regarding women politically organized as women. These newspapers proved not only a valuable source of names, dates, and quotes, but also uncovered a history largely absent from previous work on Nicaraguan women—that of women politically organized as mothers.

In the Nicaraguan press and popular texts of this period, the Nicaraguan woman as mother, particularly in relation to revolution and war, was a recurring image. Maternal symbolism was used repeatedly in Sandinista discourse in the late 1970s through the 1980s to shape subjectivities that would mobilize men and women into the guerrillas or (later) the military, encourage them to protest Somocista or contra violence, and organize politically or at least placate mothers of drafted or fallen combatants. Though less pronounced, maternal symbolism was also used in anti-Sandinista discourse to attack the Sandinista draft and to make human rights-oriented demands, such as the release of imprisoned National Guard members and contras.

Framework of Chapters

The Wide-angle Lens: This study begins with a question concerning large-scale sociopolitical processes: How are revolution, war, and democratic transitions gendered? At one level, they appear as genderless abstractions—processes governed by guerrilla warfare strategies, Cold War enmities, and civic culture. If not genderless, then they are often implicitly posed as men's affairs. I set out to reveal the distinctively gendered—and counterintuitively maternal—nature of the Sandinista revolution, the contra war, and postwar democratization. In the ideological struggles for hegemony as well as electoral victory, women as mothers were mobilized as symbols and political actors by both the Sandinistas and anti-Sandinistas.

The Microscope: This leads to further questions at a microlevel. How does a political collectivity based on maternal identity navigate the vagaries of revolution, civil war, neoliberalism, and gendered hegemonic struggle? Why did women organize politically as mothers? Were members motivated by revolutionary ideology, a sense of political empowerment, mutual emotional support, or material support? Interestingly, these were all influential in the Nicaraguan case, depending on the economic situation of individual members, the era in which they joined the organization, and the conditions under which they lost a loved one.

I alternate between these two lenses—wide angle and microscope—to capture the dialectical relationship between larger political, economic, and ideological processes and the "micropolitics" of collective action. I compare Sandinista and anti-Sandinista mobilization of mothers and maternal imagery, and in turn I analyze how a specific women's organization both adopted and manipulated maternal mobilizing identities over time through shifting political, economic, and discursive fields.

I divide recent Nicaraguan history into three periods: the insurrection and early contra war (1977–84); the contra war through the 1990 elections (1984–90); and the Violeta Chamorro administration (1990–96), with two chapters on each period. Within each period, I first analyze women's organizing in relation to dominant mobilizing identities—both Sandinista and anti-Sandinista, in addition to the political/economic contexts within the period. Then I analytically link these mobilizing identities to the specific case of the Committee of Mothers of Heroes and Martyrs of Matagalpa during that same period. As such, the Mothers' Committee is presented as an ever-evolving, inconsistent process situated in shifting power relations.

In Chapter 1, through analysis of various Nicaraguan texts, I show that despite the spotlight on female guerrillas and political leaders, women primarily organized and were organized through their maternal identity. Mothers' groups were a moral and organizational force in the revolution and contra war. Their strategies drew from their experiences in domestic labor, their goals were defined through the lens of maternal responsibility, and their resources were often symbolic in the form of "moral resources" relying on maternal imagery. The Sandinista state and anti-Sandinista groups recognized the salience of maternal identity and mobilized various images of motherhood in propaganda campaigns aimed at incorporating middle-age and older women. I outline what I found to be the dominant projections of motherhood deployed by various political camps between 1977 and 1984 with the aim of making linkages between the gendered nature of struggle over hegemony and the identity of the Mothers of Matagalpa.

In Chapter 2, I turn to the Mothers of Heroes and Martyrs of Matagalpa, building upon women's organizational history and my analysis of gendered collective identity and hegemonic struggle. I explore how individual women came to see themselves as linked by a common identity with common goals and interests. This chapter represents a shift from a focus on the construction of ideals of motherhood to a focus on the process of identity-formation. This approach allows us to see how a shared characteristic, in this case the death of a child in revolution or war, became mutually relevant for group members and how collective interests were recognized, interpreted, and doggedly pursued.

I found that the few members who joined in the first five years (1979–84) were solid FSLN supporters who primarily identified ideological and relational reasons for their participation. In these years, material benefits of membership were negligible. Rather, members stressed the importance of carrying on the struggle of their fallen children and the strong emotional bonds they formed in the group. As an auxiliary to the Sandinista women's organization, they were given little room to develop their own meanings or agendas. This relationship provided the augur for the cultivation of a collective identity, yet constricted the decision-making freedom of the Mothers.

Chapters 3 and 4 cover the next period (1984–90), during which the majority of the contra war was played out. Key changes in dominant representations of women are documented in Chapter 3, and are explained through shifts in political and economic conditions. During this same period, as I reveal in Chapter 4, the Mothers of Matagalpa initiated significant organizational changes. They established organizational independence from the FSLN in order to establish a more activist political role, as well as to better address the economic problems of its overwhelmingly poor members. Still, those who joined and remained active in this period also expressed ideological and relational factors behind their membership, attaching less importance to the small but growing material benefits.

I analyze members' collective identity in terms of the visible and latent dimensions, examining not only the organization's public actions (protests and cultural representations) but also their interactions with each other. The latent aspects of the organization—networks based on friendship and support, political discussions, and shared beliefs—involved the working out of meaning for the group, as well as the formation of a collective sense of "we." The latent dimension is important in understanding the viability of an organization and the meanings members themselves attach to membership.

Chapter 5 covers the history and mobilizing identities of active women during the Chamorro government. Despite the election of an avowed anti-feminist, this period marked a growth in feminist organizing and more diverse, less traditional popular representations of women. In Chapter 6, I demonstrate how, after the Sandinistas lost the 1990 elections, the size, strategies, alliances, and maternal identity of the Mothers' Committee changed dramatically. Now, positioned as an opposition group, the committee's appeals to the state were ineffective, yet collective action was increasingly necessary to protect the organization's and individual members' property, projects, and pensions. With NGO aid, the committee increased its income-generating projects as well as health and educational campaigns. As the violence and polarization among the general population declined, the Mothers began to accept rural women, including mothers of fallen contras, as members. Membership swelled from a few hundred in 1989 to over two thousand by 1994. Yet unlike earlier members, those who joined in the 1990s were openly attracted to the material benefits. New members were desperately poor; they were single mothers whose other support networks had worn too thin under the new administration's neoliberal restructuring.

This influx of new members seeking material aid strained the collective sense of "we" among the general membership. The committee became less a maternal community focused on interpersonal relationships and consciousness-raising, and more a bureaucratic institution concerned with distribution of material benefits. However, underneath the official committee strategy of inclusion of new members lay a submerged strategy of exclusion generated among the long-term members whose other economic support systems were increasingly strained and who now faced new competition for committee projects.

Chapter 7 analyzes the consequences of maternal collectivities and their potential for both structural and individual change. Through the notions of agency, voice, and identity, I explore both structural constraints and the manner in which the Mothers have bent the rules, contradicted previous assumptions, and creatively applied old concepts in new ways. The conclusion returns to the main arguments and findings of this study, suggesting how these contribute to larger bodies of literature, including research on war, social movements, and gender politics. It also details the decline of the Mothers of Matagalpa after 1996 and comments on the future of Nicaraguan gender politics in the new millennium.

ACKNOWLEDGMENTS

In their acknowledgments, some scholars note that their writing regrettably took time away from their children, even despite their children's clever attempts to lure them away. These scholars then thank their spouses (generally their wives) and children for their forbearance. My son, Theo, was born toward the end of this project, and for his first months of life he was content to sleep on my lap as I wrote the final pages. He was also a joyful distraction during his increasingly lengthy wakeful moments. I am very fortunate that my life partner is sincere about "dual parenting" and is living proof that men can make wonderful "mothers." But more to the point, I see this project not as something that is separate from or in spite of my child. Rather, I was drawn to this project on revolutionary Nicaragua years ago in part because of my (future) child and children everywhere. In the struggle to make the world a better place, revolution represents wonderful dreams worthy of poetry, but it also tends to result in the deaths of dreamers and poets. It generates massive unintended consequences, most notably post-triumph political violence and the empowerment of counterrevolutionaries. The mothers of this book bear witness to these consequences — providing valuable lessons on the costs of war. But they also prepared me to be a better mother in countless ways — one who does not separate parenthood from politics or political science.

I would like to thank, first of all, my mother Louise Bayard de Volo and my partner Cory Riddle. Both read this manuscript several times, and despite some self-deprecation, their comments were extremely helpful as well as supportive. My mother visited me "in the field" in 1993, meeting many of the Mothers of Matagalpa and observing their events and projects. Lengthy fieldwork in an extremely poor country—especially when much of one's research revolves around death and grieving—can be emotionally draining, to say the least. My mother arrived just in time. Cory visited Nicaragua with me in 1994; it was a joy to introduce him to the Mothers and their projects.

Daniel Levine of the University of Michigan was my advisor for the dissertation out of which this book grew. He was very supportive of my project and contributed to it in important ways, yet he always maintained that the big decisions should ultimately be my own. A heavier, more controlling hand might have crushed me early on. I was happy to learn by his example. Linda Blum, now at the University of New Hampshire, was my women's studies advisor at the University of Michigan, and her words of wisdom have been priceless. In countless ways, this project would have looked very different without her input. That is to say, whatever strengths this work might have, many were cultivated by Linda. Jeffery Paige and Kim Lane Scheppele were also on my dissertation committee. They went above and beyond the expectations for committee members, offering many critical insights. I appreciate the committee's confidence that the dissertation would one day make a good book. I hope they were right.

Steve Striffler was a supporter of this project from the beginning. He visited me in Nicaragua and later read the entire manuscript, offering rich and constructive advice from his unique perspective of a political scientist-turned-anthropologist. I am sorry that I have not managed to be as helpful on his fascinating ethnographies—from the banana industry to chickens! The following people also read parts of this book, offering support as well as constructive criticism: John Guidry, Patty Hipsher, Karen Kampwirth, Andrea Wuerth, and the students in my Women and Politics of Latin America course at the University of Kansas. I have relied heavily on them for lively and productive conversations regarding research on Nicaragua, women and politics, and the state of our discipline. I also must thank the members of the American Political Science Association, Women and Politics Section dissertation committee, who read my work and awarded it the "1997 Best Dissertation in Women and Politics." They are Laura Woliver, Kathleen Jones, and Beth Reingold. I cannot adequately express how vital such early recognition of my work was for its later incarnations—particularly this book. Henry Tom of the Johns Hopkins University Press expressed early and consistent enthusiasm for this project, for which I am very grateful.

In Estelí, Nicaragua, Egdelina Lanuza, Blanca Sevilla, and Luz Marino of the Unemployed Women's Movement were wonderful teachers who introduced me to women and politics in Nicaragua. Many, many thanks to the Cabrera family of Matagalpa, Nicaragua. They have been incredibly generous with their time, advice, food, houses, . . . well, I could go on and on. Though every member of this large, extended family should be thanked, I would particularly like to recognize the help of Martín, Gerardo, Maela, Gloria, and Martha. Through our innumerable informal conversations, these five siblings shared with me incredible insights into the beauty and pain of their distinctly Nicaraguan quest to build a new society. I should also thank their wonderful children, especially Alba Lucia and Gloria Isabel, who are growing up too quickly. Of course, I am most indebted to Esperanza Cruz de Cabrera and all the Mothers of Matagalpa. This work would obviously not have been possible without their enthusiasm for the project and their willingness to participate.

ABBREVIATIONS

AFA	Rice, beans, and sugar
AMNLAE	Association of Nicaraguan Women, Luisa Amanda Espinosa
AMPRONAC	Association of Nicaraguan Women Confronting the Nation's Problems
APMN	Patriotic Alliance of Nicaraguan Women
CDS	Sandinista Defense Committees
CENIDH	Nicaraguan Human Rights Center
CRAC	Combatant Support Regional Committee
FSLN	Sandinista National Liberation Front
IMF	International Monetary Fund
INAVG	Institute of Attention to Victims of War
INSSBI	Nicaraguan Institute for Social Security and Welfare
M22	Mothers of Political Prisoners, "22 of January"
M-6-M	Sixth of March Movement
MNC	Nicaraguan Women of Conscience
MRS	Sandinista Renovation Movement

NED	National Endowment for Democracy
NGO	nongovernmental organization
NSM	New Social Movements
OMDN	Organization of Democratic Nicaraguan Women
PLC	Liberal Constitutionalist Party
PSC	Social Christian Party
RM	Resource Mobilization
RN	Nicaraguan Resistance or *Contras*
SMO	Obligatory Military Service
SMP	Patriotic Military Service
UNO	United Nicaraguan Opposition

MOTHERS OF HEROES
AND MARTYRS

Typical of "combative motherhood" imagery as the state mobilized volunteers into the popular militias is this photograph of older women in military uniforms carrying AK-47s. Such representations shaped idealized notions of masculinity as much as femininity. Presenting elderly mothers willing to risk their lives to defend the nation made it more difficult for young men to resist military service with their sense of masculinity intact. (Photo by Maria Morrison.)

INTRODUCTION

Captured Images from the Cultural Frontline

First Image: In memory of the Nicaraguan contra war, the Mothers of Heroes and Martyrs of Matagalpa perform a dance invoking the death of their children. The song's chorus implores, "Where is the guerrilla's grave?" and on stage a mother dressed in black frantically searches among marching soldiers for her missing son. At last, his lifeless body is placed before her. In a scene reminiscent of a Pietà, she cradles this body, weeps, and searches the heavens for some consolation and meaning. The song continues, and now the lyrics comfort the mother. She is told that this fallen guerrilla lives on, embodied in all the poor and oppressed of Nicaragua. Armed with a new understanding of death, the mother stands, dons her son's cap, takes up his rifle, and marches off to join the revolution.

Second Image: In 1990, presidential candidate Violeta Barrios de Chamorro is dressed in virginal white as Nicaragua's *María* and advances through jubilant crowds in a cart reminiscent of the pope-mobile.[1] While she campaigns as the widow of a martyr and a maternal peacemaker, her family-owned newspaper describes her as "without vanity, without pride, without ambition, a home-loving woman," assuring the public that "she is not a feminist nor does she aspire to be one. She is a woman determined to support the valor of our Nicaraguan men."[2] One supporter is quoted, "Doña Violeta is capable of carrying this country to peace because she, as a woman of the home, knows what we have suffered through in our own homes. . . . The militant women only know about weapons and not about the love of the home."[3]

Third Image: In 1992, during the thirteenth annual celebration of the fall of the Somoza dictatorship, twelve girls ride through the city on the back of a parade truck. Each girl is roughly a year older than the one before, symbolizing revolutionary Nicaragua as it progressed from its 1979 birth toward a promising future. The girls look healthy and happy, with curled hair, matching dresses, and even a touch of makeup. But there, sitting beside these girls who represent the revolutionary era, is "Señora 1991"—the year after the electoral defeat of the FSLN. Representing this year of economic austerity is a sad-looking, older woman, perhaps one girl's grandmother, carrying a sign, "1991: The Year of Unemployment."

These are three snapshots of the gendered struggle over hegemony—the contested shaping of what it means to be a girl, a mother, a female politician, and an elderly woman, and the use of such gendered images to shape worldviews, alliances, and collective action. The woman on stage translated maternal grief into armed motherhood in the name of fallen children—the "good mother" carries on the struggle. The Mary-like candidate posed "woman" and armed struggle as opposites—the "good woman" stays home. Finally, the woman of 1991, long past her youthful prime, depicted despair for a suffering, perhaps dying, revolution. The positioning of an older woman to represent 1991 can be read as both a criticism of post-Sandinista neoliberalism and a definition of gray-haired women as unhealthy, barren, hopeless. Such representations of women are not apolitical, neutral, powerless, or mere reflections of "reality." Rather, these examples illustrate the constructed nature of "reality," and thus of identity, collective action, and the mobilization of a nation to revolution, war, and democratization.

Throughout this study, I reflect upon the gendered nature of "cultural politics" and collective identity in relation to the Sandinista struggle for hegemony. The Gramscian notion of hegemony insists upon the importance of ideological domination in the wielding of governmental power in modern societies.[4] Thus, it directs our focus to the cultural and political struggles in revolution, in addition to material conditions and the physical battle. More specifically, a Gramscian approach entails that economics, civil society, force, and the construction of consent be analyzed in a dialectical fashion. My addendum is that the struggle for hegemony in the Nicaraguan revolution also must be viewed as a gendered process with important implications for women.

Hegemony is often thought of in binary terms: a society relies on either force or consent.[5] With this definition, Latin American societies are commonly considered nonhegemonic, relying primarily on methods of exclusion.[6] It is important to recognize the exclusionary and too often overtly violent and repressive forms that governments of Latin America have taken. However, hegemony is more productively thought of not in terms of dichotomies but rather as an ongoing process with multiple sites of domination, popular experience, and resistance.[7] Dominant groups do not rule through force or consent but through both to varying degrees. Even the Somoza regime in Nicaragua was able to construct varying levels of hegemonic consent.[8] Indeed, instances of clear contradictions between Somoza's words and deeds—such as his misuse of international aid after the 1972 earthquake and his role in the assassination of newspaperman Pedro Joaquin Chamorro, despite lip service to the ideals of a free press—are often credited as leading to his loss of support among the middle classes and his ultimate downfall.

The overthrow of Anastasio Somoza Debayle in 1979, far from resolving the struggle over hegemony, left a power vacuum claimed by competing sectors. The Sandinistas—popularly recognized as the victorious leaders of the insurrection—prioritized the working class and peasantry, calling for a redistribution of wealth and privilege and the forging of a revolutionary "New Man." Their postinsurrection program included land reform, nationalization of some industries, and mass mobilization of society. Pro-Sandinista organizations were promoted as effective vehicles for disseminating Sandinista ideology. The FSLN was countered most effectively by another sector of Somoza's historic opposition—conservative land- and business-owners who based their interests in conservative Catholicism and capitalism. As the FSLN established control of the state, this capitalist sector resisted reforms and redistribution programs, becoming increasingly anti-Sandinista. Ultimately members of this sector formed uneasy alliances with Somocistas in their effort to defeat the FSLN. By the mid-1980s, the U.S.-financed contra war had separated Nicaraguan society into Sandinistas and anti-Sandinistas.[9]

Thus, a protracted hegemonic struggle ensued in Nicaragua, a struggle also waged along military and economic fronts. I argue here that in the case of revolutionary Nicaragua, hegemonic struggle, when analytically linked with changes in economic and political conditions, explains changes in women's collective action and identity. The flip side of my argument is that the Sandinista revolutionary process itself was born out of and fed by a distinctly gendered discourse. Images of women, particularly maternal images, were mobilized by opposing forces in the battle to capture Nicaraguan hearts and minds. Such mobilizing identities were both enabling and constraining to women. Women were organized primarily as mothers, often an empowering experience that also reshaped social views on women's place in politics. However, the maternal discourse restricted women to political action that appeared deferential and self-abnegating. Furthermore, although these mobilizing identities of the culture war channeled women into certain forms of collective action, other factors also influenced collective identity. For example, the development of identity depended upon and was shaped by economic survival. Also, government appeals for women's "patriotic" support of the war effort often fell on the deaf ears of mothers determined to protect their draft-age sons. Finally, hegemonic struggle and collective identity should be seen as dynamic. Contrary to the implicit assumptions of New Social Movement literature and despite mobilizing identities invoked through hegemonic struggle, I demonstrate that collective agents may alter the way they present themselves to the world and "reverse" from a "new" social movement expressing identity to an "old" social movement making material demands. Detecting and understanding such changes requires analytically situating a collectivity in social, economic, and political fields of force over time.

Gender Politics, Collective Action, and Hegemony in Revolutionary Nicaragua

The case of Nicaragua is compelling for its revolutionary promise and shortcomings regarding women. Because it had the distinction within Latin America of experiencing a revolution in which women played a prominent role, Nicaragua presents a rich opportunity to study the changing impact of power struggles on gender identity and collective action. The waging of that struggle must be viewed, in varying degrees over time, not only as physical confrontations but discursive ones as well. In 1969, the Frente Sandinista announced its intention to "abolish the odious discrimination that women have been subjected to compared to men," and women were recruited into the guerrilla ranks. By the time the Somoza dictatorship collapsed in 1979, women reportedly made up 25 to 30 percent of the combatants, several of whom had led troops into major battles. The following statement by the Sandinista women's association captures the optimism of the early 1980s: "[Through the revolution] women learned in practice what we were capable of doing, and our people, without much theoretical discussion, learned what women were capable of doing. That is to say, we women didn't say we were equal—we showed it on the battlefield. On the other hand, with the taking of political power, we gained the real possibility of putting into practice the objectives of the program of the FSLN, which . . . stipulated the struggle for the full emancipation of women."[10]

Women's participation did not, however, translate into a notable female presence in positions of political power. Nor did feminism flourish during the Sandinista period. In the midst of a U.S.-financed war and economic embargo, the FSLN managed to improve the everyday lives of women in terms of health care and education and increase women's political presence through its mass organizations. Yet after a decade in power, the state's failure to make much progress toward its goal of female emancipation was disturbingly evident.

Nicaragua is distinctive in the study of women and politics for another reason—in 1990, a woman, Violeta Barrios de Chamorro, was elected president. This was not widely heralded as a triumph for women because Chamorro was explicitly anti-Sandinista and antifeminist. In her six years in office, she managed to reverse Sandinista progress in economic policies, health care, and education benefiting women. Yet paradoxically, the Sandinista bust was a feminist boon, and women's organizations blossomed in the post-Sandinista period.

James Scott proposes that "a revolution is also an interregnum. Between the moment when a previous regime disintegrates and the moment when a new regime is firmly in place lies a political terrain that has rarely been examined closely."[11] Nicaragua presents a relatively unique Latin American context in which to examine gender, hegemonic struggle, and the revolutionary interregnum. *Hegemony* is often used to describe the production of popular consent for the status quo and to explain quiescence.[12] However, in the context of the Nicaraguan revolutionary interregnum, in which the old order was overthrown and hegemony was fought over by the shifting alliances of a revolutionary sector and a liberal/capitalist sector, theorizing about consent and mobilization is far from clear-cut. Because no one sector was hegemonic—rather, Nicaragua was caught in a military and ideological struggle—warring factions attempted to produce (and control) protest rather than quiescence. Their culture-laden battle was framed in terms of the consent of protesters, so to speak. For example, a lively protest march defined by one side as "the voice of the people" was dismissed by the other side as "false consciousness" or "manipulation." Both sides attempted to mobilize, but through and in support of distinct worldviews.

In this hegemonic struggle, gender identity was a key focal point. The mobilization of women was important to both sides, but their mobilizing identities (what it means to be a "good mother," for example) were distinct and changed over time in relation to economic and political change. Through extensive, open-ended interviews with members of the Mothers of Heroes and Martyrs, participant observation, and archival research, I found that participants adopted a mobilizing identity. But it was not adopted in a thorough or passive manner. In other words, women were mobilized by both sides, but they did not always say what they were expected to say. Furthermore, there were differences within the Mothers' organization based upon the strategic application of different, and sometimes contradictory, versions of the "good mother" identity.

I examine dominant representations of women over time, then place these in relation to women's collective action both nationally and in regard to the Mothers of Heroes and Martyrs of Matagalpa. I analyze actors' changes in identity and goals within a changing political, economic, and discursive environment. The Mothers of Matagalpa was a group of primarily poor women, each of whom lost a family member in the war or revolution. They evolved from a small FSLN auxiliary into a semiautonomous community organization of more than two thousand members with significant protest experience and self-help projects. Their history is linked to political and economic contexts, as well as Sandinista maternal action frames and the more fundamental gendered discourse.

In contrast to much work concerning women and politics, my research focuses on the politics of women past childbearing age. Their political acts and experiences are rarely examined in the Latin American context, but these women are politically relevant. They have formed the backbone of many grassroots human rights organizations in Latin America, particularly those focused on political prisoners and the disappeared. Furthermore, with the democratization of Latin America, they have been important as voters. In the 1990 Nicaraguan elections, the FSLN failed to capture this sector at their own peril, as women of this age group made up the largest sector opposed to the FSLN. Finally, older women must be analytically situated in relation to the big political and economic processes such as revolution, civil war, mass mobilizing, and structural adjustment. That is, not only must political research concern itself with the ways in which political changes affect women's (and men's) everyday lives, but it must also recognize ways in which they affect women differently according to race, class, sexual orientation, and age.

I proceed with the conviction that the link between gender hegemony and women's collective action warrants greater attention. The power of gendered discourse in revolutionary Nicaragua was exercised both through the centralized propaganda campaigns of two powerful parties and through political actors' internalization of, alteration of, and resistance to these campaigns. Collective actors must be recognized as products of dominant discourse. Still, key powers exercised by women through collective action are their abilities to expand the horizon of possibilities, to discover and exploit discursive contradictions, and to punch holes in widely held assumptions, scattering doubt.

New Social Movements and the Latin American Context

For over a decade of collective action research, much attention has been paid to "new social movements" (NSMs). As opposed to "old social movements," which pit workers against capital, NSM actors are said to be determined less by modes of production than by subjective identities and solidarities—"I act because of who I am."[13] The primary focus of NSM action is not directed at the state or the economic system but rather at altering social relations.[14] The new movements—feminist, gay rights, environmental, and community movements, to name a few—are thought to challenge the traditional modes of "doing politics," altering the political arena into a more fragmented space that includes a multiplicity of social actors.[15] Conflicts center on the construction of meaning, which extends beyond the workplace into everyday life and personal relationships.

Some suggest that Latin American societies are increasingly shaped by symbolic or identity struggles.[16] Indeed, some new Latin American movements, such as radical feminist and gay rights movements, seem to concern themselves less with material needs than with a struggle over meaning and toward self-realization. Even so, in Latin America movements continue to form in response to clearly material demands, and the relations of production and distribution of material goods remain central issues, often overshadowing the NSM concerns with symbolic stakes.[17] Community movements focused on obtaining goods and services are arguably the fastest-growing form of collective action in the region. The majority of participants, though not necessarily the leaders, of such barrio movements are increasingly women.[18] This contrasts with women's marked underrepresentation in "old," class-based political organizations such as trade unions and political parties, yet still their ends are more immediately material rather than symbolic.[19] Leslie Anderson, in interviews with Nicaraguan and Costa Rican peasants, found both economic and "postmaterialist" reasons given for activism.[20] Judith Adler Hellman argues that "in advanced industrial societies, movement participants struggle to overcome feelings of personal powerlessness generated by the satisfaction of material needs without a corresponding sense of full self-realization. In contrast, Latin American participants may well come to enjoy some greater sense of personal fulfillment as a consequence of their involvement in new social movements. But their struggles are principally organized around the satisfaction of basic needs."[21] Although the struggle may originally develop over material interests, outcomes such as personal fulfillment over time may become more than fortunate by-products. I illustrate a case in which solidarity and self-realization were valued, protected, and sought out by members of a women's group increasingly concerned with material demands. Furthermore, demands for material needs are often intricately wrapped up in issues of identity. June Nash, writing on Mayan communities and the Chiapas rebellion, states that the rebels "justify their recourse to war in both economic and cultural terms."[22] So NSM theory that separates such "movements reasserting their identity from the economic conditions that give rise to their actions miss as much of the dynamic as do those who reduce these movements to class relations."[23]

In sum, strict application of the NSM definition found in identity-centered literature to Latin American new movements would obscure the materially oriented aspects of collective action developing in the region. Still, the approach's focus on identity and the symbolic functions of movements as they promote alternative frameworks of meaning sheds light on the development of a collectivity.

The Process of Collective Identity

Alberto Melucci, in his analysis of identity politics, stresses that collective identity must be viewed as a process, not a preestablished, static condition. In this process, a sense of "we" is constructed through communication and negotiation of the goals, means, and the environment of action.[24] Another dimension of this process is the making of "emotional investments, which enable individuals to recognize themselves in each other."[25] By searching for the meaning members attach to their collectivity and the sense of "we" they create, this approach adds to our understanding of why actors join and maintain a political collectivity.

Viewing collective identity as the process upon which all collective action is built requires attention to the constructed and dynamic nature of identity itself—a shortcoming of much identity-oriented literature. There is nothing essential or pre-political about a group of actors' sense of "we." Rather, collective identity is a negotiated process unavoidably influenced by dominant discourse. Accordingly, I argue that the study of collective identity must include the mobilization of language, images, and dimensions of power both internal and external to the group. Furthermore, the negotiation of collective identity also involves conflict. As I attempt to show, the struggle to define identity within a group can also be a struggle over the definition and allocation of both material and symbolic goods.

As Melucci points out, collective identity and solidarity is often treated as fait accompli.[26] Through analyzing how meaning is constructed and cultural practices are organized in a collectivity, we better understand how actors represent and view their world. This poststructuralist approach historicizes constructions of meaning and relationships of power, calling universal, natural, and essentialist categories and identities into question.[27]

In instances of solidarity, individuals recognize others' social positions, experiences, rights, or physical characteristics as similar to their own. Yet the persistence of differences, in the midst of this discourse of equality and sameness, is a motor of change and a constant challenge to the fixing of collective identities. These differences must be a focal point in any analysis of collective action over time.[28] Actors' definition of collective identity and organizational goals is internally and externally contested. It is never more than the temporary result of an ongoing struggle over the distribution of power.[29] Accordingly, analyses that treat collective identities as fixed and unproblematic fail to appreciate the dynamic dimensions of power.

The maternal identities I examine here are temporary and historically specific. They are not blanket categories that fit all Nicaraguan women without regard to generation, class, race, region, and political allegiance. Rather, I track the historically variable maternal identities of older, poor, Sandinista women in northern Nicaragua who lost a child in the revolution or war. This is an identity that is differently expressed for different purposes in different contexts.[30]

I also ask some fundamental questions about political organizations. Are there internal conflicts in collectivities? Do all members have the same understanding of the collective's goals and reason for being? Do the founding members' reasons for joining mirror the newest members' motivations? Do these collectivities change over time? Such questions may seem obvious, but they are often skimmed over or assumed to be the opposite of what more careful analysis would reveal. For example, although it seems safe to assume that a collectivity's members might join for different reasons, much of the research presents collectivities as homogeneous and static. Time and power are essential components in the analysis of collective identity.

NSM theorists argue that these movements present a new form of politics, even a new way of relating everyday life and politics, linking social practices with political ideology and institutions.[31] This becomes particularly important for groups previously thought to be apolitical, politically inept, or unempowered, or simply people whose opinions do not exist or do not matter. Take, for example, the women who are the focus of this study—older, poor, rural Latin American women who embrace the identity of motherhood. Such women rarely showed up in local media or academic research in terms of their political acts or opinions until they collectively asserted an identity and a set of goals that announced to society that they have political opinions and interests.

Some scholars have pointed out that although identity-centered and the more dominant resource mobilization (RM) approaches to collective action pose different questions, each is useful in filling gaps left by the other.[32] The RM school examines the availability of resources, opportunities, and benefits in order to explain the growth and success of movements. As the RM model insists, the growth of a collectivity depends on actors' access to resources.[33] However, the RM model tends to focus on the more tangible, quantifiable resources and to overlook moral or symbolic resources.[34] As suggested by identity-oriented literature, symbolic resources—widely identifiable representations that carry a high status—can also be manipulated and mobilized.

As I argue, the identity of the Mothers of Heroes and Martyrs was first articulated from without, molded from dominant gender images by the FSLN in order to mobilize this group of women who shared an objective similarity—the death of a child. Yet these maternal images or "mobilizing identities"—Spartan Mothers, Omnipotent Supplicants, Las Continuadoras, and Madres Sufridas—should be understood as symbolic resources for women as actors, as well as characteristics imposed upon women. Mobilizing identities may be both internalized and utilized. On the one hand, they color individual women's personal identities, the way women see themselves, and highlight characteristics, beliefs, and experiences that these women share with each other. On the other hand, these identities may become instruments with which to extract public sympathy and support. In other words, identity can be a tool that cuts both ways—carving out space for solidarity within the group and waging cultural battle in the public realm.

Nicaragua, Mothers, and Identity

Clearly, Nicaragua cannot be included as one of the postindustrial societies on which "new social movement" theory is based. Nonetheless, the NSM approach's emphasis on both collective identity and struggles over the cultural domain, as well as its recognition of solidarity as not simply a tool but an end in itself, highlights new questions to be asked in our quest to understand hegemony and collective action. Furthermore, in analyzing the Nicaraguan case, I hope to add to NSM theory, broadening it to include gendered analysis that considers collective identity as a process that changes over time in relation to the political, economic, and discursive shifts of a society that is decidedly not "postindustrial."

Strategy, networks, and mobilization of resources—the focus of RM research—are also vital in any attempt to understand social movements. Accordingly, my research into a maternal collectivity in Nicaragua centers on the social construction of identity, the collective recognition of resources, and the structural opportunities and constraints within which purposive action takes place. Three questions become central. First, why did the shared characteristic of "mother of the heroes and martyrs" become relevant for the mutual recognition of members? Second, how do we explain the growth of this maternal movement? Third, why did the collectivity's identity change over time?

All these questions address the problem of collective identity, contested hegemony, and economic conditions. In the first question, one's identity is linked with the course of hegemonic struggle and one's material position in society. As NSM theorists argue, economic growth and stability in Western societies has led or freed actors to struggle for political and social recognition.[35] Similarly, structural change in a poor, agrarian society such as Nicaragua could be expected to profoundly affect actors' interpretation of their economic and symbolic interests.

The second question revolves around factors that normally interest resource mobilization theorists—strategies, organization, resources, and windows of opportunity. Changes in these factors affect the success of a collectivity. However, the notion of success is expanded here to include not only the external recognition of a group as a political actor or an increase in material benefits; success is also latent within the group itself.[36] This latent success refers to personal and collective fulfillment and empowerment. In other words, the construction of a collective identity can be a successful end in itself, apart from a collectivity's struggle against the state, economy, or dominant ideology.

The third question is approached by linking change within the collectivity to external change. Large structural change in Nicaragua—revolution, war, economic crisis and austerity, democratization, and a high-profile ideological battle—had an undeniably significant impact on social organizations and collective identities. For example, the onset of war might be expected to turn a previously material needs-oriented neighborhood organization toward an emphasis on issues such as neighborhood protection, the draft, peace, and support programs for soldiers. Similarly, a primarily symbolic-oriented Sandinista mothers' group might begin economic self-help programs with the onset of economic austerity programs.

Feminist Examinations of Revolutionary Nicaragua

In the 1980s, academics and activists enthusiastically reported on Sandinista Nicaragua's commitment to gender equality, attempts to curb prostitution, construction of child-care centers, and efforts to move women into the productive sector. Most of these texts were descriptive, persuasive pieces based uncritically on official FSLN platforms and interviews with FSLN leaders. Typical articles summarized the history of the Sandinista women's association AMNLAE (Association of Nicaraguan Women, Luisa Amanda Espinosa) and reviewed key gender debates (especially women in the military, women's double workday, and abortion).[37] They also pointed out barriers to women's emancipation: the severe poverty and limited resources of Nicaragua, the U.S. economic and military intervention, the contra war, machismo, and traditional Catholicism. As Sandinista supporters, many of the authors were hesitant to criticize and thus tip the scale in favor of the counterrevolution. The FSLN itself was rarely examined critically or in depth with regards to the lingering patriarchy in the revolutionary society. Inquiry into women's everyday experience and understanding of politics was rare. Absent, too, were the criticisms and complaints against the government readily heard at any bus stop in Nicaragua. Furthermore, the goals and raisons d'être of the mass organizations were represented as following a coherent ideology, not a complex conflict of interests, beliefs, and goals.

Although Nicaraguan and foreign feminists hailed the advent and early actions of AMNLAE, some were critical of its attention to mothers of drafted and fallen Sandinistas during the height of the contra war.[38] Their uneasiness seemed to derive from the glorification of traditional gender values that this attention to mothers entailed. However, the implication was also that AMNLAE's time was perhaps better spent on younger, less traditional women in order to keep AMNLAE on the feminist path.[39]

More critical examinations of Sandinista gender policy and practice appeared after the FSLN's 1990 electoral defeat. These criticisms, made by both Nicaraguan and international feminists, particularly concerned the hierarchical relation between Sandinista leadership and mass organizations, the failure of male leaders to apply the values of gender equality to their everyday behavior, and prioritization of other agendas over women's issues.[40] This study is in many ways inspired by these more critical reflections.

Women's Moral Framework and Ways of Knowing

In the study of motherhood and women's collective action, the "women's difference" approach is sometimes invoked. The basic argument is that women evaluate social situations differently from men. Women's sense of self is said to be characterized by an emphasis on care and connection with others, as opposed to the dominant liberal model of autonomy and the independent self.[41] This approach, however, has been criticized for being dangerously essentialist and universalizing the experiences of a relatively small subset of largely white, middle-class women of the industrialized world.[42]

Nancy Scheper-Hughes presents an alternative to the "women's difference" approach from a Latin American context. She insists that motherhood is "anything other than natural and instead represents a matrix of images, meanings, sentiments, and practices that are everywhere socially and culturally produced."[43] Scheper-Hughes's analysis is situated in a context of extreme poverty and high infant mortality, which generated a maternal reproductive strategy: "to give birth to many children and, on the expectation that only a few will survive infancy, to invest selectively in those considered the 'best bets' for survival."[44] Scheper-Hughes's work is an important cautionary note against the romantic oversimplification of women's other-orientedness and ethic of care: "The morality that guides mothers, especially poor mothers, may not follow 'conventional' wisdom or dominant moral discourses concerning justice and equality."[45]

Regardless of the status of the "women's difference" approach in academia, it is a common theme for women's movements in Latin America that women's position as "life-givers" provides them with privileged knowledge on the sanctity of life and special abilities to nurture. As one member of the well-known Argentine mothers of the disappeared—Las Madres de Plaza de Mayo—put it, "Men are perhaps more individualistic. When a woman gives birth to a child she gives life and at the same time, when they cut the cord, she gives freedom. We were fighting for life and for freedom. . . . Women, because we are stronger, and mothers, because we give life and we defend life as many times as is necessary."[46] Both the scholarly "women's difference" approach and its everyday articulations are subject to the same feminist critique—that psychological, material, and cultural contexts are collapsed to produce timeless maternal truths, drawing attention away from the construction of differences, away from a process of becoming, and into a language of essentialism and static gender opposites.[47]

Because "women's difference" implies a sense of connection and solidarity with women everywhere, the temptation to conflate gender identities into fixed, pre-political categories can be strong.[48] If women were naturally more empathetic and less individualistic, analysis of maternal collective action would also be rather straightforward. Yet women who differ from these characteristics may be judged as gender deviants and unwomanly.[49] Indeed, I present Nicaraguan cases in which such charges were leveled against women in the larger battle to shape gender identities, mobilize bodies, and minimize resistance. Such cases reveal the strategic use of "women's difference" arguments at the level of everyday discourse as well as the structural constraints posed by static gender attributes.

Thus, instead of focusing on whether women are more peace-loving, relational, and other-oriented than men, I examine when such claims are made, who makes them, and why.[50] The Nicaraguan version of "women's difference" represents an enduring, powerful, and dynamic discourse that must be grounded in actors' material and cultural contexts. In its endless variety, the myth is a source of power used by and against women. It provides mobilized women a socially acceptable cover for political work. It can also be a source of power in the claim that motherhood provides women a unique knowledge that men cannot share and therefore cannot effectively discount. It has allowed women to present a self-image of moral superiority. Finally, it can be an effective publicity tool in that, for example, the media and political figures find it hard to refuse an audience with grieving mothers.[51]

As I attempt to show, the Sandinistas and anti-Sandinistas promoted a maternal collective identity in Nicaraguan women's movements as it provided a socially acceptable means by which women could mobilize. Mobilizing mothers stressed emotions and care as opposed to aggressive ideological or physical confrontations. Furthermore, mobilizing women as mothers, positioned as men's moral superiors, camouflaged the political nature of the women's movements and allowed women to present demands in support of or against the revolution from personal, emotional standpoints as opposed to partisan ones: "We are mothers, not politicians. We want peace."

The catch is that maternal identity works against women's collective action as maternal representations become too rigid, solidifying into a language of essentialism in which shifting, fractured identities are portrayed as natural and rightly enforced attributes. Identities appear pre-political, not up for challenge or change, and categories define interests and actions without input from the categorized actors.

Engendering Protest

Temma Kaplan, in her oft-cited work on women's collective action in Barcelona, describes "female consciousness" as the "recognition of what a particular class, culture, and historical period expect from women," which in turn "creates a sense of rights and obligations that provides motive force for actions."[52] Female consciousness can have revolutionary consequences if the rights connected with this consciousness are impeded. Women's movements, according to Kaplan, follow common patterns: "They focus on consumer and peace issues and they oppose outside aggressors."[53] Thus, commitment to society's dominant notions of gender can bring women into conflict with authorities.

Female consciousness is a rather pre-political and unexamined concept in Kaplan's study. The notion of what "a particular class, culture, and historical period expect from women" is never crystal clear for actors. Indeed, it is often a highly contentious matter. Gendered discourse, like all discourse, contains gaps and contradictions that present conflict and opportunities for change. Movements and individuals alike contradict themselves and manipulate their self-representations. In the case of revolutionary Nicaragua, the ideological battle was in part waged in order to define "female consciousness" itself. Thus I stress the importance of looking for the contradictions as well as the continuities in actors' representations of themselves. The instances in which self-representations run against dominant maternal images are just as informative as when they reinforce such images and say what we might expect them to say.

This study explores the political nature of maternal identity in Nicaragua as it is constructed by the FSLN and its contenders as well as by a collectivity of actors. I trace the recent Nicaraguan history of women organized as mothers, and the central place of mothers as symbols in the ideological battle during the contra war. Although the dynamic Sandinista-guided women's organization and emerging Nicaraguan feminisms have captured more international and academic attention, this project reveals the maternalism that was so fundamental to not only women's participation but the whole FSLN hegemonic project.

The Matagalpa branch of the Committee of Mothers of Heroes and Martyrs comprised women who tended to have a rather ambiguous relation to politics—poor and working-class women between the ages of 45 and 80. These women identified themselves, and were identified, primarily as mothers whose concern for their families led them into political struggle. Their path to politics was sometimes through their children, many of whom took part in the insurrection to overthrow Anastasio Somoza. More commonly, their political participation did not begin in earnest until the death of a son or daughter in the revolution or contra war, upon which they became a "Mother of a Hero and Martyr" and were mobilized into the Committee of Mothers.

This particular Mothers' Committee grew and evolved over the years from a support group—providing symbolic and emotional support both for each other and for the Sandinista war effort—to an income-generating self-help organization. In this sense, it was atypical of Nicaraguan Mothers' Committees. The case of the Mothers of Matagalpa is offered here not so much to demonstrate the mode by which mothers of the fallen typically organized as to explore the construction of and resistance to maternal mobilizing identities. My findings are generalizable to state-mobilized collective action and even anti- or extra-state social movements.

The Mothers of Matagalpa adapted a collective identity out of dominant images of motherhood. As they applied such images to themselves and their collectivity, they also altered these images, expanded the horizons, and rewrote the possibilities. For example, as the Mothers of Matagalpa saw and presented themselves as suffering mothers, *Madres Sufridas*, they challenged the attendant notions of silent suffering, helplessness, and passive victimization. When collective action based on traditional gender identity is viewed in this light, mobilized mothers are a case of resistance as well as accommodation to gendered power relations.[54]

The creation of a collective identity is also a message to society.[55] In the case of the Mothers of Matagalpa, it was a message of the needs, hopes, and capabilities of poor, older women—formerly a rare sight outside of church, the market, and the home. More broadly, it was a message of a form of human interaction that prioritizes care, responsibility to others, and open emotion. Is the Mothers' message "cutting edge"? Perhaps not, for the Mothers' discourse reaches back into a long tradition of maternal self-abnegation and suffering. But then again, both academic and popular audiences have been fascinated for over a decade with women's communitarian leanings, their other-orientedness—call it women's different voice, a female consciousness, or women's ways of knowing. So indeed, the Mothers' message seems timely.

But it is not really such a simple matter. As is true, I suspect, with all human beings, the subjects of my study did not always live up to their own idealized images. I grappled with contradictory statements, the seemingly conflicting goals, the gaps between words and deeds, alternately ignoring them and trying to make them fit into a tidy, parsimonious explanation. Finally, I turned these contradictions into an analytical focus of this study in recognition of what complicated "beings" we humans are and with the appreciation that not even mothers are perfect.

A Few Words about "Politics"

Often in the study of politics, the "concern is with activities 'within the system'—ways of influencing politics that are generally recognized as legal and legitimate."[56] Yet to deny politics in everyday life is to imply that the processes of daily life are natural, unchangeable, untouched by, and unconnected with political institutions. It obscures the ways in which such phenomena as traditional gender relations and poverty-stricken, female-headed households are linked to and perpetuated by institutional politics. In addition, a definition of politics that extends beyond institutionally linked politics and into everyday life and collective resistance encourages a view of people in subordinate sectors of society as agents able to effect change. Research covering the methods by which people shape the world around them, despite the narrow space in which they maneuver, is sorely needed—both because political science is lacking such information and because such information is a source of empowerment.

The definition of politics I employ includes the competing political discourses aimed at certain groups. The way governments, social groups, and individuals talk about politics is itself political. The way in which identities are influenced, limited, formed, and reformed by power relations is political, as are the challenges to limits in which people define themselves and their proper mode of participation in society. Struggles to define who is a citizen, who deserves government aid, and who is a "true" Sandinista, victim of war, or Mother of the Heroes and Martyrs are political struggles. They are not just a war of words but rather are labels that determine distribution of resources and status. Discourse entails power relations that shape subjectivities, people's ways of seeing themselves in relation to society; thus, it shapes what is possible or thinkable within politics and political science.

Politics, then, is a continuous process that occurs between the discrete formal political events of elections or revolution. It seeps into and from the most nonpublic moments and the most private of spheres. For example, death in war is portrayed historically as affecting two groups: the state, concerned with the numerical loss, and the mother and/or wife who reacts in emotional terms. For one, loss is quantitative: battle statistics, body bags, the remanning of troops. For the other, loss is qualitative: love, a human life, a place in one's heart. This study examines the latter meaning of human loss in war—the family's, particularly the mother's, loss of a son or daughter. But this is not a purely domestic, apolitical matter. A mobilizing regime must fight a war on several fronts—the military and diplomatic battlefields as well as the cultural battlefield, which involves the hearts and minds of the citizenry. A regime at war seeks the support of the family (particularly the mother) that loses a loved one. Here, I look at both mothers who lost and the Sandinista state that mobilized these women as mothers to reinforce its political position.

This popular photograph was part of the discursive battle surrounding Pope John Paul II's 1983 visit to Nicaragua. It depicts distraught Mothers of Heroes and Martyrs pleading with the Pope for a prayer for their fallen loved ones. By emphasizing the Pope's response to the Mothers—"Silence!"—Sandinista media stressed the Pope's callousness in the face of maternal suffering. Anti-Sandinistas, in turn, expressed dismay that these mothers' grief was being manipulated for political ends. (Photo by Mario Tapia for *Barricada*.)

"WE WANT A FREE COUNTRY
FOR OUR CHILDREN"

1977–1984

"Bourgeoisie and traitors: Here are our women . . . standing up in tenderness and heroism, with their hands caressing the delicate skin of their children, with their eyes open and watching, with their fingers on the triggers of their guns and on their lips the war cry."[1] FSLN founding member Tomás Borge made a common discursive link between motherhood and war in a speech during the early years of the revolution. In the last decade or so, feminist scholars have become increasingly interested in such images of women and war.[2] They have explored how gendered discourse is mobilized to serve various interests in wartime and in turn have demonstrated war to be a key context in which masculine and feminine identities are polarized and solidified. Yet little has been written about how, in the language and imagery found in popular texts, Nicaraguan women were represented and appealed to in the context of revolution and war. What sorts of political claims and social identities were sustained by these gendered discourses? How did these identities change over time? Answers to such questions would illuminate the discursive context in which Nicaraguan women organized as mothers. As such, my intention in this chapter is to link gendered representations during the Nicaraguan revolution and contra (counterrevolutionary) war with an analysis of the mobilization of women between 1977 and 1984. Dominant Sandinista and anti-Sandinista representations of women shaped the process of collective identity for groups such as the Mothers of Heroes and Martyrs. These dominant representations set new gender boundaries and sanctioned certain behavior. They reinforced maternal obligations in specific political directions, channeling women into Sandinista and, to a lesser extent, anti-Sandinista organizations.

I base my argument primarily upon content analysis of Nicaraguan media and other primary sources. Despite the international fame of several Sandinista feminists and female guerrillas, I propose that women most commonly organized (and were organized) as mothers. Mothers collectively demanded an end to the persecution of Nicaraguan youth, a decrease in taxes and the high cost of living, and an end to the U.S.-funded contra war. They mobilized both in support of and against the draft, and both for and against amnesty for political prisoners. Rights were demanded through a maternal discourse based upon compassion, especially in terms of children. Protests and demonstrations were planned around women's daily routines and the domestic sphere. Through these mobilizations, participants reached back into a long history of gendered imagery in order to make appeals both against and on behalf of the state, and they planned acts of protest rich in maternal symbolism.

It must be stressed that Nicaraguan women's collective action was not always maternal, not invariably based upon traditional women's roles. Women also organized over strategic, feminist demands that extended women's identities beyond that of housewife and mother.[3] However, in this period these demands came sporadically and almost exclusively from a small subset of members in the Sandinista women's movement AMNLAE and its predecessor AMPRONAC (Association of Nicaraguan Women Confronting the Nation's Problems) under the direction of the FSLN. Although many of its leaders were sympathetic to such controversial demands as legal abortion and the drafting of women, AMNLAE worked most closely with women organized as mothers of drafted or fallen sons. Both AMNLAE's lack of autonomy from the Sandinista state and its prioritization of work with the mothers of combatants in the war effort forced more explicit and controversial feminist issues to the back burner.

Women's Early Mobilizations against Somoza

Mothers and wives of political prisoners organized on behalf of their loved ones for over two decades before the 1979 fall of Somoza. Gladys Baez, the first female FSLN guerrilla, recounted how she organized with other women on behalf of imprisoned family members when her husband was imprisoned along with many others following the 1956 assassination of the first Somoza: "I joined with the other mothers and wives and went to the prison. We brought the men food and monitored how they were being treated.... A lot of women took part. Wherever you have prisoners you generally have the mothers, wives and daughters turning out every day. Men may give money for support but women lend themselves physically."[4]

Two unsuccessful attempts were made by revolutionary parties to form women's organizations with the aim of encouraging the participation of women workers and *campesinas* in the political struggle: in 1962, the Organization of Democratic Nicaraguan Women (OMDN) initiated by the Socialist Party, and, in 1969, the Patriotic Alliance of Nicaraguan Women (APMN) formed by the FSLN.[5] Only three women attended the first national meeting of APMN; nonetheless, Baez saw it as a historic event because it was the first time in her memory that women called upon themselves to discuss their role as women in Nicaraguan society.[6]

In 1972, Santos Buitrago, mother of the famous Sandinista martyr Julio Buitrago, formed with other Sandinista mothers the Committee of Mothers for the Freedom of Political Prisoners. These mothers met secretly in order to inform themselves about the status of the political prisoners. They demanded not only their own children's release, but the release of all political prisoners, raising money and regularly visiting prisoners to monitor their situation.[7]

The Formation of AMPRONAC

By 1977, in the context of greater repression and a more mobilized population, many more Nicaraguan women were prepared to join a human rights–oriented organization. Other sectors—youth, students, workers, and peasants—were organizing, and younger women with fewer family responsibilities were joining the guerrillas. But at the time, there existed no organization for women that addressed their gender-specific experiences of the economic crisis and the military repression.[8] In March 1977, the FSLN, through Father Ernesto Cardenal, brought together a group of Sandinista and non-Sandinista women to discuss the formation of a women's organization to denounce the Somoza regime.[9] The earliest members were largely professional women or mothers of political prisoners and fallen combatants.[10] The plan was to mobilize upper-class women in hope that their social status would temper the repression directed against human rights organizations.[11] The first meeting of AMPRONAC on 29 September 1977 was overflowing. A second assembly, held in coordination with the Christian communities, attracted more than a thousand people despite the introduction of martial law.[12] Most AMPRONAC members were not affiliated with any political group. Their initial focus was on protests against the increasing human rights abuses and support for the mothers and wives of political prisoners and the disappeared.[13]

AMPRONAC stressed that because women make up more than 50 percent of the population, "no change can occur without the active participation of this half of the people."[14] Their demands drew from human and civil rights and economic and feminist goals that would appeal to a broad spectrum of women:

1. Absolute respect for human rights.
2. Freedom of political organization.
3. Freedom for all the *campesino* prisoners who are detained without charge and for the political prisoners who were submitted to unjust trials.
4. Punishment for all those guilty of crimes and barbarities.
5. An end to the rising cost of living.
6. Equal salary for equal work.
7. Repeal of all laws that discriminate against women.
8. Freedom of expression.
9. An end to the repression; no more genocide.
10. An end to the commercialization of women.

As more working class and *campesina* women joined AMPRONAC, the membership exceeded eight thousand, and the organization's acts became more confrontational. Initially, AMPRONAC focused on visiting prisons and petitioning the courts for the release of political prisoners. As the repression escalated, they moved on to hunger strikes, occupation of churches and international offices, general strikes, and street demonstrations. They also went underground, providing safe houses and first aid stations and establishing a supply network for FSLN guerrillas.

Women and the First National Strike

In January 1978, Pedro Joaquin Chamorro, the editor of the opposition paper La Prensa and an outspoken Somoza opponent, was assassinated. During the general strike that followed, AMPRONAC helped organize a takeover of the United Nations office by women relatives of political prisoners and the disappeared. The sit-in, under the theme "Where are our campesino brothers and sisters? Let the assassins respond," included four Managua women whose relatives were political prisoners, four peasant women whose relatives had been disappeared by Somoza's National Guard, and a coordinator sent by AMPRONAC. As Zulema Baltodano, one member of the sit-in, explained, "The action was a protest. We women with political prisoners had no illusions that the prisoners would be released as a result of the protest. Our major objective was to mobilize and politicize the masses. . . . That sit-in was a good experience. We were very well-organized. Chiguin's EEBI forces [Somoza's son's special branch of the military] made their debut by trying to bomb us with tear gas."[15] The women inside the offices issued a statement using a language of maternal and civil rights: "As women and as Nicaraguan citizens we support all the groups that demand the unconditional renunciation of Anastasio Somoza. . . . We want a free country for our children, where peace and justice prevail; we don't want for them a future like the past and present."[16]

The occupation lasted twelve days and culminated in a meeting of some six hundred women in front of the UN office, many of whom were upper-class women upset over the assassination of Chamorro. Lea Guido, founding member of AMPRONAC, remembered, "[Somoza] came down hard on that demonstration. Our sisters fought back. When the troops bombed us with tear gas, we threw the canisters right back at them. It was really a militant demonstration."[17] Though Nicaragua had a long history of military repression, the violence used against these women, reported by both the national and international media, was shocking. Gendered boundaries were crossed by both sides, but the women protesters gained the moral upper hand. The sight of women acting independently of men in such a defiant political manner was unusual, yet it appeared legitimate given that as wives and mothers they were selflessly defending the lives of their loved ones. In contrast, the militant crackdown on these women by heavily armed men was popularly portrayed as unnecessarily aggressive and even cowardly.

As this suggests, the women in the UN offices strategically alternated between stressing their defenseless position and announcing their bravery. In statements to a national or international audience, they deftly posed Somoza and his National Guard as cowards who preyed on the innocent and weak. For example, they sent a letter of protest to President Jimmy Carter, charging that "on the one hand you proclaim to the world your concern for human rights, and on the other hand you arm the dictator Anastasio Somoza, who yesterday sent the National Guard . . . to attack us brutally. . . . To be congruent with your proclaimed support and devotion to human rights, it is your obligation to explain before the world this campaign of arming dictators that attack defenseless women."[18]

Yet in messages aimed at participants and potential members, the women repeatedly reaffirmed their courage, as the following AMPRONAC statement shows: "NICARAGUAN WOMEN, DEFEND YOUR RIGHTS. We increase our efforts to gain freedom for our violated country and leave our children a FREE NICARAGUA. We do not frighten before the institutionalized violence; the hour of fear has passed."[19] In an article written in November 1978, AMPRONAC reported that this experience raised their consciousness and strengthened their resolve: "It was the first time the women of AMPRONAC personally experienced the repression, in which we showed in practice our determination to support the popular struggle."[20] For upper-class and professional women, the ordeal baptized them into the realities of repression that women of their class had largely avoided thus far.

The incident propelled AMPRONAC into the national and international spotlight. As the New York Times reported, "Until the National Guard made the mistake of using tear gas against a small group of women demonstrating in front of the United Nations building . . . Nicaragua's new women's movement had barely been noticed. . . . But since then, the movement has grown beyond recognition, spreading from the upper and middle classes to incorporate wives of peasants and workers."[21] Thus in subtly contradictory fashion, AMPRONAC, on the one hand, galvanized public support by posing its members as defenseless, and, on the other hand, strengthened internal solidarity as members realized that they were indeed capable of resistance in the face of repression.

Following this demonstration, AMPRONAC was contacted by *campesinas* who had also lost loved ones in the repression. Guido claimed that this "was happening all over the country. All we had to do was go and put the finishing touches on the organizations because wherever we went there were women waiting for us. That's how the association began to grow."[22]

During the same strike, women protested in other ways. A "Nicaraguan Mothers" petition calling for justice, freedom, democracy, and the renunciation of Anastasio Somoza was signed by thousands of women, and their names were published in *La Prensa*. In an attempt to shame men into opposing the regime, a group of women wrote a letter to *La Prensa* in the form of a last will and testament for a man who did not speak out against Somoza:

I leave to my brothers all the shame and hardships that I caused them through my servility and apathy. I leave my wife a broken heart and a life of misery. I leave to each of my children poverty, ignorance, brutality, and the sad memory that your father died a vile coward. I leave to society a fatal example and hateful memory.

Do you know me? I have been a conformist that has supported the Somoza dictatorship all my life. I never raised my voice in protest! If we become conscious, we might change our will and testament. It is time![23]

In working-class neighborhoods, women and children protested government repression and the Chamorro assassination by banging on pots and pans for one hour every night. Some women banged pots within their own homes, while others went out into the streets. The "protest of pots and pans" began in a few Managua neighborhoods and spread to other neighborhoods and cities over the following week. This form of protest was planned by the General Strike Feminine Support Committee as a way to involve women whose lives revolved around the home. Pots and pans were these women's tools of trade. Banging pots in unison provided a loud and undeniable sign of protest, and women could participate without leaving their homes. The National Guard, however, repressed these protests. Women were beaten and arrested, and at least one woman was killed.

In a high-profile instance of maternal protest, Albertina Serrano declared a hunger strike in March 1978 to call attention to the torture and mistreatment of her son and other political prisoners. Other mothers joined her strike, which lasted more than a month. It was frequently covered in the press, and on Mother's Day Serrano was recognized as an exemplary mother by *La Prensa*: "Few times has a mother come to such extreme sacrifice as this humble woman who has managed to move the country and gain the support of all Nicaraguans in order to win the following demand: better treatment for her son and the rest of the political prisoners. The act of love of Doña Albertina dignifies Nicaraguan mothers. She is a true representation of motherhood on this day." [24] This hunger strike was converted in April into another period of intense struggle against the dictatorship, and AMPRONAC and organized students and workers joined the striking mothers. [25]

During the same period, AMPRONAC and other groups petitioned for the freedom of María del Carmen Gomez de Palma, a Sandinista imprisoned in her ninth month of pregnancy. This campaign was carried out under the theme "All mothers have the right to raise their children in freedom." [26] They were eventually successful, marking a rare concession from Somoza to the popular struggle.

AMPRONAC Grows Stronger

Gloria Carrion, an early leader of AMPRONAC, stated in a 1979 interview that both economic and physical repression, particularly as they affected children, propelled women into the anti-Somoza struggle:

Working class and peasant women . . . have had to fight each day for the bare necessities of life. . . . And these are the conditions that pushed them to become involved in the Revolution. Women have become aggressive, developed tough characters. . . . Many women from privileged backgrounds also took up the struggle. The widespread repression, and in particular, the way this repression centered on our youth, outraged women from all classes. . . . Women took the lead in organizing in defense of the children and young people.[27]

Despite the outrage felt by women from all classes, class-based tensions over the proper goals and alliances of AMPRONAC soon developed. During its first meetings, many women of the upper and middle classes resisted extending the goals of the group beyond denunciation of the regime's human rights abuses toward building a popular women's movement that defended women's rights and supported the overthrow of Somoza. Following the takeover of the UN offices and AMPRONAC's participation in a hunger march of peasant women in Diriamba, in which two people were killed, upper-class members of AMPRONAC expressed reluctance in allying with peasant groups. Guido recalled, "There were two very different political trends developing and we would have to choose between them. One was a kind of Somozaism without Somoza that in the end would result in 'modernizing' the dictatorship. The other option was the Nicaraguan people overthrowing the dictatorship."[28] AMPRONAC members debated these positions in a series of meetings and came to a general agreement that, "due to the immorality of the dictator, our work, which until then involved the presentation of denunciations and petitions for aid, did not have an effect; therefore, our efforts should concentrate on organizing women and converting ourselves into a popular force."[29] Thus, it was decided that the association should join the United People's Movement, the umbrella organization for anti-Somoza groups, including the FSLN. Guido argued that although AMPRONAC acted with more caution in its first months, due to the hesitance among upper class members, "it was the only way to begin, because any women's movement among the poor would have been immediately repressed."[30]

Some AMPRONAC leaders later attributed the organization's success to the fact that it addressed problems specific to their gender. As Guido explained, "We always looked at the situation from a woman's point of view. If we hadn't, what meaning would it have had for us to organize as women? We might as well have been any other kind of group—a parent's association, a union, whatever. . . . None of the other organizations could provide women with the same kind of political space. . . . We had many, many women who weren't going to participate in the struggle unless we could provide ways for them to organize as women."[31]

Carrion agreed: "I don't believe, as some do, that women have no special demands of their own. . . . I think it's precisely because we've always been aware of this that AMPRONAC was able to succeed where others failed."[32] In its public statements and platforms, AMPRONAC touched on the feminist concerns of economic, political, and social equality between men and women. However, it more commonly—and more successfully—organized women through their concerns as mothers, stressing better education, health, and safety for their children. For example, an AMPRONAC statement on International Women's Day proclaimed: "Today more than ever we recognize the need to organize ourselves to search for solutions that would make our country a place where our children can grow up safe and free from oppression and misery."[33] AMPRONAC's tactics and moral resources were also gendered, highlighting the dictatorship's negative effects on women's roles and duties as mothers. For example, on Mother's Day in 1978, AMPRONAC rejected the commercial aspects of the holiday by passing out leaflets that read, "More than a gift, we want a free Nicaragua."

When Somoza raised taxes in August 1978, AMPRONAC responded with a campaign under the slogan, "Our Children Are Hungry. Bring Down the Cost of Living." Known as the "march of empty pots," thousands of women in various cities protested high prices by marching in the streets wearing aprons and carrying empty pots. Some carried signs with slogans such as "Our children are hungry."[34] In Managua, women hung aprons and empty milk containers in public places with messages denouncing the rise in taxes. As one AMPRONAC member explained to the press, "We all decided to begin this campaign because we housewives feel daily the economic crisis that this country is going through."[35] In this manner, with such domestic tools as empty pots and milk containers, women demonstrated the negative impact the Somoza regime had on women's ability to carry out their domestic duties.

Another campaign involved organizing women to write letters to wives of Somocistas, appealing to a maternal solidarity that bypassed political lines. These letters invoked traditional gender ideals of women as morally superior peacemakers and defenders of life. La Prensa published one woman's letter to Anastasio Somoza's wife, Hope:

I appeal to your sensibility as a woman and your Christian spirit, and I hope that you can use a bit of your influence from your position as first lady . . . and also as wife of President Somoza.

I cry out as a Nicaraguan mother and wife—you cannot ignore what is happening in the streets all over Nicaragua. They are massacring defenseless people, they are jailing, insulting, choking us in our homes, killing our children, our men, our brothers, they are disrespecting and committing sacrilege in the churches . . . and all this, as you know, is ordered by your brave husband of the National Guard. . . .

It is time as a woman and a mother in Nicaragua to make your voice heard and intervene in some form. Well, I have some faith and think that you cannot remain indifferent forever in the face of the pain and disgrace of a whole people.[36]

After the Sandinista takeover of the National Palace and the Second National Strike, both of which occurred in August 1978, the opposition to Somoza had grown to the extent that AMPRONAC leaders felt it necessary to concentrate on mobilizing not only women but everyone against the dictatorship. At this point, AMPRONAC began organizing civil defense committees in various neighborhoods, which after the triumph became the Sandinista Defense Committees (CDS). Due to the severe repression following the FSLN insurrection in September, core members of AMPRONAC went underground. There, they often performed rearguard tasks traditional to women. They gave first aid courses and organized houses in different neighborhoods to serve as "safe houses" and first aid stations during the war. They also established clandestine storehouses that supplied neighborhoods with basic food items, such as rice and beans.[37]

La Prensa reported that women in the neighborhoods of Managua formed mothers' committees in early 1979 "to protect the lives of our adored children against the terror which has spread throughout our beloved country."[38] Many mothers of imprisoned or disappeared children took part. One woman explained, "Before it was impossible to come together because [women] were very afraid, but now there are many women who have disappeared children or children in La Central prison and they understand that they should organize."[39] These mothers' committees demanded "respect for the lives of their children, for guarantees [of safety] for their children in the schools, in the streets, wherever they may be."[40] Women of AMPRONAC and the mothers' committees claimed that motherhood "has turned into a torture under this regime," and they pledged to "struggle against the dictator and in this struggle [focus on] the defense of the lives of our children."[41] By 1979, AMPRONAC's protest language as reported in *La Prensa* revolved primarily around children's and maternal rights—rights that were denied by the regime: "When forty, fifty youth are massacred in hospitals, schools, neighborhoods . . . then a crime is being committed against the right of all woman to maternity and of all our children to childhood."[42]

It should be noted that although many women participated in the popular struggle through maternal protests and traditionally female rearguard tasks such as preparing food and tending to the wounded, women also joined in the armed struggle. A number of guerrilla commanders were women. Dora María Téllez led a high command of three women and three men in the takeover of León, Nicaragua's second-largest city, in June 1979. Another female guerrilla commander, Mónica Baltodano, along with two male commanders, organized the final offensive in Managua. By the Sandinista triumph on 19 July 1979, an estimated 25 to 30 percent of the armed insurrectionary forces were women.[43]

Post-1979 Anti-Sandinista Representations of Women
"Depending upon the Needs of Her Family"

The ideological gap left in Somoza's wake was filled by competing counterhegemonies that were distinctly gendered. Representations of women changed in sync with the political context. In the years leading up to the triumph over Somoza, *La Prensa* portrayed women as mothers actively engaged in the struggle for a free Nicaragua. Yet after 1979, as *La Prensa* became increasingly anti-Sandinista, it focused much less on organized women than it had in previous years and clung increasingly to images of traditional feminine domesticity. Editorials and advice columns regularly referred to the Bible, stressing that a woman's most important role was within the home caring for her family. She should be a loyal, devoted, nurturing, self-sacrificing wife and mother. For example, a 1980 editorial allowed that a woman's work could extend beyond the home, "depending upon the needs of her family and the particular call that Jesus makes to her.

But she should always have in mind the words of Jesus with respect to love and balance her time so that her service outside the home does not deprive her loved ones of her services as wife and mother."[44] The editorial claimed that while men and women are equal before God, women sometimes make the mistake of imitating men, "instead of making ourselves better as we are, to be true women."[45]

These discursive efforts to redirect women's energies back into the home came during the wave of post-triumph enthusiasm and engagement in Sandinista volunteer activities. Socially conservative sectors were increasingly threatened by the new revolutionary regime solidifying its support by mobilizing citizens—including women of all ages—into various pro-Sandinista organizations. In this context, comments supporting women's divinely inspired devotion to home and family may be read as indirect responses to Sandinista women's activism. For more traditional, upper-class women, temporary activism during exceptional times was perhaps acceptable, even necessary. But as a more permanent arrangement, it threatened the entire patriarchal order.

Omnipotent Supplicants: Anti-Sandinista Mothers of Political Prisoners

From 1982 to 1986, La Prensa rarely enlisted maternal symbolism or mentioned Nicaraguan women organized in any form other than as "feminine auxiliaries" to political parties, perhaps due to censorship. Women were, of course, mentioned on an individual basis during this period, yet their gender was not a primary issue. However, in 1980–81 and again in 1987–89, images of women were common in the paper, primarily representing women as mothers of political prisoners and later as mothers denouncing the draft.[46]

In the early 1980s, soon after the fall of Somoza, La Prensa printed letter after letter from "sick elderly mothers" whose sons were imprisoned as Somocista National Guardsmen or contras (counterrevolutionaries). As editors of La Prensa wrote, "We receive dozens of letters daily from mothers and relatives of prisoners. Little by little we will publish some in order to comfort those anguished mothers and also to cooperate in an effort to improve the justice system in our country."[47] The women often proclaimed their imprisoned sons' (and to a lesser extent husbands') innocence and pleaded with authorities for a quick release because the sons were their only means of support. Other mothers charged that they were denied visitation rights and that their sons were mistreated in the prisons. The following letter was typical: "My only son has been imprisoned for one month. I plead with you for a quick investigation because I am sure of his innocence and because I am sick and old. He is my only son and he takes care of me. . . . I am afraid I will die without ever being able to see my son again."[48]

These letters were rarely accompanied by editorial comments from *La Prensa*, perhaps to avoid Sandinista censorship. Like the above letter, many were addressed to Tomás Borge, a founder of the FSLN and the interior minister; thus, it is possible that similar letters were also sent to *Barricada*, which declined to publish them. The silence on the part of *Barricada* and the emphasis on the letters in *La Prensa* are an example of the gendered hegemonic struggle being waged through the media. As a *La Prensa* editorial, enlisting the ideal of the Virgin Mary, explained, "The requests of a mother succeed in being received into even the hardest of hearts," and "The shortest road to the heart of a person is always the heart of a mother."[49] Along these lines, mothers were positioned as the Omnipotent Supplicants on behalf of their children. As sick, elderly mothers who simply wanted their beloved (innocent) sons back home, their pleas were posed as impossible to ignore. Sandinista officials, then, were cruel and heartless in ignoring the pleas of such mothers.

In response, a cartoon in *Barricada* showed an angel with a bowler hat that read "*La Prensa*" approaching a mother mourning over a grave with the epitaph "assassinated by the GN [National Guard]." The angel tells her, "Excuse me, but you are mistaken. The real victims are over there," pointing to a jail full of Somoza's National Guardsmen.[50] Through sarcasm, this cartoon articulated the Sandinista position that all political prisoners were guilty Somocistas and *La Prensa*'s concern for their mothers was simply a maneuver to divert attention from the true victims of the war—fallen Sandinistas and their mothers.

Organized Women and the State: "The Goals of Women and Those of the Revolution Are the Same"

Following the fall of Somoza, AMPRONAC changed its name to the Association of Nicaraguan Women, Luisa Amanda Espinosa (AMNLAE), in honor of the first Sandinista woman to die in combat. According to Sandinista discourse, women's participation in the economic, political, and social life of the nation would lead to a greater voice in policymaking and to greater experience and self-confidence, which subsequently would lead to even greater participation.[51] Along these lines, AMNLAE asserted that women's specific demands had also become the revolution's demands and gender equality would come through women's full participation in the revolutionary process. Accordingly, AMNLAE involved women in many aspects of the new revolutionary society, particularly in the area of volunteer work. Carrion explained in 1979, "We want our association to be an instrument for women, a guarantee to their fulfilling their life possibilities."[52]

Carrion observed that "women from the poorer sectors come to us spontaneously and enthusiastically because it is through their integration in the political process that they find personal realization."[53] Yet, looking back at the association's early years, AMNLAE member Milu Vargas argued that due to the lack of clear goals, it "became absorbed in organizing women who were working with the FSLN and we threw ourselves into the overall work of the party. Thus, we neglected our main concern to bring together and represent the large number of women who were beginning to take the first steps toward participating in the Revolution, women who were, in practice, transcending their traditional roles."[54] Because of this lack of attention to unmobilized women, as well as the top-down leadership style and lack of autonomy from the FSLN, the organization soon stagnated in some parts of the country.

Thus, while anti-Sandinista discourse increasingly stressed women's domestic obligations, the Sandinista attention to women's interests was bound up with the overall goals of reconstruction and national unity. Toward its goal of economic, political, and cultural equality for women, the FSLN abolished prostitution, banned advertising that exploited women's bodies, instituted equal pay for equal work, provided health care for mothers and children, built day-care centers, and expanded literacy. AMNLAE and some FSLN leaders asserted that men must share a larger part of domestic tasks and child care. Women not only benefited from these objectives but also played a primary role in carrying them out. They constituted 60 percent of the literacy brigades, 70 percent of the brigades for the popular health campaign, 95 percent of those working in health programs, and 68 percent of the coordinators in adult education programs.[55]

By 1983, the contra war and economic crisis had noticeably slowed the implementation of Sandinista policies regarding women. Quickly over-shadowing the goal of women's emancipation was the FSLN's desire to secure women's loyalty in the face of counterrevolutionary threats, mobilize their labor, and divert their potential opposition to the draft and economic austerity programs. The lack of basic consumer goods created many prob-lems for women and added to the time spent on domestic tasks. As their domestic burden increased due to shortages, the mobilization of young men to war opened job vacancies for which women were recruited. During the contra war, women received training for traditionally "male" jobs and came to represent up to 42 percent of the economically active sector in the cities and 67 percent in the rural areas (compared with 29 percent in 1977).[56]

As contra attacks increased, AMNLAE prioritized defense, mobilizing women into battalions of military reserves and directing women's military training.[57] AMNLAE also organized women into nonmilitary defense work, such as organizing supplies and preparing food. In 1983, the FSLN proposed a draft of men seventeen to twenty-five years of age. In response, AMNLAE argued that the participation of women in combat during the insurrection had most effectively altered society's conception of women's capabilities. Furthermore, to the extent that military defense was seen as the duty, even the privilege, of male citizens, prominent members of AMNLAE argued that this should be applied to women too. They were also concerned that military discrimination could lead to other forms as well, thus impeding the FSLN's 1969 goal of abolishing discrimination against women.[58] A common refrain was, "Women have earned the right in Nicaragua to participate in the defense of the country."[59] Accordingly, AMNLAE pushed for full inte-gration of women into all tasks of the revolution, including the draft, as essential to gender equality.

The FSLN leadership countered that social services, particularly day care, were insufficient; thus women were needed at home to care of their children.[60] Defending the FSLN's position, Comandante Doris Tijerino, the highest-ranking woman in the Sandinista army, cryptically explained that women would be excluded "because of well-known biological and

organic limitations."[61] The draft was one of the most contested issues between AMNLAE and the Sandinista leadership.[62] In the end, women were
excluded from the draft but were permitted to enlist in all-female battalions. AMNLAE was directed by the FSLN to focus its energy on mothers
of combatants. In addition to finding economic support for these women,
AMNLAE did ideological work with them, taking on the difficult task of
convincing mothers that the drafting of their sons was necessary for the
defense of the nation.

Maternal Mobilizing Identities and Cultural Warfare

In mobilizing a nation to war, differences are squelched, as the individual
voices of the nation must appear to speak as one. Since a nation's way of
life, the status quo, is to be protected, voices outside the mainstream appear
as a threat. As with representations of ethnicity and race, the most traditional and extreme representations of masculinity and femininity are often
found during wartime. As one research group put it, "A culturally produced
activity that is as rigidly defined by sex differentiation and as committed
to sexual exclusion as is war points to a crucial site where meanings about
gender are being produced, reproduced, and circulated back into society."[63]

Studies examining the relationship between discourse, gender, and war
have found dramatic dichotomies constructed between men/war/battle-
front and women/peace/homefront.[64] Narratives of men and war reject all
that is conceived of as feminine.[65] In the Western tradition of war stories,
women have been the "other"—patriotic mothers sending sons off to war,
pacifist givers and protectors of life, the civilian support network cheering
on the soldiers, or keepers of the hearth and home and all that is not war.[66]

Although images of women in war are culturally distinct, I found strong
similarities between dominant Western themes and those found in Nicaragua.[67] Analysis of the images circulated during the insurrection and contra
war leads to a better understanding of women's subjectivities in Nicaragua.
Accordingly, I probe the relationship between the gendered discourse that
evolved in the early years of the contra war and those women mobilized as
mothers for insight into the Nicaraguan constructions of "woman" and particularly "mother" that frame how women should behave. Dominant ma-

ternal images are outlined here as "mobilizing identities"—ideal types that capture basic themes and invite comparison regarding how women were appealed to and how their political identities formed.

Both the experience of the Sandinista revolution and the Sandinista vision of revolutionary society transformed some long-held notions of femininity. As with all social sectors in Nicaragua, the emergency situations created by the insurrection and contra war disrupted women's normal routines. Women who participated in the overthrow of Somoza discovered new levels of courage, stamina, and strength. Did the revolutionary process produce images of women that might enlarge the arena of opportunities for women, as FSLN discourse proposed? On the contrary, despite women's revolutionary experience and the FSLN's considerable effort to improve women's economic position, the contra war, along with a revolutionary party not fully committed to feminist ideals, led to a regression back to the safer, traditional images and roles for women. Crossing gender boundaries during exceptional circumstances, such as popular insurrection, did not secure women an equal position in the "New Society," nor did it fundamentally alter traditional notions of femininity. During the post-triumph euphoria, visions of fundamental social change, including equal rights for women, competed with a popular yearning to return to normalcy, especially within the home. With the enemy defeated, the "guerrilla girls" could lay down their weapons, return home, and bear and raise children in a new, revolutionary society.

As Miriam Cooke and Angela Woollacott wrote, "Women's inclusion as participants in wars of this century has blurred distinctions between gender roles in peace and war. War has become a terrain in which gender is negotiated."[68] Women's participation was essential to the success of the insurrection, both as guerrillas and civilian supporters, and as such traditional ideas of femininity were challenged and new opportunities were opened for women to demand greater rights as full citizens in Sandinista society.

Yet despite Nicaraguan women's unique military role, the struggle to construct women's subjectivities centered on motherhood—notwithstanding the occasional photograph of women driving tractors or working in a factory, the articles about women taking over jobs vacated by men fighting in the war, and the attempts by AMNLAE to encourage Barricada to feature women doing nontraditional jobs.[69] The image of women as mothers varied over time, depending primarily upon political and economic circum-stances. Sandinista discourse did not project a single, static, unified vision of motherhood. It exalted some traditional aspects of motherhood while it rejected others, and applied old ideas in new ways, resulting in a variety of sometimes contradictory images: combatant mothers, combatant-bearing mothers, peace-loving mothers, suffering mothers. These representations of women played a constitutive role in the structuring of Sandinista society and set the horizon of expectations for women's behavior. However, women were not simply assigned their roles, but actively contradicted, constructed, and reinforced them.

Universal Motherhood: "She Clasps to Her Breast Thousands of Hungry Mouths"

The following is a popular poem entitled "The Mother," by Gioconda Belli, a Sandinista and one of Nicaragua's best-known poets.[70]

THE MOTHER

. . . . . .

She no longer loves only her children,
nor does she give only to her children.
She clasps to her breast
thousands of hungry mouths.

. . . .

She has given birth to herself
feeling—at times—
unable to support so much love on her shoulders,
thinking of the fruit of her flesh
—far off and alone—
calling her in the night without answer,
while she responds to other shouts,
to many shouts,
but always thinking of the one and only shout of her flesh
one more shout in that clamor of the people who calls her
and pulls from her arms
even her own children.

Belli's poem depicts a common portrayal of women in Sandinista discourse using imagery of struggle, sacrifice, and universal mothering. The ideal mother acted upon Sandinista principles, supporting the revolution and the war effort, yet she never lost her maternal, nurturing qualities. Though her physical image was militarized, perhaps wearing pants and combat boots, she was still first and foremost a mother. Yet this mother did not just mother her own children. She mothered all the children of Nicaragua. The revolution that called her children away from home replaced them with thousands more who needed her mothering, her love. This required personal transformation—"she has given birth to herself"—in realizing her new politicized roles as combatant and mother to all Nicaraguan children.

I found this representation of mothers as mothering and protecting all Nicaraguan children—Universal Motherhood—in revolutionary discourse and practice from the insurrection through the contra war. It was a common image put forth to recruit women into revolutionary tasks. For example, during the literacy crusade in 1980, thousands of women were mobilized into Mothers' Committees to become "adoptive mothers" to the young teachers in the crusade.[71] Through the literacy crusade, AMNLAE organized women in remote areas of the countryside. Many mothers whose children joined the literacy crusade organized into Mothers' Committees through AMNLAE. Ultimately, there were 161 Mothers' Committees with 1,597 members. In these committees, mothers participated in vigilance programs, logistical and moral support for the crusade, and denunciations against contra attacks. Some mothers went into the countryside to raise the consciousness of women, particularly concerning the objectives of the literacy brigade and AMNLAE.[72] These mothers also countered complaints in La Prensa (by this time the opposition paper to the Sandinista government) from parents claiming their children were forced into the brigades and accusing the FSLN of intending to destroy the family.[73]

Later, during the contra war, AMNLAE and the Mothers of Heroes and Martyrs encouraged their members to again become "adoptive mothers" to soldiers hospitalized or stationed far from their own families. As an article in an AMNLAE publication put it, "United by the universal sentiments of motherhood, we make each soldier another son. . . . Let us arise in war, joining forces with our children to gain peace in Nicaragua and happiness in the future. Mothers and their children with the country forever!!!"[74]

Motherhood carried such emotional resonance that the representation of motherhood was pivotal in the battle over the hearts and minds of Nicaraguans during the contra war. For example, the Mothers of Heroes and Martyrs used the theme of universal mothering in their public condemnations of contra attacks: "In the hearts of the mothers are all the combatants as if they are our own children, and we suffer greatly when we see them fall."[75]

Translation of revolutionary tasks and condemnation of contra attacks in the language of motherhood was an effective means of mobilizing women, particularly middle-aged and older women not already mobilized as students or workers, into the revolutionary process. This appealed to many women whose own subjectivities prioritized their identities as mothers. If their positions as mothers could be broadened, if women came to see all Sandinista combatants, or all Nicaraguans, as their own children, their commitment to the Revolution would certainly grow. Self-sacrifice and concern for others, as opposed to individualism, was an important revolutionary theme, but while young men were encouraged to sacrifice their lives at the battlefront in order to save the nation, women were encouraged to mother on a larger scale by mobilizing into mothers' committees.

Combative Motherhood: "Tender in Love, Fierce in Battle"

During the insurrection and after the triumph, as contra attacks increased, the image of the mother was tied to protection, even armed protection, of the nation's children. The desire to protect one's children, even through the use of violence, was posed as a natural or divinely ordained maternal reaction. As one woman said, "When they are attacked we must defend them, like a lioness defends her cubs."[76] Women organized in Mothers' Committees during the insurrection urged other mothers to form committees with the following argument: "From the moment of conception, the mother has the obligation to protect her child, and she who does not do this is breaking divine law. For this reason, NICARAGUAN MOTHER, reflect: your mission is too great to be stifled by fear. Do not be afraid to protect your child because with fear you are not going to free him or her from death."[77] Tomás Borge, a founding member of the FSLN, stated in a 1980 speech on International Women's Day that the new Sandinista government intended to develop "women's militias and give every woman a gun with which to defend her children. Women know how to organize themselves, especially to defend the generations that are now growing up."[78] In this way, the logic that traditionally fed the image of women as natural peacemakers—givers and protectors of life—was used to mobilize women into the military and revolutionary vigilance programs.

In analyzing the representations of Nicaraguan women, I found that Combative Motherhood[79]—protection of one's children—was overwhelmingly the most common theme in Sandinista attempts to mobilize women into defense work. Gloria Carrion, general coordinator of AMNLAE, argued, "Women have earned the right to participate in the defense of the Revolution. . . . As mothers we have the obligation to fight . . . to prevent the continued killing of our children on the border."[80] Another AMNLAE leader warned women, "Today combat preparation is a necessity for the defense of the Revolution and especially for the defense of the lives of our children."[81] The caption under a photo of uniformed, armed women crossing a river, which appeared in a 1981 issue of Barricada, read, "'No more crimes against our children!' This is the combative shout of Nicaraguan women that was raised by thousands of female soldiers from León in the reserve battalion. They, like many sectors of the population, are prepared for the defense of the country. And you, compañera? Have you joined yet?"[82]

The emphasis on mothers' protective, combative role in defense of the nation's children led to some extraordinarily juxtaposed images. Among the most arresting images of Combative Motherhood, copied countless times by Nicaraguan artists, is a photograph of a young woman with an AK-47 slung on her back and a baby at her breast.[83] This image is sometimes accompanied with a slogan, such as the following celebrating women's participation in neighborhood Sandinista Defense Committees: "The woman of the CDS, tender in love, fierce in the battle!"[84] This representation of motherhood gave the message that combat, especially in the name of one's children, did not conflict with traditional notions of motherhood. Women who joined the guerrillas or, later, the militias had to leave their children in the care of others for extended periods of time. In contrast to an interpretation of these women as unfeminine or bad mothers, Sandinista discourse stressed that military women were exemplary mothers willing to offer their lives for the defense of their children and the country—the epitome of the selfless, self-sacrificing mother. Thus, the seemingly contradictory aims of motherhood and war were made complementary.

As with Universal Motherhood, Combative Motherhood was aimed at mobilizing women.[85] It undermined the traditional notions that women were naturally nonviolent or passive and that war was an exclusively male realm. Instead, women were positioned as naturally fierce protectors of their children. Women in Nicaragua were more readily mobilized into combative positions, and society's acceptance of military women more easily secured, not in terms of patriotism, bravery, machismo, or abstract political rights but in terms of maternal defense of the children. However, once women were excluded from the draft, this image of Combative Motherhood faded, eclipsed by images of women bearing future soldiers and sending them off to war.

Las Continuadoras: "Our Children Aren't Dead"

One of the thirteen points in the 1969 "Historic Program of the FSLN" is the "Veneration of Our Martyrs": "The Sandinista people's revolution will maintain eternal gratitude to and veneration of our homeland's martyrs and will continue the shining example of heroism and selflessness they have bequeathed to us."[86] A key vehicle by which this goal was carried out was the mobilization of mutually reinforcing maternal imagery and organizations. Indeed, on a certain level the two seemed to collapse into one—the mobilized mothers as a form of discourse, a message to society.

Sandinista discourse relied on the ideal of loyal and brave mothers keeping alive the memory of the fallen, thus continuing the struggle where their martyred children left off. This mobilizing identity—*Las Continuadoras*—had its incarnation in the Committee of Mothers of Heroes and Martyrs. The committee was both a central mechanism through which to articulate the goal of mobilizing in the name of the fallen and an outcome of that same discourse. As one member of the Mothers told the crowd during a 1981 protest against contra aggressions: "The Mothers of Heroes and Martyrs should be united as one fist ready to defend the Revolution and continue the struggle that our children began."[87] At the Third National Assembly of the Mothers of Heroes and Martyrs, all promised to spread the example of their children: "We fight because the blood of our children grows into

schools, highways, and roads."[88] And on Mother's Day 1984, solidarity between combatants and the Mothers was stressed, as one Mother said: "I am
ready to take up again the battle cry *patria libre o morir* [free homeland or
death] that our children shouted at the moment of their death."[89]

Sandinista discourse articulated through the Mothers of Heroes and
Martyrs stressed that the symbolic survival of the heroes and martyrs depended upon the survival of the revolution. Just as the martyred Christ
lived on in all Christians, martyred Sandinistas lived on in all free Nicaraguans. Dead combatants lived on particularly through their mothers in
the struggle. As a banner carried by Mothers of Heroes and Martyrs read,
"Heroes and Martyrs of 1970—you are present in your mothers."[90] Mothers
of Jinotega also evoked this notion, claiming that their children had not
died because "they are with us in the tasks of the Revolution every day."[91]

The Mothers were also effective in presenting the lives of their martyred children as examples to young men of draft age. One Mother who lost
two sons during the insurrection made a call to all mothers to inspire their
children to fight: "Our children aren't dead, they live on in our hearts and
the pain fills us with the courage to inspire other children to avenge their
deaths."[92]

Sandinista discourse of *Las Continuadoras* posed mothers who were resentful of their children's deaths, particularly those who blamed the FSLN,
as acting against the wishes of their children, sullying their children's memory, and even contributing to the destruction of that for which their children had died. The implicit argument was that defense of the revolution
would assure that these precious lives had not been given in vain. According to the logic that this discourse entails, to truly respect these martyrs, one
must carry on their struggle. This, in turn, presented a strong social con-
straint against mothers of the fallen who were not politically mobilized or
who espoused anti-Sandinista views.

The Mothers of the Heroes and Martyrs as *Las Continuadoras*

Though the goals, priorities, and membership of the Mothers of the
Heroes and Martyrs varied over the years, reflecting economic and political
changes, the core of its collective identity revolved around this *La Continuadora* mobilizing identity. It provided the central framework around

which the Mothers organized and publicly defined their activities. With support and direction from the Sandinista state (1979–90), the Mothers organized memorials for Sandinista martyrs, offered economic and emotional support to mothers of fallen Sandinistas, opposed amnesty for Somocistas, campaigned for the safe return of those kidnapped by the contras, and demanded an end to the U.S.-financed contra war. The Committee of Mothers of Heroes and Martyrs served as a moral resource of the Sandinista state against right-wing propaganda. They symbolized the sacrifices made and Nicaraguans' obligations to uphold the Revolution. They also conducted propaganda work with mothers of draftees and war victims to deflect resentment away from the FSLN. For its own members, the Mothers' Committee provided an economic and emotional support group.

The Committee of Mothers of Heroes and Martyrs was formed by AMNLAE soon after the Sandinistas took power. Mothers of well-known Sandinistas who had visited prisons, circulated petitions, waged hunger strikes, and demonstrated on behalf of political prisoners and the disappeared during the 1970s were the leading figures of the committee. These mothers, such as Lidia Saavedra (mother of Daniel and Humberto Ortega), Santos Buitrago (mother of martyr Julio Buitrago), and Zulema Baltodano (mother of Mónica Baltodano), were mobilized soon after the fall of Somoza to keep alive the memory of fallen Sandinistas and call for punishment for those responsible for the deaths. It was also a way to publicly recognize the sacrifices made by older women.

The Mothers as *Las Continuadoras* became for the revolution the embodiment of the sacrifices made and the keepers of public memories. On anniversaries of battles in various cities, the Mothers led marches and occupied the front rows of assemblies honoring those who died. Throughout the 1980s, committees of Mothers in various cities established permanent records of the sacrifices of their children by testifying about their children's death and constructing monuments and galleries containing pictures and momentos of those who had died.

The Mothers also provided an effective counterattack against anti-Sandinista propaganda. For example, the mothers of Somocista and counterrevolutionary prisoners in the Sandinista jails were well publicized in *La Prensa* in the early 1980s, and in response to this campaign, Mothers of fallen Sandinistas carried signs at rallies reading: "Mother of the National

Guard, your son is in jail, and my son, where is he?"[93] The Mothers of Heroes and Martyrs were also featured in *Barricada* demanding lengthy prison sentences for imprisoned ex–National Guardsmen and contras. Already by 1981, the Mothers of Heroes and Martyrs were collectively denouncing contra aggressions and U.S. economic policies.[94] They compiled testimonies on the deaths of their children and presented them to international human rights organizations. A *Barricada* headline announced this project as "Mothers Will Present Their Pain to the World," suggesting the emotional response the mobilized mothers were meant to evoke nationally and internationally.[95]

A key task of the Mothers in the struggle for hegemony was to undermine the right-wing assertion that the FSLN was antireligious. During Pope John Paul II's visit to Nicaragua in 1983, Mothers of Heroes and Martyrs stood at the front of the crowd with signs bearing photographs of their children who had died. Their requests for a prayer on behalf of their children went unanswered by the Pope, who repeatedly demanded silence from the crowd.[96] Although conservative sources described this in *La Prensa* as a demonstration of disrespect against the Pope, the Mothers through *Barricada* interpreted the Pope's behavior as a denial of their pain and lack of understanding of the violent reality in Nicaragua. As *Barricada* put it, "Clearly frustrated and with tears in their eyes, the Mothers of Heroes and Martyrs went into the street to ask the Pope for a prayer for their children and a condemnation of the aggression. . . . The people fought to be heard."[97] In this framing of the event, the FSLN was not antireligious so much as the Catholic hierarchy had turned its back on the suffering of poor mothers.

A 1984 Pastoral Letter by the bishops urging dialogue between the FSLN and the contras countered this impression by claiming, "The suffering of mothers who have lost their children, deserving of all respect, consolation and assistance, is being manipulated to provoke hatred and lust for revenge."[98] The Mothers of Heroes and Martyrs, in turn, responded that Monseñor Obando y Bravo and the other bishops were the ones being manipulated, and the Mothers insisted against dialogue with the contras. They argued that the bishops were out of touch with the daily lives of the Nicaraguan people and challenged the bishops to accompany them to the Honduran border so that the bishops might witness the contra violence. One Mother said, "The bishops should have asked the people. We say to them that no one has manipulated us but rather imperialism has manipulated some bishops."[99] Another Mother refused dialogue with the contras, asserting, "If you don't know why, it is because you haven't had a child who was assassinated by genocidals."[100]

While their externally directed efforts served to undermine right-wing propaganda, local branches of the Mothers' Committee acted as mutual support groups where members could share their pain and work to overcome an often paralyzing grief, in addition to being exposed to revolutionary ideology. These committees worked to integrate into the revolutionary process a sector that was difficult to organize—women over forty years old who did not work outside the home or worked in the informal economy—while ensuring that the mothers, in their grief, did not come to resent the FSLN. These Mothers were repeatedly exhorted to "not sit home and cry all the time but rather to remember [their dead children] by being fully integrated in the defense of the revolution."[101] The Mothers' Committees raised funds through organizing raffles and selling food and clothing. These funds went to erect signs and monuments dedicated to fallen Sandinistas, help families with funeral costs, and support mothers who were sick or whose primary means of support had been their now-deceased children. Individual mothers also received pensions and supplies, and the committees received some government funding. And as a very popular gesture, the Sandinista government sent small Christmas gifts to the Mothers every year.

Mothers were mobilized into rearguard defense work primarily through the *Las Continuadoras* mobilizing identity. As Lidia Saavedra de Ortega said at a rally, "All of us mothers should integrate ourselves into the struggle in order to defend the revolution because this is why we are the Mothers [of Heroes and Martyrs]."[102] One prominent Sandinista told the Mothers, "You should demand that the ideals of your children be carried out because you have sufficient moral authority to demand it, to criticize it, to direct this process."[103] Thus the Mothers, armed with moral authority, became *Las Continuadoras*, stepping in where their children left off and defending the revolution on the ideological front.

By the time young men began to be drafted in early 1984, AMNLAE had focused on the war effort primarily through its work with the Mothers of Heroes and Martyrs and mothers of combatants. The objective was to increase support for the war and raise the morale of both combatants and their families through working with the mothers.[104] An AMNLAE leader explained: "Our rearguard job is to support with our organized action the combatants who are in the front line of fire, so that they know that here in the city there are women, men and children willing to back them not only morally and materially, but also support solidarity with their families."[105]

Fearing the worst and influenced by the Nicaraguan bishops' 1983 statement against the draft, many mothers resisted the drafting of sons. AMNLAE enlisted the Mothers of Heroes and Martyrs for ideological work in solidifying the support of mothers of draftees and held them up as symbols of the proper revolutionary behavior for soldiers' mothers. Mothers of fallen combatants were also organized to do political work with these mothers of draftees, visiting them regularly to give them moral and economic support as well as to raise their political consciousness by explaining the necessity of the draft and the ideological aspects of the war effort.

The Mothers of Heroes and Martyrs of Matagalpa gather for their biweekly meeting in the early 1990s.

❦ 2 ❦

MOVEMENT AS SYMBOL

The Mothers of Matagalpa, 1979–1984

Interviewer: Why did the *Frente* want to organize the Mothers?
Doña Juana: Because you know that in a revolution, the Mothers are the spearhead, a force that has a morality to it with which to confront whatever situation comes about. When there is some kind of situation, the Mothers are the first there. And respect is felt for mothers.

Thus the first coordinator of the Mothers of Matagalpa described the FSLN's interest in organizing mothers of the fallen. The Mothers were a morally irreproachable cultural "force" to be harnessed by this mobilizing regime. Thus, the Mothers of Matagalpa began—symbols of patriotic suffering, followers of the fallen. Between 1979 and 1984, the Mothers of Matagalpa were unremarkable compared to groups of Mothers of Heroes and Martyrs in other cities. Yet in 1984, they separated themselves from the FSLN's mass organization for women, AMNLAE, and began to explore their own interests and set their own policies.

The Mothers' city of Matagalpa is situated in the northern coffee-growing region of Nicaragua. The mountains surrounding the city have served as the staging grounds for guerrilla warfare since the earliest years of the Sandinista revolution. The population, now estimated at roughly 100,000, grew during the 1980s as refugees from the surrounding countryside fled the contra war. Matagalpa also served as a last stop for Sandinista troops before the mountains, where much of the war was fought. Accordingly, the Mothers of Matagalpa were perhaps closer to the revolution and contra war, in both a physical and emotional sense, than those of any other Nicaraguan city its size. In the early 1990s, with the rearming of ex-contras and ex-Sandinista soldiers, Matagalpa again experienced an inordinate amount of political violence.[1] The Committee of Mothers of Heroes and Martyrs in this city was a dynamic and resilient organization that, over fifteen years, had survived such drastic political and economic change as revolution, civil war, regime change, rapid urbanization, economic crisis, and neoliberalism.

An Identity-Centered Approach

Although dominant conceptions of motherhood exist in Nicaragua, ultimately "mother" is a fluid identity with no one representation fully and passively adopted by individual women. As seen in the last chapter, revolutionary movements, the state, and contending political parties mobilized the powerful imagery of motherhood in various ways. Although the Mothers of Matagalpa worked within dominant notions of the "good mother," they applied, ignored, and interpreted concepts found within the broader political and maternal discourses in order to build a common definition of themselves and to generate self-representations and demands. Having explored the dominant maternal representations projected upon women between 1977 and 1984, here I approach the construction of motherhood through an analysis of the Mothers of Matagalpa's collective identity—the process in which individuals establish a sense of unity with others and in turn develop shared goals and strategies.

Collective identity is not assumed here to be a given or a "thing" outside of time, but rather a key process to be analyzed.[2] In the study of an organization such as the Mothers, it is important not only to determine how the collectivity grew and made gains, but also to uncover how members came to see themselves as "the Mothers" in the first place. Why did collective action in the case of the Mothers of Matagalpa develop? How did individuals recognize their common situation and construct a common subjectivity? How and why did collective identity change over time? I problematize the existence of the Mothers' movement by analyzing the process through which individuals recognized that they shared certain orientations and on that basis developed guidelines for collective action.

In the process of collective identity, a more or less stable "we" is constructed through communication and negotiation concerning the goals of action, the means to be used, and the environment of opportunities and constraints.[3] Another dimension of this process is the making of "emotional investments, which enable individuals to recognize themselves in each other."[4] By searching for the meaning members attach to their collectivity and the sense of "we" they create, this approach helps us to understand why the Mothers of Matagalpa joined and maintained a political collectivity.

However, the analysis of collective identity must also include the mobilization of language, images, and dimensions of power both internal and external to the group. Internally, collective identity involves conflict. For example, the on-going struggle to define identity can also be a struggle over the allocation of both material and symbolic goods within a group. Externally, collective identity is structured by dominant discourses in concert with political and economic contexts. The sameness recognized among members of a collectivity is not pre-political; rather, collective identity is a negotiated process involving relations of power.

In addition to ideological structures, political and economic structural shifts also shape collective identity. This and later chapters show how civil war and regime change dramatically altered the resources, strategies, political alliances, and the potential membership base of the Mothers of Matagalpa. Furthermore, economic change, and its effect on individual members and potential members, was the key factor in the committee's rapid increase in membership after 1990, which in turn reshaped identity strategies, alliances, and resources. In this case, the FSLN "made" the Mothers of the Heroes and Martyrs, but it did not make them just as it pleased. The FSLN encountered circumstances of discourse transmitted from the past, projected by contenders, and imported from beyond Nicaraguan borders.

Mothers' Testimonials of Personal Loss

The Mothers knew each other's histories well. They knew the details of the deaths of many sons and daughters. They knew the story behind each other's physical and mental scars, behind the homelessness of some, behind the orphaned grandchildren of others. Their testimonies of suffering, tinged always with dignity and sometimes with triumph, generated the first and most basic current running between the Mothers. Their stories also inevitably reflected the mobilization of narratives promoted by the FSLN. The sharing of these testimonials with each other sparked the notion that indeed they shared a common identity. The following are several members' testimonials of tragic yet defining moments in their lives.

Many of the earliest members had personally experienced the repression of Somoza's National Guard (*la Guardia*). Doña María Eugenia lived in the town of San Isidro until she was forced to flee with her family in the mid-1970s, when the National Guard killed two of her sons and her husband. She and her family were early Sandinista supporters, delivering messages and supplying food for the guerrillas hiding in the mountains. One son was captured and shot by the guard. Another was put in a sack and beaten to death. Her husband died in a confrontation between guerrillas and soldiers, at which point her family lost its land and possessions. Though she found it very difficult to discuss this episode in her life, her few words attest to its horror: "*La Guardia* threw me out. We lost what we had because my husband had already been killed. When they killed him they threw me out and only gave me one minute, no more, for me to get out of the house. I grabbed what I could. I am a mother who has suffered a lot. In my own flesh I lifted my sons where they fell."

Some Mothers actively participated in the urban insurrections or the guerrilla warfare in the mountains. Doña María O., one of the youngest members at thirty-two, was from Pancasán, deep in *la montaña*. She came to Matagalpa as a refugee from the violence during the revolution. At the time of the interview, she lived in Barrio San Francisco, a poor neighborhood on a steep hill. She was a single mother who lived with two sisters and her three daughters and worked in the Mothers' used clothing store. In 1977, the National Guard massacred most of her family. She lost her newborn daughter in that massacre, but managed to carry her two-year-old to safety. Having lost nearly everything, María, at the age of seventeen, joined the ranks of the guerrillas. Extreme scarcity and a harsh climate endangered the child, so she left him with an FSLN collaborator. The boy soon died, yet María did not find out about her son's death until a year later, when she came down from *la montaña* to run "safe houses" in Managua during the insurrections.

When they massacred our parents we didn't have any other option but to go to the mountains with the *guerrilleros* because we were collaborators and *La Guardia* killed collaborators. . . . Twenty of my family died, including one child of mine and my newborn baby. . . . So we were in the *monte* with the guerrillas for two and a half years, suffering from hunger, rain, everything that came. That's how war is. . . .

I always worked with the *compañeros*, since I was fifteen. [We] went into the cities to buy things for [the *compañeros*] during dangerous times because *La Guardia* was there. . . . Once [my parents] died, we fully integrated ourselves into the guerrilla ranks, where we went around with the rifles, knapsacks—and I also carried my son in the mountains for six months. Six months! That is, my daughter was left behind in combat. She had only been born five days earlier. My other child was bigger, and I took him with me because we were fleeing in combat. . . . We fled because there were about fifty guardsmen and we were only left with five. I carried my child for six months in the guerrilla ranks, along with the knapsack and gun, sleeping under trees with the rain, soaked, hungry—everything. I worked in this way fourteen years ago. And here I am.

Mothers also experienced the repression through their sons and daughters—youth who were under suspicion in the late 1970s simply because of their age. Many of the Mothers spoke of their fear and anger at the National Guard's harassment of and violence toward youth in the years described as the time when it was a crime to be young. Doña Ventura, who brought up her fourteen children in Matagalpa, losing two of them in the early 1980s, recalled a few of the instances in which she had to go to great lengths to protect her teen-age son.

[When the insurrection began in Matagalpa] I went to the school and asked the teacher, "Please give me my son because *La Guardia* is going to kill him." So they brought him to me, and I held him like this [she holds her hands behind her], so that if *La Guardia* shot at us, they would kill me first—so that first they would kill me and then kill him. This son, he lost half his little finger because of a bomb. The repression was horrible before against the young people. When we took him to the hospital, the doctor said that he was going to amputate the whole hand! We said, "If you do that, we're going to amputate your head!" We understood what was going on. And they didn't do it. They were afraid. It was horrible. I hope to God this never returns. I hope to God that we never go back to that. So much suffering.

Many Mothers first learned about revolutionary politics through their children as they were becoming active in the Frente Sandinista. As the Mothers often said of their children, "For us, they were our teachers." Their political consciousness continued to develop long after their children died, motivating them to "carry on the struggle" as *Las Continuadoras*. Doña María L. told of her son's influence:

We were fighters on behalf of our children—those who fell in the insurrection. We supported the struggle of our children. . . . I already knew that they were fighting because I was the best confidant for my son. He said, "Mama, some day we're going to triumph and the poor, the humble, the *campesinos* are going to be first. They're going to have a roof to live under. They're going to have their land. . . . They're not going to be marginalized. They're not going to be slaves to the millionaires." This is what we fought for. With this great love we fought and continue fighting. We know that one day, with our faith in God, there is going to be a definitive peace and each person is going to have their place—the poor, the humble, the exploited. And so our children aren't going to die. . . . They're not dead as long as we struggle.

One of the leaders of the Mothers and an active member since its beginning, Doña Elsa told the story, through a stream of tears, of her relationship with her daughter Martina in Martina's last year of life. Martina was a university student and Sandinista combatant who had died just a few months before the FSLN victory in a guerrilla attack against the National Guard in the city of León. In Doña Elsa's *La Continuadora* narrative, her daughter gives (re)birth to her mother, and she, the mother, is reborn through the ideals, examples, and lessons of life (and death) of her daughter. With brave determination, Doña Elsa secretly removed her daughter's body from the hospital morgue under the nose of *La Guardia*, which was looking to arrest whomever claimed the body.

My daughter fell right before the triumph. I went to recover her body in León. I washed her skin, closed her eyes. I didn't cry one bit. I said, "I'm not going to cry, daughter. I have to be brave like you were. You were brave. I am brave because you came from me. I'm not going to shed a tear, and I'm not going to let anyone see that I am your mother." Clearly you feel it, and you cry when no one can see you. But what would have happened if I had gone sobbing to take my daughter out of the hospital where *La Guardia* was waiting and waiting?

Three bullets had entered her. Her body was torn apart. Nonetheless, she died happy. She had a happiness about her as if she were laughing. As if she were saying, "I triumphed!" That's how it was the day she fell. She was a woman who, when she entered into something, she entered into it completely. And I knew what she was doing and why she did it. And so this courage stays with you. . . .

Some time before that, she was in an accident. She had participated in an assault, a secret operation. [During their escape] the boy who was driving the truck was wounded and he crashed. She hit her head and had two huge gashes on her face. Her face was full of glass. She didn't know if they were her teeth or glass! We were in full war. It was during the insurrections in León and Matagalpa. And there she was, soaked in blood. She got out of the truck—because I tell you that this woman had balls! She told them to leave her, and she would catch a ride [to the hospital]. When she got [there] . . . the doctor operated on her without anesthesia! I said to her, "You are a ballsy woman. I never thought that you would be able to endure this operation." When they came to tell me that she was in the hospital the woman had said, "You aren't going to recognize her. She looks like a monster." And when I arrived her face was very inflamed. I cleaned her and said, "No, daughter, you don't have anything on your face. You are fine, my little girl." I thought to myself, some day, when all this has passed, her children are going to ask why she has these scars on her face. And I am going to say that she was fighting with the Frente Sandinista, and that is why she has these scars. After that, she only lived six months longer.

Doña Elsa joined AMPRONAC after her daughter died. Stating more than once that "our children were prophets," Doña Elsa, like so many early members of the Mothers, saw her child's death as a sacrifice so that more people would organize and build the revolution. The fallen combatants were prophets, divinely inspired teachers, she explained: "Because our parents were very tame, very weak, very submissive, but our children taught us other ideas." As such, Doña Elsa not only felt an obligation to carry on where her daughter left off, but also her political consciousness was fundamentally altered through the example set by her martyred daughter.[5]

In the Mothers of Matagalpa's discourse on the revolutionary period, we find traditional gender and generational roles sometimes turned on their heads: single women who were both mothers and fathers to their children; children who gave [re]birth to their mothers; youth who were the teachers of their parents' generation; mothers who were combatants. These nontraditional gender and generational relationships demonstrate how the revolution altered people's everyday lives and identities. The new roles were described by the Mothers in a language of both obligation and empowerment. Informed by the Popular Church's theology of liberation, the discourse of the Sandinista revolution involved the shedding of the blood of innocents ("the country's best sons and daughters") to atone for sin. Death and resurrection. The sacrifice was staggering—displacement, torture, rape, killings—but it came to be seen in many Mothers' eyes as necessary: "The price of freedom is the cross."[6] The martyred sons and daughters bore the cross so that others (the "New Men" of the revolution) might teach and be taught, speak and be heard. As the FSLN reframed these relationships through its institutions (most notably its news media, schools, and political organizations), apparent contradictions settled into coexistence: grief with joy, loss with gain, death with rebirth.

Members of the committee gained fluency in the maternal discourse through the retelling of the stories of their losses and the incremental application of various interpretations of events. Such interpretations were shaped in the hegemonic struggle waged by the FSLN and the counterrevolution. Upon the sharing of testimonials, themes such as loss through gain, fallen children as prophets, and mothers as *Las Continuadoras* became more familiar to members, and thus their sense of sameness and shared experience deepened and their mobilization was channeled.

"A Mother Feels More Pain than a Father": The Construction of Specificity in Maternal Collective Identity

As Jean Cohen argues, "It is necessary to analyze those aspects of experience that shape the interpretation of interests, individual and collective, and affect the very capacity of actors to form groups and mobilize."[7] Integral to the Mothers' discourse was the notion that maternal experience uniquely shaped women's interpretation of the value of human life.[8] The maternal experience that included maternal loss fed the emotional bond between members, but at the same time it nurtured a language of maternal specificity. Their maternal identity involved constructions as to their uniqueness, thus securing a border between "us" and "them."

Such differences, although they may draw from biological differences (in this case, women's ability to bear children), are socially constructed. Furthermore, status is derived from such constructs of difference, as difference is presented as giving the group special access to knowledge. In order to explore the Mothers' notions of their specificity and uncover experiences that shaped their interests, emotions, and identification with each other, I asked, "Why were there no Fathers of the Heroes and Martyrs?"

In her interviews of mothers of the disappeared in Chile, Patricia Chuchryk asked why their organizations were comprised primarily of women:

> The women considered the question to be irrelevant. . . . Upon reflection, some suggested that above all, men are the heads of families and therefore cannot get involved for fear of losing their jobs. It was also suggested that the men who had participated during the beginning probably felt isolated, whereas the women felt companionship with other women. Furthermore, they felt that they, as women, had more time than men to devote to such activity. In any case, all of the suggestions were based on some notion of women's traditional roles.[9]

In my interviews, this question also caught many Mothers off-guard. The differences between mothers and fathers and the implausibility of having a committee of fathers seemed so obvious to them. But their responses varied somewhat from those of the Chilean mothers. Although some stated that women have more time than men because men work, and a number felt that

men are more individualistic, these responses assumed that a male companion existed in the first place and that this companion had work—an unlikely
situation for the Mothers of Matagalpa.

More commonly, their explanations centered on the question of who
suffers more at the loss of a son or daughter—the mother or the father.
While no one responded that men suffer more, a very few women argued
that fathers and mothers suffer equally at the loss of a child. Doña Bibiana,
one of the oldest members at eighty-one, lost one son and three grandchildren in the contra war. She explained: "A father is the same as a mother;
they suffer. My son has three fallen children, and he cries when he remembers them. It afflicts him completely. . . . He is like a mother, I say, because
he has suffered." Yet, as her response reveals, the term *father* does not evoke
images of suffering and grief quite like the term *mother*, and so this motherlike father is more the exception to the rule in Nicaraguan society.

Several other Mothers stressed that the father's suffering depended upon
his relationship with the rest of the family. A father's involvement in and
dedication to the home and family life will lead him to grieve the death
of a child. However, in the common case of an absent or detached father,
the death of a child will have a much greater impact on the mother. Doña
Teofila, who was abused and abandoned by her first husband, deliberated
over the issue: "If the father loves the child, he suffers because my [second]
husband suffered for his child. But in analyzing it, it is clear that it is harder
on the mother because in this country the majority of the mothers raise their
children almost alone. The man only gets her pregnant and then leaves.
And so it is clear that here the mother suffers more. The mother serves as
both mother and father."

Published interviews of mothers of the disappeared in Argentina and El
Salvador reveal that these women avoided the debilitating anguish they saw
in their husbands by actively searching for their children and then mobilizing with other mothers, always vocalizing their demands and communicating their grief with others.[10] Although the fathers were also deeply hurt by
the disappearances, the women claimed that the fathers dealt with it in an
individual, inexpressive, isolated manner.

Similarly, the Mothers of Matagalpa sometimes explained that although
fathers suffered when their children died, they hid it because of machismo.
These Mothers criticized the system of machismo that forbids men from

showing grief and crying. A mother's response to loss—open grieving—was considered to be more legitimate, honest, and healthy. Doña Chepita told me that her husband—who was not the real father of her eldest son—suffered so at the death of this son that he drank himself to death:

Men aren't like us women. It is easier for us to release all our grief. A man can be crying, but he doesn't let others see him cry. Men always want to hide their feelings. And we do not.... [And so] to say that the mother suffers most is untrue. It's like I said—the father always hides [his feelings]. They don't connect with others; they don't feel comfortable showing their feelings, unlike us. Men never want to lower themselves. They never want someone else to say, "He's not a man because he cries." And this is not true! I tell you, the man who cries from pain is the better man. [Men] deal with their pain in a different way. They drink in order to forget. And perhaps this is worse. We women come together, perhaps we have some activity. We feel in the middle of everything. We trust each other. We laugh, perhaps we sing a song. And men don't.

Doña Ventura described how her husband sank into a deep depression and went to live alone in the mountains following the death of their two sons. "When we lost our [first] son, he lost control. He isn't right in the head." She asserted that the machista belief that men are emotionally stronger is false. Women, she believed, are able to suffer through and survive much worse episodes in life than men. "Men are different, like I was telling you. Men suffer alone. . . . Men are weaker, I say. And I have suffered through more. But that's the way it is—we have to suffer more, we mothers." Referring to this perceived male weakness, she laughingly added, "We Mothers say we don't have husbands for this reason!"

These Mothers of Matagalpa described the difference between mothers and fathers in terms of their ability to deal with strong emotions. Although men grieved alone if they grieved at all, women gained strength by openly expressing and sharing their grief, and they united on that basis. This is also similar to the responses of Chilean mothers of the disappeared described by Chuchryk, who suggested that while men felt isolated, women felt companionship with other women.[11]

Among those I interviewed, however, the clearly dominant view was that mothers suffer more than fathers at the loss of a child. Genera, who lost her brother in the contra war and worked closely with her mother in the Mothers' Committee, explained the dynamics of grief in her own family and Nicaraguan families in general: "[The death of a child] is harder for the mother. It seems that mothers are more emotional. They have more love for the children. This is because of their experiences. There are fathers who care little if their child dies or leaves or whatever. But the mother isn't like that. A mother hurts more for the children. It is true that the father works, but it is the mother who feels more for her child."

Doña Josefina, a single mother normally shy and soft-spoken, was adamant on this point. She used specific examples to make her case that the mother-child bond and sense of responsibility was stronger than between father and child, leading mothers to suffer more upon losing a child. She recalled trips she took into the war zones to see her son, zones where ambush was always a threat and where in 1985 a group of mothers and family members (all female) traveling to see men in the army were brutally attacked and killed. This tragic incident touched Nicaraguans deeply, and several Mothers referred to it as an example of mothers' devotion to their children.

> The father isn't going to suffer like us mothers. For example, if my son hasn't come by 8:00 in the morning, I am thinking all sorts of things. "What could have happened to my son?" The father isn't like that. During the war we didn't sleep, thinking about what could have happened to one of our children. I went to San Jose de Bocay, to Cua to see my son [in the army] when the war was in full swing. They told me not to go [because] something could happen to me, but I didn't pay any attention and always went to see him under any condition. I went with other mothers. There were no buses. It was prohibited because [the contras] could lay down mines. I refused to be held back. I always went, and the father didn't. He didn't worry. Only mothers went. Nobody is going to tell you that fathers died going to see their children. Only mothers died.

Mothers also spoke of the gendered division of labor to explain the lack of activism on the part of fathers. For example, when asked why the committee was composed of only women, some women pointed out that many of the fathers worked in the countryside or worked less flexible hours and were thus unable to attend meetings. For example, Doña Leonor, one of the few middle-class members (her husband was a self-employed car mechanic and several children lived in the United States) commented: "The fathers always have more problems with their work. Since they are the ones that work, they can't form an organization. And we mothers—women—are different. After working we can go more places. We have more time to be organized." Yet this is more of a middle-class ideal than reality for most members. The majority of Mothers were either widows or single mothers, unemployed and/or living with men who were unemployed.

Doña Esperanza C., who became the coordinator of the Mothers in 1984, added that only Mothers were actively organized by the FSLN when a soldier fell. Fathers were virtually ignored in this respect.

> It is desirable to involve fathers also. . . . Perhaps it's an error because the children didn't come just from us. . . . Always there was an invitation to the mother and not to [both] the father and mother. I believe that it came from political principles. Politics had something to do with this, it seems to me, in that only the mother was recognized and not saying, "The son of this father fell." The father was separate from it all.
>
> I don't know . . . if it was due to too much machismo that men always have some of. So it is like it would be a big leap to say "mother" and then "father" also. Understand? That is what it seems to me. But some women—it's like she's looking for some way to leave [her house] and have her own place, to have a little more freedom.

Thus, the absence of fathers was in part due to deliberate political design—which in turn reinforced a traditional gendered division in Nicaraguan society. But there was some ambivalence among the Mothers as to whether fathers should participate more in the committee, which offered women a special place of their own.

The Pain of Childbirth and the High Cost of Raising a Child

Sara Ruddick presents an analysis of women's thinking as it develops out of the work that mothers do—feeding, clothing, nurturing, protecting, and training their children.[12] According to her, this "maternal thinking" offers an alternative reasoning that does not separate truth from bodies or reason from feelings.[13] Although women do engage in and promote war, Ruddick claims that "maternal practice is a 'natural resource' for peace politics."[14] Thus, "a pure maternal peacefulness does not exist; what does exist is far more complicated: a deep unease with military endeavors not easily disentangled from patriotic and maternal impulses to applaud, connect, and heal; a history of caring labor interwoven with the romance of violence and the parochial self-righteousness on which militarism depends."[15] As we have seen, mothers in Nicaragua promoted and even fought in the revolution and war. Nonetheless, my interviews with the Mothers also revealed a narrative that privileged mothers' labor (both birthing labor and the labor of raising a child) as an exclusive source of knowledge concerning the costs of war.

In explaining why they believed that mothers suffered more at the death of a child than fathers, and in turn why they developed an organization to deal with this singular pain, the Mothers often stressed the importance of pregnancy, birth, and raising a child in creating an incomparable mother-child bond. As Ruddick wrote of the mothers of the disappeared of Chile and Argentina:

[They] invariably evoke an experience of mothering that is central to their lives, whatever other home work or wage labor they engage in. Repeatedly they remember and allude to ordinary tasks—clothing, feeding, sheltering. . . .

As these women honor mothering, they honor themselves. The destruction of the lives of their children, often just on the verge of adulthood, destroys years of their work. . . . Yet there is something misleading about this way of talking. The women do not speak of their work but of their children; they carry children's photographs, not their own. The distinctive structuring of the relation between self and other, symbolized in birth and enacted in mothering, is now politicized.[16]

This passage also speaks to the experience of the Mothers of Matagalpa. They repeatedly alluded to an emotional and physical bond between mother and child, melded through the dependence, pain, and regular contact in daily maternal labor. Doña Geronima, who was separated from her husband, explained to me, "[The death of a child] is more painful [for the mother] because the father creates the child then goes off to work. He isn't seeing the children all day. But the mother lives her life giving them food. She lives cleaning them."

The Mothers' responses often dealt explicitly with the body, their gendered, female bodies, and their (socially constructed) emotional responses to embodied experiences. Many spoke of the fetus's dependence on the womb and the painful birth: "For the mother, the child was in her womb; she felt the pain of giving birth to the child. And so perhaps [the death of a child] is harder for the mother" (Doña Carmen). "Clearly a mother suffers more because the child was in the womb, and you felt the pain of mothers [giving birth]. And you were raising that child" (Doña Rosaura). To the Mothers of Matagalpa, the experience of pregnancy and the pain of labor left an indelible emotional mark and an unbreakable bond that gave them privileged knowledge about the cost of bringing a child into the world.

Olive Schreiner, a South African pacifist-feminist, wrote, "No woman who is a woman says of a human body, 'it is nothing.' . . . On this one point, and on this point almost alone, the knowledge of woman, simply as woman, is superior to that of man; she knows the history of human flesh; she knows its cost; he does not."[17] This notion of superior maternal knowledge that in part defines "woman" and differentiates her from "man" is a dominant theme in the maternal discourse of the Nicaraguan Mothers. The Mothers of Matagalpa spoke of the "cost" of human flesh, making three distinctions as to the nature of these costs: the physical costs involved in pregnancy and giving birth; the labor and emotional costs invested in the raising of a child; and the monetary costs of feeding, clothing, educating, and protecting a child. The following statements by Doña Lourdes and Doña Esperanza R., both single mothers, testify to the costs of children in these three terms.

> *Doña Lourdes:* The one who feels [the loss of a child] is the mother. It is a feeling that is never erased. Every minute we remember because we mothers are the ones that gave the child its food, loved it. In reality, a child costs the mother more than the father. . . . You raised that child! You gave birth to it! And as it left the womb, you felt it!
>
> *Doña Esperanza R.:* The child costs the mother more than the father [because] the fathers don't carry the child in the womb. The father doesn't feel the pain of childbirth. The father gives the money that he gives and goes off

to work. And the work of raising the children, of cleaning them, attending to them is done by the mother.

Doña Esperanza R. here makes a gendered distinction between the three "costs" in raising a child: the father's financial costs and the mother's physical and emotional costs. According to this narrative, although a child might cost a father financially, the loss of the child does not imply the heavy emotional toll felt by mothers.

Some Mothers did speak more directly about the intensive amount of labor and financial resources mothers invested in children. Such investments were seen as particularly relevant to single mothers, such as Doña Chepita, who supported herself and her young children by working a plot of land she received through the Mothers of Matagalpa. She described how she tried, against her sons' will, to get him out of the draft because she had raised him alone under extremely stressful economic circumstances, alluding to her expectation that he would take care of her in her old age: "I would say, 'Look son, you're the only one. I raised you with so much sacrifice.' He was little, about three years old, when his father died, so I would say, 'Look son, I sacrificed so much to raise you. I'm going to look for some way so that they don't recruit you.'" Her son Ulises joined the Sandinista army at the age of fifteen and died at seventeen.

The Mothers invariably spoke of sacrifice, of investment, and of love. They spoke of the grief they felt at the loss of a life that they had created and nurtured. In this maternal discourse, individuality gave way to a self/other bond created through blood shared in pregnancy and blood shed in birth — a bond that was only strengthened in the raising of a child. Through this fusion of self and other — to destroy fruit of my womb is to destroy me — the mother was destroyed but went on living.

The importance of the link these mothers made between pain at the birth of a child and suffering at the death of that child, and in turn the link formed between mothers of the fallen by their shared experience, was uniquely illustrated by Doña Juana C. She offered that perhaps mothers who gave birth through caesarian sections did not suffer as much to lose their children: "I believe that the pain [of a mother upon the death of a child] has to be the same pain, independent of the position of each mother because I believe that to give birth to a child—well, perhaps those that have a caesarian don't feel this pain of natural childbirth, I don't know—but I say that if they are born by natural childbirth, one feels the same pain. Perhaps these mothers who had their children by operations don't feel the same pain." In other words, if the pain of natural childbirth is the same for all mothers, the pain of losing a child must be the same, regardless of each mother's individual situation. As a rule, the Mothers stressed their sameness, their equality in this respect.

In sum, because fathers had not physically experienced pregnancy and the birth of their children, and, if present at all, were less involved in the daily domestic life and had less contact with their children, most of the Mothers interviewed said that fathers felt the death of a child less intensely. The daily routine was less disrupted for the father and his emotional ties to his children were weaker, so the sudden severing of those ties was less dramatic. Men were also less economically dependent on adult children, while many women of this class considered their children as their future providers—a traditional form of social security. Indeed, upon the death of a soldier, the pension was received by the mother and/or the wife, not the father. Moreover, according to the Mothers, men's incapacity or unwillingness to express emotions over the loss of a child also inhibited their ability or likelihood to organize. As such, men generally did not seek out a forum such as the Mothers' Committee to help them deal with the death of a child.

Perhaps most importantly, as the Mothers' responses imply, "father" did not represent a strong individual identity for men of their class background in Nicaragua, nor was the experience of fatherhood—which lacked a physical experience comparable to the intensity of pregnancy and labor—as fundamental to men's interpretations of their interests. The manner in which Father's Day is celebrated in Nicaragua reveals the lack of status given to fatherhood and the failure of most fathers to live up to paternal ideals (which are less demanding than maternal ideals). Although Mother's Day in Nicaragua is celebrated with flowers and odes to the endless love and sacrifices of mothers, Father's Day provides an opportunity to discuss fathers' shortcomings. On this day in the early 1990s, fathers commonly were reminded of their obligations through various media. In 1992, television advertisements encouraged fathers to spend time with their children, children prepared skits in school on paternal neglect, and newspapers published articles criticizing absent or abusive fathers. For example, in Barricada's Sunday supplement for children on Father's Day, a cartoon portrayed children putting on a play that was critical of fathers. This cartoon addressed paternal abuse and neglect, men's unwillingness to communicate, and the strain these placed on family stability. In the first act of the cartoon play, a father yells for his lunch and brusquely tells his son not to bother him. In the second act, once the father has left for work, the following dialogue occurs:

> *Boy:* "I don't think that he loves us."
>
> *Mother:* "What are you saying, son! Of course he loves us."
>
> *Boy:* "What a way to show it! Shouting, hitting, mistreatment, and whatever he feels like."
>
> *Mother:* "It's because your father has many problems."
>
> *Boy:* "And who doesn't?"
>
> *Mother:* "You're right! Your father only knows how to shout. He never says what is wrong so that we can help him."
>
> *Boy:* "Yes, but who can put up with such a grouch?"
>
> In the third act, the father returns from work.
>
> *Father:* "I'm home and I'm hungry!"
>
> *Mother:* "Sit down, I'll serve you."
>
> *Father:* "How many times do I have to tell you . . . !"
>
> *Mother:* "Don't say another word. That's it. I won't support this anymore. You're on your own. We have put up with enough!"

The curtain closes and the children clap. Then a girl addresses the children in the audience: "Do you like this? Are there papas like this? How would we like our papas to be? I would like it if my papa were affectionate. And you?" The children answer:

> "If he was loving."
>
> "If he didn't shout."
>
> "If he was good."
>
> "If he was nice."
>
> "If he didn't hit."
>
> "If he understood us."
>
> "If he didn't mistreat us."

The girl responds, "OK then, all together!" And the children in the audience, with certain irony, yell in unison, "Happy Father's Day!"[18]

Clearly, in many homes, there was estrangement and even animosity between fathers and their children. Thus, while mothers were put on a ped-
estal, fathers rarely measured up to the fuzzily developed paternal ideal.
Within the system of machismo, which prioritizes sexual conquest and
virility over paternal responsibility and affection, there was little status to
be attained through this paternal ideal and not much of a basis upon which
to build a collective identity based on fatherhood.[19]

Beginnings of a Collective Identity and the Goals
of Consolation and Propaganda

The Committee of Mothers of Heroes and Martyrs of Matagalpa formed
in the first week of December 1979. As noted, the Mothers' Committee
was not simply a spontaneous collective reaction to Somoza atrocities or
the result of a collective maternal instinctual desire to carry on where their
fallen children left off. Although the Sandinista media tended to present
the Mothers of Heroes and Martyrs as a group that arose "organically" from
the members themselves, they were originally created by the FSLN, particularly through AMNLAE and its predecessor AMPRONAC.[20] Indeed, the
Mothers' Committee of Matagalpa did not even have its own coordinator
until 1983; before then, its meetings were presided over by an AMNLAE
representative. Analysis of Sandinista documents as well as my interviews
with party officials who worked closely with the Mothers reveals three primary objectives in organizing mothers of the fallen. First, the FSLN sought
to draw a group of grieving and potentially resentful mothers into the Sandinista fold, allowing AMNLAE to give them "special attention" (emotional
and some financial support as well as consciousness-raising and ideological
training). Second, like all FSLN mass organizations, the Mothers were to
provide a communication link between this sector of women and the party.
Third, the Mothers were seen as an effective vehicle through which to mobilize the imagery of motherhood in FSLN propaganda efforts.

Doña Elsa A. spoke of how she became active in AMPRONAC and,
in turn, participated as one of the first Mothers of Heroes and Martyrs of
Matagalpa who set out to gather more Mothers into AMNLAE. As Doña
Elsa notes, in the early years of the revolutionary regime, AMNLAE home

visits provided valuable information concerning who was pro- and anti-Sandinista.

> When my daughter fell, I joined AMPRONAC. I went to a number of meetings. So it was easy for me to continue being organized [after the triumph] since I was organized from the start. . . .
>
> *Interviewer:* What did AMPRONAC do?
>
> Meetings, and analyzing the situation, seeing how it was. How the *muchachos* were dying. And [it worked] to better prepare the mothers who had lost their children. To prepare them and visit them, to not forget them. That's how I met many Mothers, *many* Mothers. And this made me want to visit and get to know the families—[to find out] who was the mama, who was the papa, what did they think? We buried [their children]. And this way you hear things and analyze the situation. And you find out who is in agreement [with the FSLN] and who isn't. So I knew many Mothers, and after the triumph, all we had to say was, "Over here there is so and so." . . . After the triumph, when it was AMNLAE, that's how we went about collecting the Mothers. Some wanted to participate; others didn't because they didn't see how it would benefit them. That's how it is.[21]

Through visits, talks, and even help in burying the dead, contacts were made and alliances were established as it became known who was for and against the revolution. The Mothers' Committee was first formed in this way—through the dedication of AMNLAE women who were also Mothers of Heroes and Martyrs and who went door to door to learn about, comfort, and recruit new Mothers.

With the intensification of the contra war, the Mothers gained new purpose. As more youth died, the FSLN, through the media and grassroots organizations, saw to it that Mothers' anger was channeled, their resentment redirected, their protests planned for them, and their image appropriated, all for the larger purpose of winning the war.[22] Doña María L. was one of the founders in 1979 of the Mothers' Committee in the nearby city of Jinotega and later became a core member of the Mothers of Matagalpa: "Then we were about six mothers; we joined together as Mothers in AMNLAE. That's where all the work of the Mothers began. And then the war started— or continued. Each time a *compañero* fell, we worked hard in persuasion [of the mother], collecting together all these mothers to our organization. We had to look after them, to accompany them in their suffering."

Doña Juana, the Mothers' coordinator when it operated under AMNLAE, described the early years of the committee:

[In the early 1980s] the committee was formed with very few Mothers because the insurrection had just occurred. Then we saw again that it was necessary to organize because the North American government was financing [the counterrevolution], and . . . so more boys had fallen. So the committee started growing. At this time the committee was directed by AMNLAE, and the Frente had its hands in it. There wasn't freedom for the organization. . . . I believe that we worked as women there, representing other women, no more than that.

Here, Doña Juana touched upon an important contradiction within the FSLN's framing of its mass organizations. On the one hand, these organizations were to promote participatory democracy by communicating the concerns of the masses to the party. On the other hand, they were to obediently promote the political projects of the FSLN in order to protect the revolution.[23] In instances in which these two goals conflicted, the stability of the revolution always took precedence. As Katherine Hoyt explained, "The organizations were to represent the aspirations of their members but at the same time make those members understand when the higher interests of the revolution as decided by the leaders might supersede their interests and needs."[24] This prompted Doña Juana to assert, "There wasn't freedom for the organization."

As an auxiliary to AMNLAE, the Mothers of Matagalpa could be depended upon to support the demands of other pro-FSLN organizations, to stage demonstrations against contra atrocities and civilian counterrevolutionary claims, and to recount the tale of the death of their loved ones to foreign delegations and the media. As then-coordinator Doña Juana explained: "When solidarity brigades came, we had to give testimonies so that the brigades knew the truth that we had suffered and so that they knew what a revolution was—what had been fought for and why we were organized, in order to continue the struggle of our children."

Their grief was recognized, yet as Doña Gregoria recalled, they were regarded more as objects to be mobilized than as subjects with their own needs and ideas:

> *Interviewer:* What did you do in the first years with AMNLAE?
>
> Nothing. Best to say nothing because there were only meetings.
>
> *Interviewer:* What did you talk about?
>
> Politics. The fallen *muchachos*. The contra. At first with AMNLAE there were only about ten of us, no more. And so perhaps we were together to lessen the pain. They invited us to meetings, to protests. We went to protests in the streets against the Honduran government and the U.S. embassy in Managua. We would go in a bus. We went all over.

Doña Lourdes and Doña Berta spoke of AMNLAE's dependence on the Mothers to fill rallies and marches: "AMNLAE, they needed the support of the Mothers for their activities, marches, protests—for whatever. And so we were organized as Mothers in AMNLAE" (Doña Lourdes). "It was necessary to go when there were demonstrations in the streets. When we worked with AMNLAE, we had a lot of work to do, we met often. Many delegations from other countries came and we had to receive them and have interviews with them" (Doña Berta). The Mothers' recollections of this period generally reflected a lack of agency—they were followers rather than leaders. In sum, the focus of the committee in this period was on consoling Mothers and mobilizing them as Sandinista combatants on the propaganda frontline. As such, the Mothers had their agenda planned for them and were invited to their own protests.

Until 1984, the Mothers of Matagalpa, along with mothers of draftees, were given talks about the current economic and political crises and were placed at the head of marches and rallies to represent revolutionary sacrifice. Before the counterrevolution turned into a full war, only a few core mothers of fallen children were fully mobilized into projects or propaganda campaigns. Most mothers of the fallen were expected to attend meetings and rallies, and little else. Indeed, the most active and politically conscious Mothers focused their efforts outside of the Mothers' Committee on AMNLAE, Sandinista Defense Committees (CDS), or the pro-Sandinista popular church—organizations with projects that they felt made a more direct impact on the community.

Doña Elsa explained the Mothers of Heroes and Martyrs' slow start as having to do with the Mothers' political inexperience and lack of education. When she joined the Mothers, it was as a student of sorts.[25]

> We were mothers who didn't know how to read, write. We were like new-born infants being taught how to eat, being taught how to walk, being cared for. And so we were some mothers who knew nothing about organizations, about what was the Frente, what the party was about. We joined to know, to see why our children died. . . . They said that those who caused the war were the same *Guardia* [of Somoza], that we shouldn't allow the enemy to pass. They told us where so-and-so fell, where a mobilization was, when we had to go.

This suggests the important role both AMNLAE and the Mothers of Heroes and Martyrs played in disseminating party ideology and the mobilizing identities. For example, Mothers who attended to learn "why their children died" also learned why and how they should carry on the struggle. As such, members did not necessarily join because they already saw themselves as *Las Continuadoras*. Rather, in this period it seems that women were often first mobilized because AMNLAE and other Mothers of Heroes and Martyrs actively recruited them through visits and invitations. In the process of attending these, they were exposed to a Sandinista ideology that included a maternal mobilizing identity that helped them both make sense of their loss and develop a sense of solidarity. Thus, through the process of joining and participating, they became *Las Continuadoras*.

Mothers: Messengers of Death and New Life

In my interviews with the Mothers, they stressed the healing effects of their committee and spoke of how they urged other women to join them—to leave the house and discuss their loss with mothers who shared their pain. The importance of this contact with the Mothers' Committee was not lost upon the Sandinista army. In the early years of the contra war, the FSLN recruited Mothers of Heroes and Martyrs through AMNLAE to deliver the news of war deaths and comfort the grieving family, hoping to lessen resentment and check counterrevolutionary propaganda. The Mothers, it was believed, had the moral authority both to give sympathy and facilitate consciousness-raising with the family. The Mothers of Matagalpa explained this process in their 1984 progress report sent to the Matagalpa FSLN: "Each time that there are fallen *compañeros*, we accompany the new mother of this movement in this difficult moment, but we also prevent the enemies of the Revolution from taking advantage of the family's grief. We work to rescue all the mothers whom we find isolated or resentful until we convince them that we confront problems better united."[26] In Doña Nacha's words,

> Wars are horrible. AMNLAE would come in the middle of the night—those who collected the dead and brought notice. We delivered so many dead. They would come to [us] and say, "We are going to deliver some bodies that are going to arrive at, say, one or two in the morning." [We went ahead to notify the family.] And do you know why we did this? Because . . . we knew how [the mother's] heart would stop as we told her, "The one that we bring is your child." We were sent ahead of the rest to prepare her, to cry with her. . . . We went first to accompany her as other mothers. And also to talk with her. We cried as much as she did! The death hit her like it hit us because to deliver the dead child was like the delivery of our own dead child. And so we tried to make things easier on her, telling her, "Pray to God to give you strength so that you can go on because if you only cry, nothing else is going to get done."
>
> When you lose your child it seems to you that you're the only one that this has happened to. And you ask, "Why? Why?" You stop eating because of your nerves, and so you become depressed. But later you begin to reflect and see that they had to die so that many things are gained.

Here we find the theme of losing in order to gain, which was key to Sandinista discourse on martyrdom. Doña Nacha touched upon the development of this political consciousness encouraged by reflection upon the meaning of the death. The Mothers of Heroes and Martyrs were an effective conduit through which to carry out the construction and dissemination of the meaning of death in war in a manner conducive to Sandinista victory.

As such, in addition to emotional support, the aim of the visit was political as well. During the visit the Mothers, as representatives of the FSLN, helped the family make wake and burial arrangements and informed the mother about government benefits and pensions. If the mother of the dead soldier showed resentment toward the FSLN—and many did—the visiting Mothers tried to refocus her anger on the contras.

> *Doña Leonor:* They called on me many times to visit these mamas and it was very hard to go to a house and tell a mama, "Your son fell." . . . Now many mamas blame the Frente, but the Frente never was to blame because the Frente never said, "Kill them." It was the contra that killed them. . . . At least ten died every day. . . .
>
> [The mothers] would start to cry and they would ask how could it be that their children died. Some reacted badly. They would say, "This isn't my son." And, "It's the Frente's fault that my son fell." In this work we would say to them that it wasn't the Frente that was killing them. It was the contra. If the contra weren't in the mountains, they wouldn't have died.
>
> *Doña Carmen:* A group of Mothers would go to talk with a mother whose child had just died, to unite her with our organization, because many were left resentful because their child had died. We knew how to talk with her, to tell her that the same had happened to us. Then we would bring her to the committee.

Through consoling so many grieving mothers, this small group developed a stronger sense of what it meant to be a Mother of the Heroes and Martyrs. In this visit they acted out the role of "Mother of Heroes and Martyrs," thus both constructing and solidifying their own sense of a maternal collective identity. In acting out an identity, putting image into practice, individual members had to clarify to themselves what the identity involved, and they were forced to fill in the blanks, to bridge the gaps left by inevitably incomplete and contradictory discourses. The Mothers infused their message of death with Virgin Mary–style suffering and revolutionary-style sacrifice for a higher cause. The Mothers/messengers became the prototypes for future *Continuadoras.* In the delivery of their message, stronger bonds were developed both between the Mothers/messengers and those receiving the news and among the Mothers/messengers as they traveled, sometimes for hours, to deliver bodies.

Yet this task also involved a high emotional toll for the Mother/messenger, creating ambivalence among the Mothers concerning this task, as it did with Doña Elsa. She spoke of both the benefits and costs of Mothers act-ing as the messengers. Mothers recognized the need to support and set an example for a new Mother, and this task was also a new challenge—deliv-ering the news required strength and courage. Yet it was almost unbearably painful.

> We told [the army] that if they deliver a child, they didn't know the pain that the mother was going through while other Mothers do. This is what we did—we went to inform the mother, to deliver him, "Here is your son." . . . It is different talking from one mother to another. You have to have great morale, great courage. Here many mothers ask me, "Do you remember when you brought me my son?" "Yes," I say, "I remember." It is one of the tasks that we carried out, and it took a lot out of us.

Such a difficult job, which many believed required maternal empathy, also involved a measure of self-sacrifice because the Mothers, in delivering the news of death, relived the day they received news of their own child. As Doña Nacha said earlier, "We cried as much as she did." Sometimes, as in the case of Doña Esperanza R., the stress built up to the point of illness.

> When the draft started, the Mothers went to leave the dead with the family and to talk with the mother. It was very hard for us. . . . The Frente came and said to deliver a *muchacho* who had fallen. And so we armed ourselves with courage and went to take the body. . . .
> [One time] Doña Juana arrived with some other Mamas, and they said, "Look, you have to deliver this cadaver. But I cried because [Doña Teresa, the mother of the fallen soldier] is a good friend. . . . I said to her, "Doña Teresa, you're a good Christian, you have a lot of faith. You have to be strong be-cause I am going to give you some bad news." And so she says to me, "Why?" "Look," I say, "the dead boy is your son." . . . And I remember that she grabbed me and embraced me. She said, "Ay, Doña Esperancita, what can I do? My son has died." "Yes," I told her, "It is your son that died. But you have to be strong. We mothers," I said to her, "We have to suffer. For us, this world is for suffering." . . . We passed the whole night with her. This was one of the many cadavers that I had to deliver.
> Another time was in Waswali. . . . On the way, I was praying to God,

"*Señor,* give strength to this woman so that she doesn't become ill, so that she doesn't suffer so much, so that she accepts the death of her son." But *gracias a Dios,* the *muchacho* didn't have a mama! He only had a father! And it is never the same. *Never.* . . . I felt so relieved that this *muchacho* didn't have a mother.

I became [emotionally] ill, and so I said, "Look, I'm sorry, but I'm not going to deliver any more cadavers because this work is hard on us." And so they didn't ask anymore. They got other people to deliver the cadavers. It made me ill delivering the cadavers. But always when someone fell, we were there.

The *Comite Regional de Apoyo al Combatiente* (the Combatant Support Regional Committee, or CRAC) was created in 1984, and it took over this daunting task. CRAC worked as a liaison between families and soldiers, arranging visits between mothers and soldiers, facilitating communication, and delivering bodies to the families. Though the Mothers were no longer obligated to deliver the news, many worked closely with CRAC and continued to accompany mothers when they received their child's body, to help with wake and burial arrangements, and to encourage women to join the committee.

This first contact with the Mothers was an important recruitment method. In this visit the Mothers emphasized, or rather demonstrated, the new identity the grieving mother now shared with so many other Nicaraguan mothers. As Doña Elsa explained, "We just hugged her and transmitted to her the strength, the love, the courage. It was necessary to demonstrate at those moments the pain that we have had and how to bear the pain upon seeing our children destroyed." They invited the mother to participate in the Mothers' Committee, stressing that contact with other Mothers with whom they could share their feelings was vital to her emotional health. Mothers spoke fondly of their first contact with the committee, describing members as "affectionate," "attentive," "loving," and "people who care." Two Mothers, Doña María Elsa and Doña Nacha, remember it this way:

Doña María Elsa: [The Mothers] came when they brought my son. They told me, "We have an office where the Mothers meet, and it is a distraction." Because this was very hard on me. . . . [They said] that we can't stay in the house all day thinking about our dead children because it tortures us. And so they came and comforted me. . . . I felt a friendship with all of them.

Doña Nacha: Doña Berta came to me. I was grieving, very sad. She told me to meet with [the Mothers] and talk in order to understand my pain and the pain of others—to know that you lost as I lost, that your pain is the same as mine. . . . This way you can be consoled. If you stay inside your house, you are suffering. You are remembering things and thinking that you are all alone. "In order to overcome the pain," she said to me, "come to the meetings, Nacha."

Here, Doña Nacha directly addresses a key component in the development of her sense of collective identity with the Mothers' Committee—"to know that you lost as I lost"—and the emotional benefits to be gained from it. Members saw their committee during this period more in terms of emotional support than political goals or propaganda work. Many mothers did not find the comfort and understanding they needed within their own homes, sensing an emotional gap between themselves and the rest of the family. It was important for them to connect with others who "have the same pain" in order to feel accompanied in their grief. The notion of shared pain as the bond that united the Mothers was a common theme throughout the interviews. The shared experience of pain in both the birth and death of their children was fundamental to the emotional investments individuals made in the collectivity, allowing them to see themselves in others.

The Mothers who made this "first contact" on behalf of the FSLN saw it as a maternal mission, therapy for the grieving mother, reassurance that she was not alone. As such, planting the seeds of this new identity—"Mother of the Heroes and Martyrs"—for a grieving mother was more than a means toward the political ends of the FSLN. With the sense of a shared identity came a sense of accompaniment, love, understanding, sharing—"I am not alone." This was a benefit, a "good," a reason for being a member of the committee of Mothers. The importance Mothers accorded to this intangible benefit challenges economic or "rational choice" approaches to social movements based upon individualist, isolated actors. Here, individual actors joined a collectivity in part to overcome isolation. This does not mean that they acted irrationally, or that they had no sense of their own individual interests. Rather, the point is that they prioritized community, friendship, and affective relationships as benefits, something in their own and others' best interests. Conveniently, the idea that mobilizing as Sandinista mothers was in their own best interests also fit well with the hegemonic project of the FSLN.

Shift toward Autonomy

The Mothers of Matagalpa's auxiliary relation to AMNLAE and their largely symbolic role in the revolutionary process began to change in 1984 when the Mothers gained a new coordinator, Esperanza Cruz de Cabrera, whose son had recently died. In that year, under her leadership, the Mothers decided that their symbolic role and dependence on AMNLAE were too restrictive and contradicted other Sandinista and liberation theology discourses promoting participatory democracy and active social struggle. Coordinator Esperanza C. envisioned a more active role for the Mothers in the revolutionary process and was also concerned that the basic material needs of the Mothers were unaddressed by AMNLAE. As she recalled:

When I joined . . . I noticed that invitations came to us to participate in some activities, so I went. But they didn't invite all the Mothers. They invited Elsa Alemán, Haidee Miranda, Juana Centeno and me.[27] A group. We went to the activities, and they put us in the front row of the crowd. "The Mothers of Heroes and Martyrs!" [she claps] and they would applaud. And the other Mothers? No, they only invited a few of us to represent the committee. The gifts, the participation—only for this little group. And the rest got nothing. So it was like a decorative representation.

Also, the Mothers didn't decide what they were going to do. It was AMNLAE that decided. I didn't like this. I'm not saying I didn't like the AMNLAE organization, just their form of working, the way they presented women. The Mothers went everywhere doing work [for AMNLAE], but they weren't permitted to represent their work personally, and I don't agree with this. It's like if I, as the coordinator of the Mothers, presented the work of the Mothers of barrio Otoniel Arauz. That would be wrong. It's important to show that the Mothers of Otoniel Arauz themselves are doing the work. It is a little more democratic this way. . . . We are AMNLAE women, but we have our autonomy. We remain in harmony with AMNLAE, and they always invite us. But we make our own decisions in our organization.

The earliest members of the Mothers' Committee echoed Doña Esperanza's concerns about the lack of autonomy and representation. Some recalled how only the better-dressed or more articulate—those who best conveyed the Sandinista maternal images of *Las Continuadoras*—were chosen to represent the rest in marches and assemblies.[28] The group's accomplishments were not recognized as the work specifically of Mothers of Heroes and Martyrs but rather as the work of AMNLAE—a disempowering experience in which the Mothers were only recognized as victims, not as doers or agents of change. They also spoke of AMNLAE's failure to respond to their material needs. Single mothers who had lost a significant portion of their present and future income when their children died were in particularly desperate circumstances. In addition, many Mothers had taken on the responsibility for raising their orphaned grandchildren. In part, the Mothers represented the issue of their economic needs as a matter of dignity, drawing on revolutionary discourse. A common refrain in the Mothers' literature explaining their shift to autonomy was "Our children didn't fight, didn't die so that we would go begging door-to-door." Instead, Doña Esperanza promoted discussion among the Mothers as to how they might help each other help themselves.

In addition to their economic needs, they also wanted to more rigorously address their emotional problems. These problems were symbolically recognized within AMNLAE, yet they were addressed largely by calling the Mothers together only to deliver a body or go to a meeting or a protest: "We only met in order to meet. . . . Our own needs were never addressed." In other words, they were spoken to but rarely listened to or solicited for input. Doña Lourdes described the one-way nature of the relationship: "We were organized as Mothers in AMNLAE, but you couldn't see a future in any of it. . . . Doña Esperanza told me, 'Lourdes, we're going to have a meeting . . . and if you have Mothers in your barrio, invite them. . . . We want to form [our own] committee.' With AMNLAE, when they called us it was when they needed our support. They needed our support as Mothers. But we were never strongly organized as women of AMNLAE. It was only the support that they needed from us."

According to Doña María L., the coordinator of the Mothers of Jinotega, and Doña Juana, the 1983–84 coordinator of the Mothers of Matagalpa, the Mothers put aside the maternal image of self-abnegation, insisting on their independence and the right to organize over the issue of their own survival. Doña María L.: "We never got much attention. If AMNLAE needed us to work, we were there. But in looking for solutions for us, it was difficult. We never had anything. No one responded to our needs. But if they invited us or needed us to support them, we were there to support them." Doña Juana: "There wasn't freedom for the organization. It was all within the circle of AMNLAE, the Frente, and you worked in this way. We didn't have the right to a more independent organization.... There were no [income-generating] projects because with AMNLAE there was no independence."

Although active membership in the Mothers at this time was still quite low, Esperanza and other Mothers went from barrio to barrio, spreading the word that the Mothers of Matagalpa was forming as a separate organization designed in part to better recognize and address the needs of its own members. They managed to gather many inactive Mothers together for discussions on the future of the committee. Esperanza described the first steps toward a feeling of unity and shared purpose within this larger group: "When I organized, we were about 70 people . . . and we met and talked and talked as if we were in the same route that each one has in her own home—only talking and talking and nothing else. But because of this, the group felt more initiative, and we came to an understanding amongst ourselves that we had to go forward from there, with more projects. And with this work that we were developing, we learned more—knowing more people, we have shared our lives and our experiences very much."

It might at first have seemed that they were "only talking and talking and nothing else," but as Doña Esperanza C. implied, this was how their collective identity was strengthened and deepened. They shared thoughts, experiences, and emotions with each other, coming to recognize these could also be found in others.

In meetings first held in Doña Esperanza C.'s home, they explored the Sandinista ideals for which their children died as well as the teachings of liberation theology—particularly the role of Mary, mother of Christ, as a significant actor in her son's struggle and the popular church's preferential option for the poor. In turn, they looked for ways in which they, as a group, might both carry on their children's struggle and address their own economic problems. Subsumption under AMNLAE and the FSLN was now interpreted as restricting their ability to recognize and carry out their own interests. They formed a separate organization in which they could blend the goals of self-help and Sandinista-style social justice.[29] As Doña Esperanza C. recalled in a 1991 speech during the national celebration of Mothers of Heroes and Martyrs, "Let's remember when we began. We didn't have anything. We didn't have anywhere to meet, we didn't have houses, we didn't have money, and to us it didn't look good that we would have to go about begging from everyone. . . . We came to an agreement, and we united and began to work, working at making things that were useful for our own members, and this was our first form of reaffirming our condition as Sandinistas."[30] This was a new experience for Mothers who had previously been assigned tasks, spoken to but not listened to, and obligated through the maternal discourse to practice self-abnegation. They renegotiated their collective identity and goals, opting for a group subjectivity that involved agency over victimization, democracy and action over—as Doña Esperanza C. put it—"decorative representation." It was as if the FSLN and AMNLAE, in the mobilization and empowerment of the marginalized, had let the Mothers—middle-age and older, poor women—slip through the cracks in Sandinista ideology. In a time of increasing contra attacks that seriously threatened the revolution, the subordination of this group's needs to the broader needs of the revolution set a tone of top-down politics with little real input from the average member. Revolutionary practice did not meet up to revolutionary ideals, and the contradiction led to reflection by members on the need to establish independence. Thus, the Mothers wrote themselves out of their muted position as AMNLAE's humble, obedient *mamas* and into the narrative of the "New Man" of the revolution. As the Mothers wrote in a 1991 historical summary:

> Our organization had its basis in a small group of five to eight Mothers who were present as mothers of fallen children since the end of 1979. Nonetheless, their participation was relegated to the act of symbolically representing the struggle of their children. In the beginning of 1984, our organization took a new tone and dynamic when it determined through analysis that our participation should not be one of representing as a symbol the struggle of our children, but rather to dynamize our participation and continue the struggle initiated by our children for the salvation of the exploited and oppressed and to carry through the social justice, peace, and construction of a new society.[31]

Stressing the need to look after their own survival as well as that of the revolution, they now expressed as their common goals "to support our members in confronting their individual situation and to involve ourselves as activists within the context of our national situation."[32]

To conclude, the Mothers did not spontaneously unite one day, drawn together out of common maternal grief. Rather, they were encouraged to form through a prefabricated (though shifting and contradictory) maternal identity presided over by various Sandinista organizations. The Mothers developed a public identity based upon the images of *Las Continuadoras* as they were repeatedly presented through Sandinista institutions. The recruitment process was also key to members' adoption of a collective identity in this period. Media images, the educational system, revolutionary art and literature, the popular church, and the Sandinista mass organizations all worked to draw people into the Sandinista project through the notion that the goals of the revolution and the people were one and the same. The Mothers' identity involved intricate arguments as to their specificity based upon pain and maternal labor. But the *La Continuadora* mobilizing identity did not encourage reflection on women's own needs or pride in their own accomplishments. During this period, members followed directives more than they planned their own strategies, and they adopted images more so than they forged their own.

But collectivities are a process, rather than a static "thing." Key factors driving change within the committee were the shifting political and economic contexts as well as the contradictions and gaps within Sandinista discourse. Working within the broad parameters set by Sandinista ideology, the Mothers reinterpreted the meaning and implications of *La Continuadora* and thus inserted themselves more actively into the revolutionary process.

One of the most common Sandinista representations of "combative motherhood" was this depiction of a young woman with a baby at her breast and an AK-47 slung over her back. In this case, AMNLAE of Estelí used the image on their banner.

THE PRIORITIES OF WAR

Deferring Feminism, (Re)drafting Motherhood,

1984–1990

Gender identity politics in the period 1984–90 revolved around the U.S.-financed counterrevolutionary war. The war both distracted the government's attention, time, and resources from gender equity issues and heightened the potential political threat (and thus political importance) of mothers of draft-age sons. The FSLN admitted in its 1984 electoral platform the need for "greater efforts to overcome social problems so that women can achieve full equality with men."[1] Yet at almost every turn, in the eyes of the FSLN leadership, the war and the draft demanded other priorities. Thus, AMNLAE, working closely with the Sandinista army, continued organizing mothers of combatants in order to neutralize the counterrevolutionary campaign aimed at mothers' distress over the drafting of their sons.[2] The Nicaraguan right wing and the U.S. State Department also mobilized mothers and maternal imagery. Mothers of political prisoners organized against the Sandinista government using symbols, methods, and discursive claims surprisingly similar to those of the Mothers of Heroes and Martyrs.

This chapter details the Sandinista and anti-Sandinista cultural war to capture hearts and minds as the contra war raged in the mountains. Striving to convince mothers of draft-age sons that their interests and the military's were one and the same, the FSLN mobilized imagery glorifying women giving birth to future combatants and later sending them off to war. Anti-

Sandinista discourse, in turn, portrayed the FSLN and its draft as the antithesis of maternal love and liberty.

AMNLAE and the War Years

During the most intense war years, the Mothers of Heroes and Martyrs and mothers of combatants consumed so much of AMNLAE's time and energy that AMNLAE was said to be virtually personified by these mothers.[3] Indeed, in its public statements, AMNLAE sometimes deployed a maternal collective identity. For example, an AMNLAE declaration addressing "North American Mothers and the Mothers of the World" included five statements denouncing U.S. support of the counterrevolution, each prefaced with "We, the Nicaraguan mothers, say enough. . . ."[4]

However, despite its appeals through more traditional maternal discourse and the common Sandinista portrayal of feminism as "an imported fad," there was an undercurrent of feminist discourse within AMNLAE.[5] In 1985, AMNLAE formed women's organizations within trade unions and professional associations that articulated both the gender and class concerns of their members. They also helped bring such controversial issues as abortion, birth control, and domestic violence into the public discourse and challenged the FSLN to become more responsive to such issues.

Through their publication *Somos*, AMNLAE regularly discussed issues such as sex education, domestic violence, and women's double workday. The articles could be classified as feminist in the sense that they worked to undermine male dominance and improve women's lives—though never in a way that contradicted the FSLN's war priorities. A regular theme in the magazine in the mid-1980s was men's refusal to share in housework, despite women's increased participation in the paid labor force. *Somos* cartoons depicted exhausted women frantically doing housework and tending to children as their male companions relaxed.[6] Articles discussed the country's need for women in the labor force, particularly as men were mobilized for war, and the harmful effects on children and ultimately the nation if only the working mother attends to their needs. As one article put it, "The Sandinista People's Revolution needs to develop healthy and strong men and women for the construction of a new society. This is difficult to attain when only one of the parents maintains the household."[7] In 1985, AMNLAE proposed that the new Nicaraguan Constitution contain the following: "The work in the domestic sphere that permits the reproduction of the workforce should be socially recognized and carried out by all members of the family."[8]

Popular discussion of controversial gender issues occurred the following year, between May and July 1986, as over seventy town meetings attended by an estimated 50,000 were held to discuss the new constitution.[9] Although five meetings had been planned especially for women, women took an active role throughout the process in asserting demands that closely affected their lives. Issues raised by the women at the meetings included the right for women to be considered heads of households, sex education, and the right to abortion. These assemblies helped popularize feminist discourse, yet they also highlighted the tensions between the FSLN, AMNLAE, Nicaraguan feminism, and poor and working-class women. For example, in a "Face the People" meeting between women and President Daniel Ortega in 1987, the great majority of the women's concerns involved issues such as electricity and water—issues that affected their daily lives and ability to carry out domestic tasks. This dismayed some feminists who felt such issues would be more appropriately discussed in the unions or community movements.[10] Ortega, in turn, responded to the feminists' demands by dismissing them as petit-bourgeois.

The FSLN issued a "Proclamation on Women" in 1987, which many in AMNLAE hailed as a landmark action because it argued that women's struggle for gender equality could not be put off until the end of the war.[11] Through the proclamation, the FSLN recognized the specificity of the oppression of women and stated that "to move forward, we need some mechanism that will enable us to identify the obstacles to emancipation, to identify women's most pressing problems, and to propose practical solutions." Declaring AMNLAE as "precisely that mechanism," the FSLN clarified what types of feminists they were willing to work with: "We reject any group that proposes the emancipation of women through a struggle against men, as an activity exclusive to women. This position divides and distracts people from the tasks at hand."[12]

By 1987, AMNLAE increasingly emphasized sector-oriented work in the mass organizations that would link women's concerns as students, agricultural workers, blue-collar workers, or professionals with their gender-specific demands.[13] Lea Guido explained, "We don't aim to organize women in a

separate sectarian organization. AMNLAE draws together [women's] movements in each social sector, each of which has to develop its own struggle
based on our general program."[14] AMNLAE changed its name from the
Luisa Amanda Espinosa Women's "Association" to "Movement" in September 1987, to reflect its new method of organizing. Previously, as a female
member of the Sandinista Workers Federation explained, "AMNLAE existed as a parallel structure to the unions, and that prevented the evolution of an awareness by means of which the working class as such would
take on women's demands as its own."[15] The shift to a women's movement,
then, was intended to promote awareness of women's concerns in the workplace, with each labor organization—including teachers, health workers,
industrial and agricultural workers, professionals, and campesinos—acting
as women's secretariats through which to formulate their specific demands.

In 1988, AMNLAE moved toward further decentralization by setting up
fifty-two "women's houses" that became AMNLAE's primary base of operation.[16] These functioned as training and counseling centers, offering vocational training, ideological and women's legal rights workshops, and sex
education. The national office began to function as a research, information,
training, and project management center.[17]

Women's demands made through women's sections of Sandinista unions
and mass organizations in the late 1980s highlighted the tensions within
AMNLAE, which were later attributed to AMNLAE's continued lack of
autonomy from the FSLN.[18] Milú Vargas, a feminist member of AMNLAE's
executive committee, explained, "AMNLAE was the presence and representative of the party within the movement. Its leaders were imposed by the
party; they were often unfamiliar with the movement's situation and in addition were charged with the mission of fulfilling party tasks over and above
having the mentality for responding to the genuine demands of women at
the grassroots."[19] The lines between the party and the women's movement
remained blurred to the point that AMNLAE leaders were essentially in-
capable of acting outside of or against the party line. As it became clear that
AMNLAE remained a creature of the FSLN rather than an organization
by, for, and about women, membership and participation declined.[20]

As it followed FSLN directives during the war, AMNLAE maintained
an ambivalent position on feminism. A number of high-profile Sandinista
women identified themselves as feminists. Furthermore, AMNLAE valued

consciousness-raising among women to combat sexism and gain dignity. It also weighed in on the gendered division of labor at home. For example, AMNLAE's full-page ad on Mother's Day read, "The care of children—everyone's responsibility."[21] Nonetheless, it consistently stressed that the struggle against sexism must be undertaken by men and women together, as opposed to a struggle of women against men—a tendency they associated with First World feminism.

Throughout the 1980s, AMNLAE hesitated to embrace feminism as a necessary component in bettering women's lives. Within the discourse of the FSLN and AMNLAE, the word *feminism* generally functioned as an epithet for "elitist" and "out of touch with local reality."[22] When Lea Guido was asked in a 1987 interview whether AMNLAE was a feminist organization, she replied, "It is an organization that deals with women's problems and defends their demands. There is [a] whole gamut of feminist movements in the world; ours is immersed in a revolutionary process, in a revolution that is in power. On the other hand, one shouldn't forget that there is a war here. . . . Our priority was to attend to the problems of the mothers of the combatants, and those who have been killed in battle. However, at the same time we see that it is also necessary to deal with the obstacles that prevent women from participating in the national undertakings. For that reason, we will continue working in both areas."[23] Here we see an interesting discursive practice among AMNLAE representatives, in which the problems of mothers of combatants and the fallen are positioned as distinct from feminist goals. AMNLAE, as Guido put it, worked in "both areas." As AMNLAE struggled against obstacles to women's emancipation, it was also channeling maternal grief into tightly defined revolutionary identities. The one goal aimed to expand women's opportunities and consciousness, viewing women as agents of change. The other goal purposefully narrowed women's choices and posed grieving mothers not as agents so much as victims acted upon.

Its lack of autonomy and contradictory goals kept AMNLAE from fully appreciating the activities of the women's sections established in Sandinista unions and other associations. That it would not, or could not, prioritize women's demands over defense or the economy did not lead such demands to disappear, of course. Nor did many women voluntarily defer their most urgent economic and social needs in order to participate in rearguard defense work.[24] Despite some changes, AMNLAE remained an organization with a top-down leadership style whose effectiveness was eventually eclipsed by the more vibrant and assertive — and more independent — women working in the women's sections of other Sandinista organizations.[25] As a result, these sectors pressured for autonomy from both the FSLN and AMNLAE, and when this was refused, they began to set up independent activities. Rosa Ceballo, a Sandinista community activist, explained that because of AMNLAE's close ties to the party, it "has stayed above everyone. Women can accomplish more and are better represented by the Community Movement, which doesn't distinguish between women — whether we are feminists or nonfeminists."[26]

The Sandinista loss in the 1990 elections was a crippling blow to AMNLAE. Ceballo recalled, "Of all the mass organizations, AMNLAE was the most dependent upon the party, so that when the FSLN lost the elections in 1990, AMNLAE was devastated the most."[27] It was not clear whether AMNLAE would disappear or become increasingly bureaucratized and isolated from the growing independent women's movement. Moreover, the deferral of the demands prioritized by many women, explicitly feminist or otherwise, created space for the right, which in organizing for the 1990 elections courted women through propaganda focusing on safe, familiar gender images.

"For Every Boy Drafted, A Mother Turns against the Sandinistas"

The FSLN's interest in mobilizing mothers into mass organizations and attending to them through AMNLAE is easier to understand in light of the maternal draft resistance,[28] particularly the protests in 1984 (the draft's first year of implementation) and 1987–88 (when La Prensa reopened and the state of emergency was lifted). In various cities in 1984, groups of mothers protested the drafting of their sons. In public meetings with recruiting officers as well as in interviews with journalists, mothers articulated a variety of reasons for draft opposition. Some were explicitly opposed to the Sandinista government, while others were more concerned with the methods employed by the military and its recruiters.[29] The recruiters conducted draft sweeps, picking up all men without draft cards on buses or outside movie theaters if they appeared to be of draft age. Mothers claimed their sons were drafted indiscriminately, despite legal exemptions for the physically unfit and those who were their family's sole source of support. Some were concerned that young men were given inadequate training before being sent into battle—that in effect their sons were being used as cannon fodder. Furthermore, many mothers lost contact with their sons once they were drafted—not knowing whether they were still alive, where they were stationed, or when they would be discharged.[30]

Public meetings called by the army to calm mothers' fears sometimes turned into shouting matches between army officials and worried mothers. The army's initial response was to warn mothers that such sentiments only helped the counterrevolution. Sandinista security chief Lenin Cerna told reporters that fomenting draft opposition was "one of the most important aspects of the CIA campaign" against the Sandinista government.[31] A mother from Matagalpa recounted a turbulent meeting between more than one hundred mothers and party officials that she attended: "We kept asking why the kids weren't being trained well and why we could never find out where they were being sent. We were only told that we should stop playing into the hands of the enemy, and to be proud of our sacrifices."[32]

In April 1984, some three hundred mothers rallied against the draft at the San Francisco Church in Granada.[33] In the town of Tisma, army recruiters ran into an angry group of seventy mothers in place of the draftees they had summoned for induction.[34] Witnesses said that after some shoving and rock throwing, the recruiters fired shots into the air in order to disperse these angry mothers.[35] Four hundred women reportedly gathered outside the recruitment office in the town of La Paz Centro to protest the drafting of their sons.[36] One of the most violent protests occurred in December 1984 in the small city of Nagarote. Barricades were erected and street fighting ensued as residents tried to prevent army recruiters from entering town. More than fifty people were injured, including mothers of draft-age sons who figured prominently in the protest.[37]

Conservative members of the church hierarchy helped generate antidraft sentiment before the draft even became law. The Nicaraguan Bishops' Conference in 1983 condemned the draft, labeling it "totalitarian."[38] They issued a letter published in La Prensa entitled "General Considerations on Military Service," claiming that "the army will become an obligatory center for political indoctrination in favor of the Sandinista Party."[39] Arguing that nobody can be required to take up arms for a political party, the letter went on to urge young men who did not support the Sandinistas to resist the draft.[40] Monseñor Silvio Selva spoke at mass in Nagarote following the draft protests there: "Do not be afraid. The church is with you, the Bishop is with you, I am with you."[41] In response, the FSLN accused conservative priests of encouraging draft resistance among young men and their mothers as a means of undermining the revolution.[42]

Rerouting Maternal Anger and Facilitating Military Recruitment

By mid-1984, the FSLN, recognizing some legitimacy in the mothers' protests, actively searched for ways to address their concerns. Generating acceptance for the draft became a Sandinista priority and a massive propaganda campaign was launched, much of it focused on mothers.[43] As one Sandinista comandante remarked, "These protests reflect reasonable concerns on the part of the mothers. We have not handled the military call-up in the best way."[44] Another Sandinista official told a reporter, "We are now trying to counter the propaganda of people who want to manipulate the sentiments of mothers."[45] The military shifted away from its harsh recruiting methods.[46] Barricada featured stories on the big community send-offs, as boys "voluntarily" went to war and mothers sadly yet proudly bade farewell to their sons. Their recruits were said to be "graduating into manhood."[47]

Another response to such draft resistance on the part of families, particularly mothers, was Apoyo al Combatiente, or "Combatant Support," a government organization that supported mothers of combatants as much as the combatants themselves. The first director of Apoyo al Combatiente explained the hegemonic intent behind the organization: "The cult of the mother is strong in Nicaragua. The mother and the family had to be made aware that the draft is a sorrowful necessity imposed by outside aggression against our revolution."[48] A significant aspect of its work involved facilitating communication between soldiers and families. As Major Victor Moreno, a subsequent director of Apoyo al Combatiente, explained, "We misinterpreted the mothers' attitude. It wasn't really a protest against military service. It was a communications problem. We cut them off from their sons and gave them no information about what was going on."[49] Apoyo al Combatiente ran its own mail service to carry letters and packages to and from combat areas in the mountains. It organized bus trips to the mountains so that mothers might visit their sons, bringing home-cooked meals and little gifts. Apoyo al Combatiente also raised consciousness with the families of draftees: "We have tried to convince parents that the best school [the draftees] could have is in the mountains." [50]

In addition to new recruitment techniques, the reframing of the draft through Sandinista institutions, and the improved relations between the military and mothers of draftees, the FSLN also created material incentives for obeying the draft law. Apoyo al Combatiente worked to ensure that former soldiers got jobs or scholarships to resume their studies. Young men were required to show draft cards to register for school, hold a salaried job, get a passport, or sign a legal document to own a house or buy a car. A mother who had been involved in the 1984 Nagarote antidraft protests explained the relative quiescence in 1987: "If you don't sign up [for the draft], you have to wander around like an outlaw in your own country. You can't work. You can't study. All you can do is run like a fugitive." [51]

In the Gramscian sense, the rethinking of draft policies represents a more concerted Sandinista shift from rule by force to rule by consent. As evidenced by the maternal protests, rule by force generated resistance, which in turn required more repressive and costly use of force. By 1987, the head of the anti-Sandinista human rights commission Lino Hernandez recognized that "the Sandinistas have learned to avoid massive confrontations over the draft." [52] A Sandinista official put a more positive spin on the matter: "Without a popular political base, this war would be a lost cause. The army needs this solid link to the community. We cannot afford a professional army. It must be sustained by political conviction." [53] The Sandinista state's shift to generating consent (backed by force) for the draft suggests its recognition that hegemony is more efficient and stable. One international observer reported the general acceptance of—or at least resignation to—the draft by 1986: "The draft itself has disappeared as a contentious public issue and become a grudgingly accepted institution." [54] Young men who did not fully embrace the idea that their own interests were represented by the Sandinista military at least recognized their interest in avoiding a draft-dodger's life of public scorn, economic repercussions, and pursuit by recruiters.

Mothers as Ideological Combatants in the Contra War

As mentioned, AMNLAE's energy and resources were devoted to organizing work with the Mothers of Heroes and Martyrs and mothers of combatants during the war in the mid-1980s. The top priority given to these
mothers helped establish their allegiance to the FSLN and convert them
into political capital. As the Mothers of Heroes and Martyrs of Matagalpa
put it in their 1986 "Work Plan," one of their main objectives was "to convert each Mother into an ideological combatant who defends the principles
and justice of the Sandinista Popular Revolution."[55] The Sandinista hegemonic project relied upon the Mothers to support key Sandinista policies,
to make rousing speeches to bolster the war effort, and to give moving testimonies to journalists and foreign delegations. The FSLN requested the
Mothers' participation in a 1989 celebration of the Constitution, explaining that the Mothers would "symbolize the heroic sacrifice of our people
in defending with weapons in hand the legality of the revolution and in
confronting the anti-patriotic work of those who are playing up to U.S. imperialism."[56]

Often the Mothers were quoted urging other mothers to encourage their
sons to defend the country. One Mother told the *Barricada*: "We have
to support our children so that they are stronger and more combative."[57]
Another opined, "I believe that one of the best [Mother's Day] gifts that
all mothers should hope for from their children is that they be good Sandinistas, good combatants to defend our country."

Mothers, through AMNLAE, were also encouraged to denounce contra
atrocities and U.S.-financed aggression to the national and international
press. Their emotional pleas to the Reagan administration and contras for
an end to the aggression were internationally appealing. Indeed, photographs of the Mothers demanding peace frequently appeared in foreign
newspapers and pro-Sandinista literature.

With the violence in the countryside and increased hardships brought
on by the war, many mothers were unable to visit their wounded sons in
far-off hospitals. In response, AMNLAE set up support networks between
these mothers and members of Mothers of Heroes and Martyrs in which
the latter became "adoptive" mothers to soldiers, visiting them, entertain-
ing them, bringing them gifts, and generally "mothering" them. This show

of support, framed through the mobilizing identity of Universal Motherhood, increased morale among soldiers and eased their way back into active
duty. Furthermore, such solidarity encouraged Mothers to view FSLN combatants as their own children and thus strengthened their commitment to
the revolution as well as gave them a sense of empowerment and usefulness.[58] Psychologist and AMNLAE member Vilma Castillo explained the
benefits: "AMNLAE has . . . greatly helped the mothers of those who are
fighting or have fallen in battle by bringing them out of their solitary and
self-destructive depression to establish a movement for political action and
social and individual transformation."[59]

Patriotic Wombs and Spartan Mothers

As discussed earlier, the Sandinista mobilizing identity of Combative
Motherhood was deployed in the early 1980s to mobilize women into
defense work—voluntary militias and neighborhood vigilance programs.
However, once young men were required to register for the draft in 1983,
gendered mobilizing identities underwent a marked transition. Because the
army no longer relied primarily on volunteers and women were excluded
from the draft, FSLN maternal imagery turned from mothers as combatants
to mothers as homefront war supporters. The two most common mobilizing
identities employed in the war effort were "Patriotic Wombs" and "Spartan
Mothers."[60]

"Patriotic Wombs" refers to the popular depiction of mothers as bearers
of future soldiers.[61] The following is a selection from a Gioconda Belli poem
that frames revolutionary motherhood as women's ability to carry on the
struggle through their reproductive role.

"WE WILL BEAR CHILDREN"

. . . .

We will bear children,
for every man or woman whom they kill,
we will give birth to
hundreds of children
who will continue in their footsteps.[62]

The theme of revolutionary struggle through childbearing, viewing women as "patriotic wombs," was often expressed by both Sandinista leaders and mothers of combatants. The *Barricada* quoted one soldier's mother, "Aggressors should know that with each of our children that they assassinate, more are born to fill the ranks of the army of brave and honored members. We will continue giving birth to children in order to defend the conquests reached at the cost of our blood."[63] Carlos Nuñez, member of the FSLN Directorate, used similar imagery to praise mothers on International Women's Day: "We celebrate women, saying that today you are a thousand times mothers because you gave birth, leaving to the country so many children to defend it and liberate it from the oppressive yoke of tyranny. Because with this act, you participated in the birth of history when the womb contracted to give birth to the Sandinista Popular Revolution."[64] In 1984, AMNLAE in the city of Rivas celebrated Mother's Day with the Mothers of Heroes and Martyrs and mothers of mobilized sons under the theme "Blessed is the womb of the mother that gives birth to a combatant."[65] And in another example framing women's role in reproducing Sandinismo, a popular Sandinista slogan throughout the contra war was, "As long as Nicaragua has heroic mothers, it will have sons and daughters to defend it."[66]

As contra aggression intensified, the FSLN directed AMNLAE to focus on raising moral and economic support for the mothers of combatants and discouraging them from impeding their sons' military recruitment.[67] Toward this end, AMNLAE and *Barricada* portrayed women as patriotic mothers who were prepared "to offer to the nation their lives' most valuable treasures, their sons and daughters, in order to obtain our liberty."[68] This representation of motherhood runs close to that of Plutarch's Spartan mothers who raised their sons to be warriors ready to die for the country.[69]

One member of the Mothers of Heroes and Martyrs who lost two sons told the press, "I feel proud to have two Sandinista children and prouder to have given my children to this Revolution."[70] And in a letter from the Sandinista Army addressed to "Heroic Mothers," on Mother's Day, a celebration was given to honor "the Mothers of our Heroes and Martyrs who offered to the country their most loved ones in order to gain freedom."[71] A mother who had already lost one child told *Barricada*, "I am ready to give all my children and die with them rather than be under the boot of imperialism."[72] Note that these "Spartan Mothers" were portrayed and saw themselves as taking an active part in the enlistment process. They did not simply support their sons' enlistment—they offered or gave their sons to the country. Through this sleight of hand, these mothers were not victims so much as warriors once removed, and the conscious, deliberate act of sacrifice was more the mother's than her child's. This "transfer of ownership" of a young person from mother to state, when posed as conscious and voluntary, implicates the mother (at least indirectly) in her child's death. With the weight of this responsibility, the mother may still renounce the state and see her child's life as wasted and death as a mistake. But it is far more comforting to take "solemn pride" at so "costly a sacrifice upon the altar of freedom."[73]

Although mothers seen as givers and protectors of life might evoke images of war as destructive, in Sandinista discourse over and over again I found mothers espousing an image of war as creative: "I'm proud of my son, because he gave his life for the life of the people."[74] At the funeral of one soldier, a Mother was quoted as saying, "This is painful for all of us, but we know that each loss is a seed that will germinate and multiply into thousands of sons and daughters of our country who will know how to defend it."[75] One Mother sent a message to mobilized youth in the Barricada: "That blood [shed in the insurrection] germinated into all those who carry on. Now, these young people volunteering are the fruit of that sacrifice."[76] In 1968, FSLN founder Carlos Fonseca wrote to Nicaraguan mothers on Mother's Day, saluting "Mothers of glorious martyrs who have offered their lives for the liberation of Nicaragua. . . . Let the best consolation for the mothers who carry a tortured heart be that their children are the honor of Nicaragua in these times. If in Nicaragua not everything is selfishness, avarice and darkness, it is because the martyrs have shed their blood."[77] In this discourse, Sandinista blood is not spilled in vain but rather fertilizes the revolutionary process, eventually germinating "fruit": new combatants and a new society.

The Mothers of Heroes and Martyrs, and the aura that surrounded them, were enlisted to convince mothers not to stand in the way of the drafting of their sons. The following is a typical plea by a Mother: "They killed my son but he died like a man. . . . To mothers all over the country, I beseech you, do not revert to the selfishness that at times characterizes us—don't cut off the dreams of your children to go to the borders to fight for the country. Let them go."[78] Here, a mother's desire to protect her children is translated into "characteristic" maternal selfishness. In other words, if a youth is willing to sacrifice his or her life for the good of the country, the mother should also be so generous with that life.

In gearing up for the expected U.S. invasion of Nicaragua, Sandinista discourse sometimes settled upon middle-age and older mothers of combatants pledging their readiness to fight alongside their children. At a meeting of mothers of combatants, one mother was quoted, "We take pride in feeling ourselves to be at the war front where our sons fight because if the invasion comes . . . as mothers we also should be prepared to die alongside our children." Another mother agreed, "We also have to be ready to take up the gun."[79] In stressing the obligation of all Nicaraguans to take part in defense, one elderly mother of a fallen combatant told the press, "Even my wrinkled hands are able to hold a gun with which to defend the country."[80] Such bellicose statements by older women inspired combatants and directed public anger toward young male draft dodgers.

Through the Patriotic Womb and Spartan Mother mobilizing identities, Sandinista leadership at times presented an explicitly pronatalist stance. President Ortega told an audience of women celebrating AMNLAE's tenth anniversary that sterilization and abortion must be viewed in terms of U.S. imperialism, which involved halting the population growth in third-world countries "to avoid the risk of an increase in the population that could threaten a revolutionary change."[81] Nicaragua had a small population, he argued, and was subject "to a policy of genocide" through the U.S.-supported contra war. "The ones fighting in the front lines against this aggression are grown men," he continued. "One way of depleting our youth is to promote the sterilization of women in Nicaragua . . . or to promote a policy of abortion." The speech relied upon a rather regressive gender discourse to support the mobilizing identities of Patriotic Wombs and Spartan Mothers: while men fought imperialism at the battlefront, one of women's roles in defense was to ensure the supply of future soldiers. Because it denied women control over their own reproduction and restricted access to political and military ranks that conferred the highest status and power during the Sandinista regime, this way of thinking ignored women's history of guerrilla struggle and contradicted the FSLN policies meant to ensure women's emancipation.

In sum, the image of Patriotic Wombs and Spartan Mothers defined the good, patriotic mother as bearing and raising future Sandinista soldiers. Women's primary role in Sandinista society as presented in this discourse was as a combatant-bearing vessel who later enthusiastically sent her children off to war, an image that eclipsed that of the glorified Combative Mother popular during the insurrection and predraft years of the revolution. The effort put into constructing and reinforcing the myth of Patriotic Wombs and Spartan Mothers attested to the actual (and potential) resistance on the part of mothers to the war and the draft.

Madres Sufridas and Mary, Mother of Christ

The most enduring maternal image I came across from the late Somoza era through the post-Sandinista era was the reference to mothers of fallen combatants as *"madres sufridas"* (suffering mothers). These Madres Sufridas were often compared to the Virgin Mary, particularly as the Mater Dolorosa at the crucifixion of Jesus. In the periods of intense warfare—the late 1970s and much of the 1980s—it was consistently framed in such a way as to recognize women's grief yet also dissuade them from being too protective and impeding their son's or daughter's political struggle. For example, during Holy Week in 1979, a few months before the fall of Somoza, La Prensa carried a series of articles comparing the stations of the cross with the Somocista repression in Nicaragua. In one, the Virgin Mary was compared with the experiences of Nicaraguan mothers:

Mary is the strong woman of the Gospel. She had to live through many hard experiences at the side of Jesus, but none was so terrible as that of the Calvary. In spite of her grief, Mary was always at the side of her son, knowing that he did the will of his Father, and she did not oppose him.

Like Mary, many mothers today know that their children have a mission to carry out, and they are always there sharing their life of struggle and suffering. Her heart is always at the side of the imprisoned child, the lost child, the suffering child. Like Mary, many have witnessed the greatest suffering: the assassination of the child of their wombs.

Like Mary, all mothers can understand that their children are carrying out the will of the Father.[82]

Thus, the good mother was strong despite her pain and obediently supported her child's divinely ordained anti-Somoza mission.

In 1983 as contra attacks increased, the Jinotega Mothers of Heroes and Martyrs held a silent march with the message, "The Passion of Christ is being imitated by our brothers, husbands and children who walk with the cross on their backs, practicing love for the people and the country, and they are being assassinated as innocents." [83] In another example, when a conservative priest refused to bless dead Sandinista soldiers in the late 1980s, mothers responded in the press by comparing themselves to the Virgin Mary. One mother whose fallen son was refused a blessing told *Barricada* that she was at the side of the Virgin "because she is also the mother of a martyr, crucified for love." [84]

Later, the *Madre Sufrida* imagery was used to encourage Sandinista women to carry on the struggle despite the end of the war and the loss of the 1990 elections. The following was a sermon delivered by Father Arnaldo Zenteno and dedicated to the Mothers of Heroes and Martyrs. It was written following the 1990 elections to urge these mothers not to despair that the sacrifice of their children was in vain: "Don't say, Mother, with grief: 'So much for nothing. . . .' Don't say it, Mother, even though perhaps you feel it, nailed to the cross with your child, for you well know that the life delivered is so much for so many. . . . Don't say it, Mother, Mary of Nicaragua, because it wounds the soul, and we both know very well that for him, for his life, for his blood, for his hope—and your hope—our hope is alive." [85]

Comparison of mothers and their fallen Sandinista children with the Virgin Mary and Jesus Christ raised the Sandinista struggle to the irreproachable level of a holy war. The image of *Madre Sufrida* and the Virgin Mary of Nicaragua undermined the counterrevolutionary discourse that presented the Sandinistas as godless. It also posed mothers of the fallen who opposed Sandinismo as diverging from the ideal of Mary. The Virgin Mary, already established as the ideal of womanhood in Nicaragua, stood by her child and did not waiver in her faith even when she lost her son or daughter to "the will of the Father" (or the will of the FSLN).

Images of Motherhood: Old Roles and New Connotations

A 1986 Mother's Day letter from the National Directorate of the FSLN published in the *Barricada* described the many roles that mothers took on: "MOTHERS have played a heroic role not only in sending their children to battle against Somocismo and for the defense of the revolutionary gains of today, but also in being the *guerrilleras* of the army defending national sovereignty, clandestine militants and FSLN combatants and sacrificing for the achievements made by our people in these seven years. The MOTHER is the model of bravery, strength, capability, self-sacrifice and love."[86] This operated less as a description of reality than as a normative statement in the competition to influence women's subjectivities. During the war, women were not invariably presented through FSLN discourse only as mothers. They were also "patriotic Nicaraguans" volunteering their labor in the tasks of the revolution, workers dedicated to raising production levels, militia members defending the country, and young women in bathing suits participating in beauty contests "to raise the morale of the troops." Some women, such as Nora Astorga, Dora María Téllez, and Doris Tijerino (all of whom had proven themselves militarily during the Sandinista struggle against Somoza), were depicted as capable, intelligent, and brave revolutionaries occupying important positions in the insurrection and the Sandinista government.[87] Yet even within the roles of worker, soldier, and politician, it was difficult for women to escape the pervasive identity of mother.

Through new applications and reinterpretations of traditional maternal images, mothers were expected to take on new, politicized responsibilities. Women were consistently portrayed in Sandinista discourse to be militant mothers, Spartan Mothers, nurturing mothers to all, Patriotic Wombs, and *Continuadoras*. Such portrayals did not necessarily confine women to the domestic realm and traditionally female tasks. Rather, women as mothers were encouraged to take an active part in the construction of a new society and enter traditionally male activities such as grassroots politics, productive work outside the home, and the predraft military. Women could now take on the identity of political actors and try to affect Sandinista-sanctioned change. As AMNLAE director Doris Tijerino put it, women were encouraged to believe that they were "not only someone capable of reproducing life, but also capable of transforming it."[88] Yet women should still be fundamentally mothers, sacrifice their own interests, and make demands on behalf of others, particularly their own families and the "Nicaraguan family."

Analysis of this pervasive maternal representation provides new insight into the FSLN's failures on the road to women's emancipation. Previous studies on women in Sandinista Nicaragua have focused on the economic constraints that arose from the contra war and argued the financial impossibility of creating new programs or even continuing current ones aimed at improving women's position in society.[89] Here, in contrast, I have focused on the manner in which the FSLN fought the war through deployment of discourse, revealing its reinforcement of traditional gender roles through maternal images that surrounded the public on an everyday basis. The FSLN recognized that women who identified themselves primarily as mothers would be potential war dissenters due to the drafting and death of sons, severe inflation, and scarcity of consumer goods. Accordingly, they appealed to these women through an image virtually all Nicaraguan women were comfortable with—the mother—redefining old dichotomies, such as motherhood and militancy, so that they complemented each other. However, as is typical in male-dominated societies, the most respected traits, those that conferred status and power, were those associated with men, and the glorification of stereotypical feminine traits actually worked to keep women in their separate and unequal places. It also discouraged the development of a feminist analysis and political strategy within the FSLN and AMNLAE.[90]

The Sandinista images of mothers masked a more complex reality. They were ideals meant to influence, models of behavior constructed for emulation. The maternal images found in *Barricada* and elsewhere marked the Sandinista struggle to construct the arena of proper maternal behavior, altering women's subjectivities in the context of their participation in Sandinista organizations such as AMNLAE and the Mothers of Heroes and Martyrs. Yet as the FSLN presented ideals and models of behavior that benefited its own political goals—such as Patriotic Wombs and *Las Continuadoras*—and presented these as the true Nicaraguan reality, they alienated many women. On the one hand, women whose subjectivities went beyond the traditional feminine lifestyles, particularly those who leaned toward feminist interpretations of society, found their options restricted. On the other hand, many women who still perceived themselves to be on the losing end of the revolution—either economically or through the loss of loved ones—despite Sandinista propaganda attempts to draw them in, turned a sympathetic ear to anti-Sandinista discourse. Ironically, the Sandinista representation of women as mothers indirectly helped pave the way for the Sandinista loss of the presidency to Violeta Chamorro, who arguably made the most politically effective use of the powerful images of motherhood.

Refusing to Forget: The Mothers of Heroes and Martyrs Confront Amnesty

As in the waging of war, mothers also figured prominently in the construction of peace. During the series of Central American peace talks in the late 1980s, the Mothers of Heroes and Martyrs mobilized for the return of those kidnapped by the contras and against amnesty for imprisoned counterrevolutionaries. Groups of Mothers met outside Cardinal Obando y Bravo's curia in Managua every Thursday for months, hoping to discuss the case of the kidnapped and ask him to carry their messages to the peace talks. Although Obando met with mothers of imprisoned contras, he refused to meet with the Sandinista mothers.

In 1988, when the contras presented their list of the kidnap victims in their custody, all of whom were to be released in compliance with the peace accords, the list contained only sixty-six names. The Mothers insisted on the return of all six thousand of the kidnap victims documented by the Sandinista government's human rights commission. The Mothers of Matagalpa sent the following letter, prefaced by a biblical passage, to Cardinal Obando in response to his perceived failure to press the issue of the kidnap victims:

> *I am the good shepherd*
> *The good shepherd*
> *lays down his life for his sheep*
> *He who is a hireling, and not a shepherd,*
> *who is not the owner of the sheep*
> *flees from the wolf, abandoning them,*
> *and the wolf grabs them and scatters them,*

because he is no more than an hireling,
and the sheep are not important to him.
John 10: 11–13

Your Eminence, Cardinal Miguel Obando y Bravo,

We address you again with the hope that this time our voice will find a place in your shepherd's and Christian heart and you will know to take a just and dignified position towards our request. . . . Again we ask that you intercede before the high officials of the counterrevolution. . . . Do not leave us with 66 "prisoners of war." Our disappeared and kidnapped are thousands and now we know that the majority have been killed and disappeared. . . . Do not leave us alone in this hard road to peace and life: Unite with us; JOIN HANDS AND HEARTS WITH US; JOIN TOGETHER OUR LOVE AND FORM A WALL AGAINST THE HATEFUL IMPERIALISM. LET US DESTROY A POWER WITH OUR UNION.[91]

The Mothers thus positioned the cardinal as a "hireling" of U.S. imperialism, arguing that instead he should "lay down his life for his sheep" by demanding the full return of the kidnapped.

During the peace talks, some Sandinistas argued that the Mothers' relentless demand for the return of all six thousand whom they considered kidnap victims and their protests against amnesty impeded the peace process. The Mothers responded: "We ask of you that our children be returned to us. If they are not alive, let them return their cadavers. . . . We will not stop fighting until we have them. To fight for our children is to fight for peace."[92]

Obando and others asserted that the mothers of the kidnapped acted out of partisan rather than maternal concerns and that their pain was manipulated by the FSLN. The Mothers responded through a comparison of their own plight with that of the Virgin Mary: "Let our determination to find our kidnapped children not be interpreted by your eminence as a political matter because then the Virgin Mary who is the Mother of Jesus was also political because she went looking for her son."[93] They also countered accusations of being politically manipulated with the charge that it was actually the cardinal who was acting out of political rather than Christian motivations. Hundreds of Mothers planted crosses representing recent victims of contra attacks in front of the cardinal's curia, challenging him, "Here is part of your Christian people, Monseñor. We wait for you to act with justice and love and not out of partisanship."[94] One Mother was quoted in *Barricada* as saying, "It seems that Cardinal Obando is part of the contras since he doesn't want to help us rescue our children because when the Mothers look for him to help us, he hides."[95] The Mothers called on Obando to accompany them to the contra camps in Honduras to investigate the cases of the kidnapped and asserted that he received CIA funds: "We have sustained this struggle through our own efforts, without receiving financing from anyone. . . . We don't need financing from the CIA like the Cardinal does."[96] The expected mode of conduct for both mothers and priests was to act unselfishly, show concern for others, promote peace, and act outside of political concerns. In this propaganda battle, the most self-sacrificing, apolitical, and truly Christian party would have the moral upper hand. In their weekly vigils outside Cardinal Obando's curia, the Mothers of Heroes and Martyrs and mothers of the disappeared both publicized their case and called Obando's credibility into question.

Nationally, under Sandinista directives, the most public role of the Mothers was as symbolic leaders of various demonstrations, posing as figureheads and symbols of suffering in marches and assemblies. They were also an effective moral counterforce to the powerful cardinal and conservative church hierarchy. However, although the FSLN ultimately agreed to total amnesty in peace talks, the Mothers' protest against amnesty marked a more independent or politically conscious period for the Mothers in which they set out to influence FSLN policy rather than simply follow its directives. Groups of Mothers from various cities traveled to Managua to call for peace and at the same time aggressively protest total amnesty. Mothers' statements to the press were unusually virulent and uncompromising, stressing punishment and vengeance rather than forgiveness. One Mother asserted, "I don't know what would happen . . . if one day in the street I met the contra who killed my son. . . . I'm sure I would take justice into my own hands." Another explained, "To accept that the guardsmen go free . . . to forget the past . . . I would have to forget that I had ever given birth."[97]

M22: Mothers of Political Prisoners

In January 1987, ninety-six women sent a letter to the secretary general of the United Nations denouncing "unjust and cruel" prison conditions and calling for a general amnesty for political prisoners.[98] Several days later, they gathered in the offices of the anti-Sandinista Social Christian Party (PSC) to create an organization: the Mothers of Political Prisoners, "22 January" (M22).[99] The leaders had met while waiting outside prisons during visiting hours and approached attorney Enrique Sotelo for assistance in developing an organization.[100] Within months, the movement was estimated by the U.S. State Department to have grown to at least 1,500 members.[101]

M22 depicted itself as a politically independent human rights organization, though it opposed the Sandinista government, was presided over by the very partisan Sotelo, and was advised by the U.S. embassy, which arranged financing through the U.S. National Endowment for Democracy (NED). The U.S. State Department featured M22 in a May 1987 issue of its *Latin American Dispatch*. The article apportioned more space to photos of grieving women than to written text, suggesting the emotional impact of M22 on which the State Department hoped to capitalize. Fact-finding delegations of U.S. elected officials met with M22. Members of M22 also toured the United States accompanied by a State Department representative.[102] In September 1987, M22 was granted $20,000 by the NED.[103]

In 1988, after Congress denied further contra funding, U.S. foreign policy focus shifted from guerrilla warfare toward the struggle for ideological hegemony. The U.S. embassy advised the State Department that loss of contra funding "has placed the internal civic opposition on center stage in attempts to bring democracy to Nicaragua. [Aid to the civic opposition] would not only have the effect of supporting and galvanizing the opposition, but also would place the Sandinistas in the position of either allowing the strengthening of the opposition or showing their anti-democratic colors by blocking aid."[104] It then named M22 as a key organization that merited such support. In detailing M22's importance for its plans, the embassy argued, "This organization presses the Sandinistas on one of the most neuralgic and potentially explosive issues, general amnesty. Even while operating on a shoestring budget, this group has attracted considerable media attention, to which the Sandinistas have responded with considerable harshness. The movement needs assistance in renting its own office, producing its own pamphlets, organizing rallies and marches, and developing international connections."[105] Predicting that the Sandinistas would not permit direct U.S. government funding for M22, the embassy advised, "We must be prepared to use NGOs when the expected denial is received."[106]

In May 1988, *Barricada* carried stories of CIA destabilization efforts through NED funding, specifically focusing on M22.[107] When President Ortega declared such funding illegal, the U.S. embassy told the State Department, "The strong Sandinista reaction is an indication of the potential effectiveness of this type of support for democratic forces."[108]

M22 received ample coverage in *La Prensa* as competition for public sympathy developed between M22 and the Mothers of Heroes and Martyrs.[109] Each side struggled to appear as the "true" victims. The two held similar protests and utilized similar techniques, slogans, and symbols. As the anti-Sandinista strategy shifted from rule by military conquest to rule by consent, M22, *La Prensa*, and the U.S. State Department captured the powerful image of the protective mother used so frequently by the Sandinistas and turned it against them.

The emotional issue of amnesty reached a peak when the Mothers of Heroes and Martyrs clashed—both symbolically and physically—with M22. A physical confrontation occurred in October 1987 outside the church where M22 held its meetings. There, the two mothers' groups and their supporters exchanged heated accusations. One member of the Mothers of Heroes and Martyrs argued, "They might also be mothers, but they are mothers of [Somoza's National Guardsmen] who have assassinated our children. If [these prisoners] are let go, they would act the same, continuing to assassinate the people."[110] During this confrontation, the Mothers of Heroes and Martyrs and their supporters were shot at and two people were wounded. The Mothers of Matagalpa issued a press release: "Mothers and relatives of Somocista prisoners should realize that their sons were responsible for the torture, death and disappearance of our children. Their children are in prison paying for the crimes committed and our children are dead for having fought against death and oppression."[111] Reversing the claim that the FSLN manipulated mothers of the fallen, an editorial in *Barricada* referred to M22 as an "artificial 'movement'" created by the American embassy that "intends to manipulate the mothers of some counterrevolutionary prisoners."[112]

M22 denounced the poor prison conditions and called for a general amnesty, an end to the five-year state of emergency, and abolition of the People's Tribunal responsible for the guilty verdicts of their relatives. The NED officially funded M22 "to increase public awareness within Nicaragua and abroad of the plight of those incarcerated for allegedly violating the country's security laws, and to provide improved legal services and material assistance to the families of Nicaraguan detainees."[113] Communication between the U.S. embassy in Managua and the U.S. State Department reveal the centrality of M22 in U.S. attempts to undermine FSLN legitimacy during implementation of the Central American Peace Accords.[114] In November 1988, the U.S. State Department identified M22 by name in advising the Nicaraguan opposition (through the U.S. embassy) on how it could "actively and aggressively capitalize on several Sandinista weaknesses."[115] Yet in order to do so effectively, M22 needed to appear as *Madres Sufridas* above messy partisan politics—something that it never quite managed to do.

Employing gendered discourse similar to that honed by the FSLN, *La Prensa* couched M22's demands through politicized maternal symbolism. The government reacted through a variety of tactics. Sandinista police impeded the official signing of M22's constitution by blocking off the streets leading to the meeting place and intimidating the women.[116] According to M22, government agents harassed members, threatening to arrest them and punish their imprisoned relatives if they continued to organize.[117] One member was told that a special prison wing was being prepared "for all you crazy ladies."[118] Her imprisoned husband told her that he was isolated and put in chains for three days as punishment for her activism. On 8 March 1987, M22's attempt to hold a third meeting was unsuccessful, as government forces again blocked road access.[119] In June 1988, about thirty members, in commemoration of Father's Day, unsuccessfully attempted to deliver a letter to Interior Minister Tomás Borge calling for general amnesty in compliance with the Esquipulas Accords. According to *La Prensa*, a "human chain" of Sandinista police prevented the women from entering the building and numerous police and state security vehicles surrounded M22's meeting place.[120] By February 1988, the Sandinista government was sufficiently threatened by the symbolic power of M22 to arrange for a group of pro-government female relatives of political prisoners to present themselves at the pro-government daily *El Nuevo Diario*, praise prison conditions, and denounce M22 for trying to manipulate them.[121]

Wearing "distinctive white handkerchiefs" reminiscent of the world-renowned Argentine Madres de Plaza de Mayo, M22 headed marches protesting the Sandinista government, held weekly protests to publicize the plight of the political prisoners, and gave testimonies to foreign delegations, politicians, and journalists. In attempting to influence the Central American peace talks, they sent letters to the wives of Central American presidents: "With all due respect we address you in your double roles as WOMEN AND AS MOTHERS to beseech you to intercede in the presence of your illustrious husbands so that the GENERAL AMNESTY becomes effective in Nicaragua. . . . Thousands of Nicaraguan homes suffer spiritually and financially over the years due to the imprisonment of their most loved ones."[122] Here and in other communiqués, M22 stressed the financial as well as the emotional problems that arose when a male breadwinner was imprisoned.

Just over a year after it formed, M22 began to experience serious internal conflict, and the movement soon split. Members of M22 told embassy officials that partisan figures such as Sotelo and Erick Ramírez (leader of one faction of the PSC) had exploited M22 to advance their own political ambitions in the midst of the ongoing power struggles within the opposition.[123] As amnesty was granted and political prisoners were released, the immediacy of the issue dissipated. M22 public gatherings and protests grew less frequent, despite the U.S. embassy's numerous attempts to resurrect M22 and resolve the split.[124] Infighting degenerated to the point that various factions were accusing each other of being clandestine Sandinistas.[125] One of the M22 factions briefly reorganized in August 1988 to become the Sixth of March Movement (M-6-M), named after the date of the 1988 antidraft "March of Sorrow" in Masaya that was broken up by Sandinista police.[126] This attempt to replace the increasingly less relevant amnesty issue with the issue of the draft was ultimately unsuccessful. *Barricada*'s front page in September 1988 declared M22 a "crumbling puppet of the U.S. embassy."[127] As M-6-M leaders and Sotelo requested additional NED funding, the U.S. embassy privately expressed doubts and advised NED to reexamine its support.[128] By December 1988, the U.S. embassy expressed dismay that M22 failed to develop independently from partisan politics: "The appropriation of rival civic opposition factions has dealt a blow to the already foundering M22 movement."[129] In the end, due to the split within M22, its inability to stay above the fray of partisan power struggles, and the possible misuse of NED funds, the U.S. embassy and NED discontinued its support for M22/M-6-M and the organization folded.

A former leader of M22, Tomasita Hernandez, formed a new organization, "Women of Masaya," to protest the draft and poor economic conditions, and she approached the U.S. embassy for support.[130] In her conversations with a U.S. embassy officer, Hernandez expressed frustration at the divisions within M22 and the inability of anti-Sandinista parties to focus on upcoming electoral issues due to internal bickering. In part because she had a son approaching draft age, she had expanded her political focus beyond political prisoners to primarily focus on the draft. Her group also protested Sandinista economic policies that, according to them, had eroded health care and nutrition for Nicaraguan children.

To replace M22 in the post-amnesty context and mobilize the women's vote for Violeta Chamorro in the 1990 elections, the NED (through Delphi International) founded the Nicaraguan Women of Conscience (MNC). After the elections, the MNC continued to attract money from the NED, and it turned its attention to civic education and outreach to single mothers and unemployed women. With its U.S. funding, much of MNC's efforts were dedicated to promoting a socially conservative worldview aimed directly at women. According to the MNC, the problems women were experiencing as women included sexual promiscuity, domestic violence, abandonment by men, and lesbianism, all due to the FSLN's contempt for Christian morals. This group aimed to "rescue religion and the family from the libertine philosophy of the Sandinistas" and positioned women as the pillars of their vision of the new social order. Ironically, NED discovered that approximately $10,000 donated to the organization was unaccounted for and several office machines were missing.[131]

Mothers as Victims of the Draft

As the case of M22 implies, *La Prensa* depicted mothers as the primary victims of the war and the draft. As in *Barricada*, *La Prensa* was filled with references to the *Madre Sufrida*. Yet while *Barricada* blamed the contras and U.S. imperialism for maternal suffering, post-1979 *La Prensa* positioned the FSLN as the guilty party. One 1989 editorial argued that Mother's Day should disappear in Nicaragua because in each home "there is mourning, sadness, and depression for the death of a son or because they are in the mountains or out of the country. . . . To be a mother, in any epoch, has signified love, devotion, renouncement, sacrifice, and now in our beloved Nicaragua, we must add one more phrase: Sorrow and Suffering for the Absence of Our Children."[132] Antonio Lacayo, soon to become Chamorro's minister of the presidency, was quoted on Mother's Day as saying, "I am sure that never has there been so much pain in the hearts of Nicaraguan mothers," pointing the finger of blame at the Sandinistas.[133]

After an interlude of relative maternal quiescence on the draft issue, opposition was reactivated as a result of the political openings signaled by the signing of the Central American Peace Accords in August 1987. Most important, *La Prensa* reopened in October 1987 (this time without government censorship) after fifteen months of enforced silence, and the six-year state of emergency was lifted in January 1988. In 1987–89, images of women filled *La Prensa*, primarily represented as mothers of political prisoners and mothers denouncing the draft.[134] *La Prensa* used mothers' testimonies to protest repressive recruitment tactics and demand an end to the draft. These mothers testified to the forced recruitment of their underage sons—sometimes as young as twelve and thirteen years old. Sons were often taken off buses or picked up on the street by the army, and their mothers were unable to prove their young age because, as was so often the case with poor, rural families, they did not have birth certificates. Other mothers protested to *La Prensa* that recruiters had forced their deaf or mentally retarded sons into the army. A group of mothers denounced the draft in general: "We want to live in peace. We reject the war . . . when boys are taken by force to die for a cause that is not theirs."[135] As in the case of political prisoners, mothers were portrayed as heroic protectors who, in their condemnation of violence, "bravely refuse to hand over their sons to the SMO [*Servicio Militar Obligatorio*—the draft]."[136] There were even reports of mothers presenting themselves at the recruitment offices in place of their sons, indicating that "they would hide their sons so that the military does not take them away."[137]

In their letters to *La Prensa*, mothers repeatedly called for an end to the draft. For example, a group of women wrote in 1988: "We mothers can no longer bear the pain and sadness of seeing our humble and simple youth leave our homes to be sent to their death, being used as cannon fodder. . . . We humbly ask Daniel Ortega and the rest of the military leaders that for the love of God they agree with us and all Nicaraguan mothers by putting an end to the recruitments because the life of our children does not have a price." [138] Mothers' opposition to the draft was a powerful counterattack on Sandinista hegemony. It portrayed FSLN leaders as needlessly prolonging the war and sending youth to their deaths. In contrast, mothers were positioned as universally peace-loving, thus competing with the Sandinista models of Spartan Mothers and Combative Mothers by using the age-old wisdom of women's "natural" pacifism.

In 1988, despite past censorship and threats of closure, *La Prensa* became increasingly bold in its condemnations of the draft. Mothers, not draft-age men, were presented at the forefront of the antidraft campaign. One 1988 article on International Women's Day told readers of a mother whose son was killed by military recruiters after he refused to be drafted, contending that "Nicaraguan mothers should fight with true love for their children, regardless of political ideas, and they should try to preserve their children's lives and not be influenced by foreign ideologies." [139] The article then claimed that "women feel more womanly fighting like a lioness for their children, fighting so that they leave us to live in peace alongside the children who are the future of the country." For the ideal mother of anti-Sandinista discourse, "true" maternal love was more important than, and contradictory to, political ideas.

(Im)mobilizing Identities

Discourse on both sides of the ideological war focused on women as mothers, overshadowing other women's voices, other stories. The mobilizing images were alluring yet suffocating. Women who followed the ideal gained admiration within the Sandinista or anti-Sandinista community, yet an ideal based almost exclusively upon maternal self-sacrificing restricted women's life choices. More independent roles for women, which the FSLN had originally supported, were not effectively promoted by Sandinista and anti-Sandinista war discourse.

During the contra war, Sandinista and anti-Sandinista discourse presented women as mothers acting in political, patriotic, and morally irreproachable ways in order to bolster political support and prepare a nation for war. Some tinkering was needed to allow for images such as Patriotic Wombs and Spartan Mothers, yet essentially women were mobilized through images that reflected their own preexisting visions of ideal womanhood—the suffering, loyal, selflessly protective mother. The difference lay in that these images came to have an explicitly political content.

Sandinista and anti-Sandinista maternal imagery during the war did not simply mirror reality; it helped constitute it in an attempt to secure women's political support. In turn, through use of this maternal imagery, women themselves reinforced and legitimated their own political activism and agenda in both the public's eyes and the eyes of the state. Women themselves forged, reinforced, and challenged the dominant maternal imagery described above. Women writing poems, giving speeches, creating slogans, writing letters, and speaking to the press turned to maternal images to make a point, sway the audience, and even legitimize their right to speak out.

Mothers of Heroes and Martyrs of Estelí stand beside their display of weapons used by FSLN combatants to overthrow Somoza, including paving stones used to construct barricades, molotov cocktails, and hunting rifles. Elsewhere in their Gallery of Heroes and Martyrs is a display of the much more sophisticated and lethal weaponry of Somoza's *Guardia*.

❧ 4 ❧

THE LATENT AND THE VISIBLE

The Mothers of Matagalpa in Two Dimensions,

1984–1990

> My value to the group was not calculated by the physical items I brought to it. These people included me because they wanted me to be part of their circle, they valued my participation apart from the material things I could offer. So I gave of myself to them, and they gave me fruit cakes and dandelion wine and smoked salmon, and in their giving, their goods became provisions. Cradled in this community whose currency was a relational ethic, my stock in myself soared. My value depended on the glorious intangibility, the eloquent invisibility of my just being *part* of the collective; and in direct response I grew spacious and happy and gentle.[1]

I begin with this passage, in which Patricia Williams speaks of the joy and self-worth involved in simply belonging, to launch a difficult navigation between the instrumental and relational benefits of collective action and the latent and visible dimensions of collective identity. There are instrumental reasons for belonging to a collectivity—so often the focus of social movement research. But as the most active Mothers of Matagalpa insisted, it was the intangible sense of community, shared emotions, and purpose that kept them coming back week after week, year after year. This nonmaterial benefit is linked to, and reliant upon, the Mothers of Matagalpa's shift from passive, symbolic representation to active explorers and champions of their causes. This shift, however, was never complete but rather a constant negotiation.

Doña Esperanza Cruz de Cabrera's story of her political awakening and involvement in the Mothers, though in many ways unique, is a good introduction to how members understood and portrayed their own activism in terms of material, political, and relational ends. As she raised eight children she did not concern herself much with politics until, as the revolution against Somoza accelerated, she became involved in the struggle through her children. Her eldest son Ernesto, a student activist and clandestine FSLN collaborator, introduced her to revolutionary politics, and this eventually led her into the Mothers' Committee:

> [Ernesto told me,] "Look, the situation is very serious. There have been many young people disappeared who were active in the student organization because they don't support this dictator." I saw that what Ernesto was saying was true. . . . With time they got me more involved. . . . I was his messenger in that if there was a very clandestine plan, I had to go and be under his orders. . . . In this way I began to learn. . . .
>
> After I lost my son, it impacted me quite a bit. He was like a part of my life. Each child that is lost is like losing a part of your own life. And it was like I needed more love—to give more love and also to receive more love. So I decided to join with the Mothers. . . . We visited barrio by barrio, and in each barrio we encountered women who had lost a child. So we organized some 80 mothers. . . . We didn't have anything, nowhere to meet, and since we didn't have anything, we had to sacrifice more.
>
> With this blow of losing a child, afterwards another and another, I was left with an emptiness that is not filled with food, that is not filled with money, that is not filled with clothing. Rather, it was an absence of giving love. But then again, giving love was not an easy road to travel because I had to sacrifice more of myself each day because each day new obstacles appeared.

The Mothers of Matagalpa, 1984–1990

The period 1984–90 was one of both war and new collective beginnings for the committee. The Mothers spoke of it as a time of strong unity, a time of working together for a common cause—the survival of the revolution.

Their language privileged notions of extreme suffering, *La Madre Sufrida*, but also of support and solidarity. Doña Juana described the changes she perceived soon after Doña Esperanza C. took over as coordinator: "[We] felt that the organization was becoming a more solid organization, or rather, we began to work in a more united way. . . . It was very nice because . . . I felt more love, more warmth, because we were just beginning."

The shift in strategies and goals from symbolic representation to social action on their own behalf as well as others broadened the potential base for membership. It attracted new members and encouraged many of the early members to redirect their time and energy away from other grassroots organizations (especially the Sandinista neighborhood committees, AMNLAE, and neighborhood religious groups) toward the Mothers' Committee. Doña Haidee, previously active in AMNLAE, described the new attraction she felt to the committee; "There were many boys dying and the mothers went looking for Doña Esperanza so they could join the committee because we found more warmth with her—in the way she spoke with us. She gave us hope. She encouraged us to overcome our problems [and] look for a way to console ourselves." New members were recruited to temper maternal resentment toward the FSLN but with a more pronounced emphasis also on what might be called internal benefits—to offer mutual aid and emotional support, to educate each other, and even to provide themselves with an alternative mode of living and interacting. As such, during this period the collective identity of the Mothers evolved from Mothers as *Las Continuadoras* to also focus on stronger emotional bonds and their greater potential as women. The committee was developing an organizational form that was not simply instrumental to their political goals (ending the contra war, promoting social and economic justice, creating self-help projects); it was a goal in and of itself.

Their alliance with the FSLN and AMNLAE remained after the Mothers established some autonomy from the party. Both did political work with the Mothers, speaking to them about the contra war and the draft and emphasizing the Sandinista ideals for which their children fought. Doña Haidee explained that during the mid-1980s, "AMNLAE advised [the Mothers] of activities that they wanted us to participate in. They would tell Doña Esperanza, and she would send representatives from the committee. In this way they would always come looking for us, so that we would give more strength to AMNLAE." The relation between AMNLAE and the Mothers was still rather one-sided, with AMNLAE asking for support for their demonstrations and activities more so than giving support to the Mothers' own plans and projects.

The Mothers also continued to serve as symbols of revolutionary suffering. Both the potency of and the FSLN's need for such symbolism increased as the debate over the contra war and the draft became foremost in the public's mind. Taking a prominent role in the ideological battle against counterrevolution, the Mothers of Matagalpa issued press statements and met with international groups in support of the FSLN and the war effort. Indeed, their first major project involved fund-raising to build a memorial to the revolution. This memorial—large and centrally located—consisted of three figures, two young men and a young woman, frozen in the act of firing their weapons.

The organization grew steadily during this period, thanks in part to the hard work of its core members. Doña Leonor recalled the organizational journey from a small group of Mothers accustomed to following directives to a dynamic group learning to plan, fundraise for, and execute its own projects: "We began to work to make the organization bigger. We had food sales, sold enchiladas, *atol* [corn-based drink], *elote* [young, tender ear of corn]—we sold everything. The monument was our first project, then the houses, the office." Doña Adela, the committee *responsable* for her barrio, described their new recruitment process. Members reapproached women whose children had died perhaps years earlier and documented their individual situations: "I didn't know how many Mothers there were. So I looked for Mothers whose child had fallen, or their husband. . . . I brought them to the committee. . . . This was the job of all the *responsables* of barrios, to make the committee bigger. If we had not worked like this, the committee would not be as big as it is. We all worked by barrio, [asking] how many Mothers were in each barrio? And each Mother filled out a form . . . [noting] what battalion her son was in . . . [and] where their son had fallen. And so the Mothers, here in my house, came to fill out the forms. . . . I gathered together 18 Mothers."

These forms helped the committee petition INSSBI (the social security and welfare office) for members' pensions. The information and aid offered in the pension application process was one of the committee's first concerns. Through interaction with Mothers in filling out the forms, barrio *responsables* amassed feedback on what the new members themselves saw as their needs. Core members were struck by the difficulty so many mothers of the fallen had in making ends meet. Their desperate economic situations were often exacerbated by their advanced age, abandonment by male companions, loss of income-earning sons, and loss of homes and livelihood in the war-torn countryside. This information inspired a more concerted attempt by core committee members to aid the poorest Mothers. The committee began to monitor its members' financial situations and redistribute government assistance, and later international aid, accordingly. As coordinator Esperanza C. explained: "We began to know what it was the Mothers needed. There were many Mothers who had come from the mountains. They didn't have anywhere to live. So we started building houses as our first [large-scale material aid] project. . . . It wasn't an effort to enrich ourselves; rather it was an effort to share, like Christ did in sharing the bread."

The Mothers, both collectively and individually, received financial support from the Sandinista state. The assistance was limited, but became essential to many members and their families. Aid to individual members included a monthly pension, rice, beans, and sugar packages (*arroz, frijoles y azucar,* or AFA), exemption from taxes, priority consideration for health care and scarce goods, occasional housing supplies and land, and a yearly Christmas present.[2] With inflation, the U.S. embargo, the growing casualty rates, and the redirection of state funds to defense, these state benefits were increasingly inadequate. But according to coordinator Esperanza C., their needs were by no means only material: "[Our effort] above all was to give life to the Mothers . . . because they didn't laugh, they didn't talk when we met with them. But now there is a fantastic change. When the Mothers began to work, creating the projects, it's like they changed. They were women who began to smile, began to chat. They began to set an important example. People came from other countries, and they met with us. Mothers gave their testimonies, spoke of their needs, spoke of their gains, spoke of the revolution. They said that the revolution gives a space to them as women, because this is also very important."

The Mothers' Committee sought support from nongovernmental organizations (NGOs) in 1985 and received donations of used clothing, which they sold to fund other income-generating projects. Through these donations, the Mothers began a close relationship with the Instituto Juan XXIII, a Nicaraguan Catholic NGO, and the U.S.-based Quixote Center. The majority of the NGO funding and clothing donations the committee received over the next ten years came from the Quixote Center in cooperation with the Instituto Juan XXIII.

The Mothers' Committee presented their change in focus as a corrective measure so that their ideology and actions did not contradict. No longer maternal figureheads who passively received state handouts, they became creators of income-generating projects through reference to the ideals of their fallen loved ones: "Our children didn't fight, didn't die so that we would go begging door to door. They died, they gave their lives, so that we would all live better. This is what we are trying to do ourselves—to gain a better life. In this way, this committee has gone from being a group that received federal assistance to an economically active women's group."[3]

Many members lived on the outskirts of town and the hills surrounding Matagalpa. These neighborhoods lacked the infrastructure and services of the older neighborhoods—water, electricity, sewage, garbage collection, paved roads, and gutters. Many others, refugees from the countryside, were homeless, moving between houses of relatives and friends and living in terribly overcrowded conditions. Such conditions have generated female-dominated collective struggles in cities throughout Latin America.[4] It is not surprising, then, that these conditions also affected the goals and strategies of the Mothers of Matagalpa. The following is a list of the committee's projects begun during this period. Although at first the projects reflected a priority in honoring the fallen, later projects all concerned the welfare of members and their families: monument of the Heroes and Martyrs (1984); two committee offices (1985); gallery of the Heroes and Martyrs (1986); forty-two houses in Barrio Juan XXIII (1986–91); a community building in Barrio Juan XXIII (1989); five popular eateries—income-generating (1985–91); four sewing cooperatives—income generating (1986–93); and skill and health workshops (1985–95).

In a 1987 report, committee leaders pointed to a new emphasis for the Mothers. From 1984 to 1987, the committee had focused on finding new mothers of the fallen, particularly the most marginalized, and registering them so that they might receive pensions and other economic benefits. With more Mothers formally organized, the committee could better look after and represent these women's rights as mothers of the fallen. Yet after 1987, the committee focused less on recruitment and increasingly on the education and well-being of the organized members and their surviving family members.[5] The skill and health workshops listed above represented their shift in this direction, a trend that accelerated after the contra war.

In addition to their community and self-help projects, the Mothers became prominent in the mobilizations against contra aggression and U.S.-funding of the contras. As one of their contributions to the war effort, the Mothers attended to mothers of mobilized soldiers, including them in activities as well as doing the ideological work of convincing these mothers that the draft was necessary and good. The Mothers worked with AMNLAE and Apoyo al Combatiente as a link between the army and mothers of soldiers, arranging trips to visit soldiers in the mountains, facilitating communication between families and soldiers, and visiting soldiers in the hospital. Doña María L., the leader of the Mothers in the nearby city of Jinotega, invoked notions of Universal Motherhood in describing her work with mothers of soldiers: "We formed the Committee of Mothers of Mobilized Soldiers so that they could visit the front where [their sons] were fighting. We were growing and growing by including these mothers of mobilized sons. They learned to share also among all those combatants—who for us were like our own children."

Core members of the Mothers of Jinotega began to work more closely with the Mothers of Matagalpa, traveling by bus to the meetings and activities. As the Matagalpa organization expanded beyond city limits, the committee increasingly concerned itself with helping rural Mothers obtain pensions by aiding illiterate women in filling out forms and cutting through bureaucratic red tape. In trips organized by the regional FSLN, the Matagalpa Mothers traveled to small communities in the countryside to help with projects and develop solidarity. These trips were also promotional in the sense that the Mothers presented themselves, and were presented, as the Sandinista maternal ideal—politically active *Madres Sufridas*.

With the example set by the Mothers of Matagalpa, mothers of the fallen living in the countryside were also coming together to address their own economic and emotional needs. Doña Teofila lived in the rural community of Rancho Grande, which in the mid-1980s was under constant threat of contra attacks. She worked closely with the Mothers of Matagalpa, establishing regular communication between the two Mothers' organizations and producing joint efforts:

> I helped [Mothers in Rancho Grande] go through the process . . . to get their pension. We as Mothers knew that our children had died, but none of us knew that we had the right to a pension and other aid. . . . So I brought these Mothers [to Matagalpa]. It was necessary to bring a birth certificate and information on [the son's] battalion and to fill out many forms. I told the National Assembly that . . . the Mothers were very poor and couldn't come [to Matagalpa], or they didn't have the papers. In the countryside, mothers don't register the births of their children, so they don't have their birth certificate with which to claim their rights. So I demanded that they be helped. . . . And things became easier. The war zones were prioritized and birth certificates weren't required. So problems were resolved little by little.

In the late 1980s, the Mothers of Matagalpa were active in the debate over amnesty for political prisoners (Somoza's National Guardsmen and contras, as well as civilian counterrevolutionaries), insisting, "The amnesty should be partial. . . . Our government cannot decree total amnesty, much less sit down to dialogue with the counterrevolutionaries who are nothing more than the servants of the North American government. Why negotiate with puppets?"[6] The committee also regularly participated in demonstrations and wrote communiqués condemning contra attacks in the late 1980s.

In this period, the Mothers were no longer an auxiliary group, but it is not easy to define what they became—a social movement demanding peace, social justice, and economic benefits for the poor and victims of war; an economic and emotional mutual support group; a community movement struggling for goods and services in poor neighborhoods; a loyal Sandinista mass organization; or a distribution center for international donations. These are not mutually exclusive categories, and the Mothers became in some sense all of these. The key, however, is that they were no longer simply *madres sufridas* mobilized as a vehicle for propaganda or an obedient group silent about its own needs. The importance of the organization's move toward autonomy and shift in focus from symbolic representation to activism cannot be overemphasized. It marked a fundamental change in how core members viewed themselves and their work in the committee. They evolved from symbolic, isolated figures that were celebrated and cared for into a larger, more independent organization with a maternal collective identity that made demands and formed projects on behalf of its members.

Exploring Economic Needs and Incentives to Join the Mothers

What attracted members into the committee during this period? How can we account for its growth from less than ten active members in 1984 to hundreds by 1990? One obvious factor was that the potential base for membership grew rapidly in this period due to the rising mortality rate in the war. Two other factors were the gradual decline in state benefits and programs due to the rising costs of war and the flow of war refugees into Matagalpa and surrounding communities, both of which resulted in a greater need for additional sources of economic support. Clearly, the economic benefits offered by the committee would seem to be a primary factor in its growth. However, the issue is complicated by the words of the core members themselves, who stressed political ideals and emotional/relational benefits and often denied the attraction of material benefits.

Before turning to core members' explanations for their activism, I first present the Mothers in demographic terms through an analysis of data gathered from the Mothers of Matagalpa's 313 membership forms. These forms documented each member up through 1989. Although the results do not readily apply to the very small group of active members prior to 1984, they are relevant to the 1984–90 and even the 1990–94 period, given that almost all the core members I interviewed had joined in the 1980s. My own demographic data from the fifty-five interviews conducted in 1992–93 closely resembled the larger sample from the 1980s. These data indicate that the Mothers shared a socioeconomic position that left them not only poor, but also with weak support networks and few economic options.

The majority of the Mothers of Matagalpa were middle-age women and older. Class was an important social distinction for the Mothers. In the interviews they invariably described themselves as poor, though they recognized several levels of poverty. Unemployment and underemployment were very high within the Mothers' households. Of the fifty-five I interviewed, only seven members could be described as working poor and only six as middle class.[7] The forty-two others lived a stressful, tentative existence in which either no one in their household had regular employment, or perhaps one or two individuals had low-paying jobs, often in the informal sector, and supported a household of five to ten people.

The average member was in her mid-fifties, with members' ages ranging from thirty-two to eighty-one years at the time of the interviews.[8] The average Mother had seven children who survived infancy.[9] Although virtually every Mother lived with at least one of her children, over 70 percent of those interviewed did not live with a male companion, describing themselves as separated (6 percent), single (33 percent), or widowed (33 percent).[10] Female-headed households are a growing phenomenon throughout Latin America, and women's lesser earning power condemns many such families to extreme economic marginalization.[11]

Studies of women's movements in Latin America describe problems male companions have posed for women's political participation.[12] Husbands often complained about gossip concerning their wives' attendance at meetings and claimed that because of their wives' political activism, domestic chores and the husbands themselves were neglected. Men can be resistant, if not hostile, to their wives' devotion of time to nondomestic activities, and this resistance obviously inhibits women's political mobilization. The generalizability of this problem is supported by my finding that over two-thirds of those I interviewed—often the most active Mothers—were separated, single, or widowed. Those women without male companions were free of barriers men sometimes impose on women's political activism. Interestingly, in the process of conducting the interviews for this research, the majority of which were done in members' own homes, I observed tenacious resistance to women's activism outside the home more from sons than from male companions (in part because male companions were relatively rare). While daughters served refreshments and tried to keep the children quiet, more than a few adult sons would interrupt to demand attention (an answer to a question, some coffee) or to "correct" their mother's responses. One simply remained in the room muttering about how the Mothers' Committee was "vagrancy" (*vagancia*). There were, however, several very notable exceptions among sons and husbands—those who were loyal Sandinistas or at least committed to carrying on the struggle of their fallen sibling or child. These men showed great respect and affection for their mother or wife, and helped out the committee by carrying out heavy labor, for example, or driving members around.

The absence of a male companion also tended to increase the precariousness of the household's economic situation. The lack of a male companion as breadwinner left a woman more financially dependent on her adult sons and daughters as well as herself for survival. As such, to a poor member in her fifties or older, the number of surviving adult children (particularly sons) was a vital factor in her ability to make ends meet. Repressive regimes, revolution, and war in Nicaragua, with their disproportionate death toll on young men, severely threatened women's traditional support networks and financial stability.[13] Accordingly, the death of an adult child who was a single mother's main provider was financially devastating. Of the Mothers interviewed, all had lost at least one loved one in the revolution or contra war, but 49 percent had lost more than one member of the immediate family. Almost 18 percent had lost their husband as well as at least one child to political violence. So for many, the absence of both a male companion and at least one adult child translated into a more tentative, fragile economic safety net that might have led them to seek out the support network of the Mothers of Matagalpa.[14]

Members' limited household incomes came from those family members who could find work, in addition to a small income (on average $20 per month in 1992) from Mothers who received a government pension as the mother of a victim of war. Most of the Mothers did not work outside the home. On their committee membership forms, 61 percent described themselves as housewives. Some of these housewives still carried out income-generating activity within their homes, such as taking in washing and ironing or selling cold soda and ice to neighbors.[15] Another 6 percent described themselves as unemployed or too old to work, leaving 33 percent of the membership with work outside the home. Many of those who worked outside the home (approximately 12 percent of the total membership) earned money in the informal economy, for example by making tortillas, selling food in the market, or sewing clothes. Six percent worked in private homes as domestics, and another 4 percent had a small family business, such as a bakery or a neighborhood store set up in their house.[16] The distribution of work for the members interviewed, those most active in the committee, was similar, except that 20 percent of these women worked in the committee's income-generating projects: corn mills, popular eateries, and a used clothing store.[17]

Roughly 40 percent of the Mothers of Matagalpa I interviewed were originally from the countryside, having been displaced by either the spread of war or the growth of capitalist agriculture before 1979 or after 1990. These were the poorest and least literate members, and they had often lost the most family members. Several of these women personally suffered torture and imprisonment at the hands of Somoza's National Guard or the contras. These Mothers lost not only family members but also their material possessions in the war, arriving in the city middle-aged or elderly, illiterate, unskilled in nonagricultural and nondomestic labor, responsible for their younger children and grandchildren, homeless, and often penniless.

In sum, the women who joined and remained active in the Mothers of Matagalpa were generally the poorest mothers of war dead; only a few active members could be described as middle class, even though many sons and daughters of the middle-class also died.[18] Members were largely unemployed or underemployed single mothers, almost half of whom had lost more than one close family member. Because the FSLN and AMNLAE and later the Mothers' Committee itself targeted the most marginalized for distribution of material aid, such women could expect to benefit financially from collective organizing. In light of their precarious financial situation and the material support available through the committee, we might from the outset view the Mothers of Matagalpa as a mobilization over the satisfaction of basic needs, a movement concerned with material demands more so than political ideals, symbols, personal relationships, or self-realization.

Nevertheless, although receipt of material benefits was an obvious incentive to participate, this was very rarely the reason the core members expressed when asked why they joined the committee. More commonly, those interviewed spoke of the bonds they formed and solace they found within the collectivity, the opportunities for personal growth, and their political commitment to carry on where their children left off. Although their economic situation may have predisposed many to join the Mothers of Matagalpa, the meaning core members attached to their organization was based on two other incentives—the political goals that propelled their visible actions and defined their public statements, and the latent emotional/social relationships.

Visibility: Political Paths to the Mothers' Committee

The Sandinista revolution first broadened citizenship to include many previously marginalized groups while still recognizing separate identities — women, *campesinos*, indigenous communities, youth. Yet with the contra war, identities were leveled through Sandinista institutions such as schools, the media, popular organizations, and the army into one primary identity — a Sandinista-style, nationalist "New Man." Women's identities and interests were shaped and mobilized with the aim of winning the war and securing a more equitable economic system. There was a relative absence of women's voices that expressed feminism, abortion rights, draft opposition, or even the demand to include women in the draft.[19]

The Mothers' separation from AMNLAE can be taken as a form of resistance to this leveling of voices and identities. The Mothers insisted upon their difference, their specificity. While supporting the war effort, they also demanded that their self-defined needs be recognized and addressed. Separation allowed for a securing of both public and private spaces for exploration of their needs and interests. However, dominant political discourse privileges some options and actors while hindering or excluding others. For example, in Sandinista Nicaragua, those deemed to have suffered were discursively privileged, particularly when this suffering was presented as having political causes — Somoza's repressive regime, the contra war, and, in the 1990s, the economic policies of President Violeta Chamorro. The Sandinista political discourse continued to shape the collective identity of the Mothers after they became autonomous, and the Mothers clung to images such as *Madres Sufridas* and *Las Continuadoras* throughout the 1980s.

One way of examining how the Mothers themselves viewed politics and their own activism is through two gendered concepts of morality: a morality of rights involving abstract laws, autonomous individuals, and universal principles; and a morality of responsibility and care involving connection with others, inductive solutions, and situatedness.[20] The Mothers confronted the crisis of the contra war using the latter language of responsibility more than liberal notions of individual rights. They appealed to emotions and emphasized emotional and physical trials of the family, community, and nation. When they did discuss rights, they emphasized the right to peace and the right to survive. Most strikingly, when circumstances compromised the right to survival, they spoke of their own acts of caring and their right to be cared for. Thus, the language was one of interconnection and reciprocity in which obligations flowed two ways—to care and be cared for, to have responsibility toward others, and to have others be responsible for them.

Their language in the interviews relied heavily on two words: *deber*—duty, debt—and *compromiso*—obligation, commitment. The force of duty and obligation ran strong in the Mothers' Nicaragua, in which individual rights were eclipsed by responsibilities to others. The FSLN used this moral force effectively. Sandinista rhetoric mobilized many women by emphasizing what was owed in the memory of "our heroes and martyrs." The logic went as follows: "So that blood was not shed in vain, the best way we can pay homage to our fallen children is through participating in the revolutionary process."

But the direction of this language of responsibility and debt was easily reversed. Mothers of fallen children—sons and daughters who had supported them economically or were expected to do so in the future—turned to the Sandinista state for economic support. Because their children gave their lives to the revolution, it followed that the revolution should assume the family economic responsibilities of the fallen. With over 80,000 deaths resulting from the insurrection and the contra war, the Sandinista state was heavily indebted according to this maternal balance sheet.

Yet despite their lobbying for economic support and their demands for an end to the U.S.-funded war, the Mothers of Matagalpa were ambivalent about describing theirs as a political organization. Rather, they situated themselves above politics in the realm of loyalty, patriotism, community, and emotion. In their understanding of the intersection of motherhood and politics, women truly acting as mothers out of love for their children should not involve themselves in the complicated, competitive, greedy world of politics. But they could involve themselves in marches, hunger strikes, Sandinista meetings, ideological workshops, and community projects. This type of activism, to them, was *Sandinismo*, but it was not really politics. Politics for the Mothers was distinctly individualistic, a lack of concern for others. It connoted competition, greed, looking out for oneself, ingratiating oneself to the right people, and manipulation. It also seemed to require military experience, education, or wealth. Many insisted they were not in the committee "*por interes*" (for their own self-interest or profit). Rather, they defined the committee as helping other people, supporting the causes of their heroes and martyrs, and struggling for the Nicaraguan people. As such, to struggle for change did not necessarily mean to act politically. Doña Elba told me, "One of the wonderful things about the Revolution was this: we learned to organize and to share the little that we had." In her view they learned to act not in a "political" manner involving greed and competition, but rather to act in a nonpolitical, communitarian manner. Similarly, Doña Juana defined the struggle: "To struggle means to learn something new everyday. To struggle means to not just accept, to not sell out for the gain of others. . . . But the sad thing is when the people only know to keep silent." As such, politics and struggle were separate concepts: politics was greed, hierarchy, something for the elite, whereas struggle implied sharing, social change, something of the people.

However, as Doña Elba spoke of the material benefits of the revolution, in this case some land, she revealed both the negative implications and the necessity of "politics": "[Receiving land through the revolution] was a great thing because we didn't have anywhere to live. . . . With the revolution everything changed. . . . There are many people who say they're not political, but I think that everyone uses politics. If not, you're not going to get anything." Another Mother, Doña María Elena, deliberated over the word "politics" and whether she had engaged in it. She decided that indeed she and the Mothers were political, but she took care to qualify what Sandinista politics meant: "In part we are political because we are Sandinistas and without politics we wouldn't be anything. We have the goal to continue struggling. . . . How many thousands and thousands of young people have fallen? We can't just sit around. . . . You always have your own politics because you know how to defend yourself. But I didn't fight for material gains. I never liked this. I'm upright. Fighting for personal gain isn't *Sandinismo*." To be sure, for the Mothers interviewed, "politics" was not a clearly defined term. They did not spend a good deal of time thinking about "politics" and reconciling the various contradicting images and concepts the word conjures up. But generally, it was a concept employed to help define what they were not.

The Mothers' sense of collective identity as it related to politics and struggle developed around the obligations they felt toward their heroes and martyrs and the *Frente Sandinista*, which these women believed took good care of them while in power. The popular image of mothers carrying on the struggle where their children left off—*Las Continuadoras*—was embraced and acted upon as a maternal duty. Mothers repeatedly expressed their determination to carry on the struggle of their children through the Mothers' Committee. Though their motivations were political in the sense that they struggled on behalf of social change, these were not the traditional politics associated with political parties and elections, and they were quick to differentiate themselves from *politicos*.[21]

Statements made by the long-term members reflected the deep sense of connection and responsibility they felt toward their dead family members and how this influenced their political ideals, goals, and alliances. "Obligation" and "commitment" to the fallen were mentioned again and again as members explained why they took up the struggle. The following comments by Doña Juana and Doña Rosaura were typical: "This struggle of one's children was also an obligation . . . signed with pain and blood. And so this struggle, I believe, is unbreakable, and it is a struggle that we won't betray, not even for a minute" (Doña Juana). "Like we say, if our children died for a free Nicaragua, so that everyone would be free, so that they would have food, . . . we have to be united to fight for all this. . . . If my son died for this [cause] and my husband is handicapped, I don't see how we can think differently" (Doña Rosaura).

Struggle through the Mothers' Committee was a mode of paying respect to the heroes and martyrs and an obligation inherited from them. Drawing from the familiar Sandinista theme of losing in order to gain, these deaths were sometimes presented as an opportunity for the Mothers to learn more about Sandinista ideology. Coordinator Esperanza C. spoke of the death of combatants as a new beginning for their mothers: "Losing a child was not the end of the world; rather, it was the start of a new life in which we could live and reflect upon what they had done. They were young people, full of hope, full of ideals." During meetings the Mothers discussed Sandinista ideology and drew links between the Mothers' goals and those of the revolution. As Doña María L. explained, "We fought because we knew why [our children] were fighting." Projects and protests were planned around the Mothers' interpretations of their children's goals.

Ironically, this sense of obligation to the fallen, framed through Sandinista discourse, motivated the Mothers' separation from AMNLAE. Act-

ing only under FSLN and AMNLAE directives had limited the Mothers'
struggle to tearful testimonials and behind-the-scenes, unrecognized "revolutionary tasks"—traditional forms of women's work, such as cleaning the
neighborhood or the cemetery. These tasks were not intended to empower,
and they did not challenge limiting images of women. As the contra war
intensified, many members were ready to support the revolution in more
challenging ways and to have this work explicitly recognized as accomplishments of the Mothers of Heroes and Martyrs. The strength and urgency of
this obligation to carry on the struggle was illustrated by Doña María L.:[22]
"We Mothers never rest because our children didn't rest. This is the example
they left for us—to continue fighting until we conquer definitive peace,
until everyone is equal, and until everyone has and is able to defend their
homes, defend their land, defend their health, defend everything that would
be good for the exploited classes. In all, we are *las continuadoras*. This is the
goal of the Mothers. It is the continuation of what our children left behind
when they died."

The goal of keeping alive their children's ideals was extended by the committee into creating and maintaining physical representations of their children. There were plaques and monuments celebrating Sandinista heroes
and martyrs. Some Mothers lived in neighborhoods named after their fallen
child. Schools, offices, streets, and public spaces bore the names of martyrs.
Mothers spoke of their children as embodied in and their children's ideals
represented by structures built in the effort to carry out the revolution—
for example, a school named after a fallen guerrilla, or a rural health clinic
that a soldier died defending. The presence of the fallen was felt by the
Mothers as they visited sites rich with personally relevant symbolism and as
they carried out political work in their children's memory. Doña María L.
put it this way: "[Our work with the mobilized soldiers] helped us not forget our children. Rather, we felt that some combatant who was there, some
wounded *compañero* who was in need of our help, that these were our children." Doña Chepita, whose son was missing in action and who for that
reason described herself as a Mother of the Disappeared, explained: "One
carries on in order to conserve their ideals—to continue forward; to struggle
like they struggled; to feel that one's child is still here, that they haven't
died."

In a more general sense, the survival of the revolution symbolically meant the survival of those they lost—martyrs only really die if the revolution dies. As Doña María L. explained it, "As long as we participate . . . [in] our revolution, our children haven't died. Our children continue to live because they fought so that we would know our culture, so that the poor would have land, so that the poor would have a house. . . . And so we can't stop struggling for land for the campesino, for housing, for health because for all this our children died. . . . The important thing is to keep alive the memory of the heroes who loved us. . . . As long as we struggle, they haven't died."

Christian discourse melded with and supported revolutionary discourse as the Mothers sometimes compared their child's death with the crucifixion of Christ and themselves with the Virgin Mary. With such an equation, to abandon the struggle would mean a betrayal of both one's martyred child and one's religious faith. Doña Esperanza C., in an interview with a nun who worked closely with the Mothers in the mid-1980s, discussed her commitment to political struggle as having intertwining maternal and religious roots:

When the news arrives "your child fell" . . . it is a moment of desperation, of anguish, of grief, but also . . . one remembers when Christ was crucified, Mary felt this same pain. . . . Crucified Christ, his decision was a great sacrifice, a change. Jesus saw the injustices during the time in which he lived preaching the word. So we also think of our children at this moment: they shed their blood for a change, a change of humanity for the poor. So this brings us closer to our faith in Christ. But then what is it that brings us closer to our faith? Continuing the doctrine of our children, filling ourselves with courage and faith because one day our people will be free, there will be no wars. . . . So we can't turn back, we have to continue this message . . . of faith that Christ left us and that our children continued.[23]

The morality they applied to politics relied heavily on a sense of connection with others, obligations, and care—a morality that research has found to be more often expressed by women.[24] Debates within feminist theory continue over the extent to which this is innate, socially constructed, or inscribed in the subconscious through the mother-child relationship. While it is outside the scope of this research to settle this debate, arguments presented here are based upon a notion of gendered constructions through state-generated discourse. As I have documented, the FSLN spent considerable effort fine-tuning women's morality to reinforce Sandinista hegemony.

The salience of this maternal identity demonstrates the importance of looking to discursive resources in understanding the construction of collective identity. Through countless discursive vehicles—for example, the media, revolutionary art, and especially Sandinista popular organizations—the FSLN constructed the Mothers' identity by employing such themes as losing in order to gain, mothers of the fallen as modern-day Marys, and mothers' obligation to carry on the struggle. In an official sense, women became Mothers of the Heroes and Martyrs upon the death of a combatant child. Yet the identity of a "good" Mother of the Heroes and Martyrs who "truly loved her fallen child" entailed the adoption of certain Sandinista-prescribed behaviors and attitudes. Primary requirements included active participation in the Mothers' Committee, self-abnegation, and open grieving. This prepackaged identity, defined and spread by the state and attached with a high status, facilitated the collective identity process. The *Las Continuadoras* mobilizing identity provided a foundation upon which the Mothers of Matagalpa constructed their own personally relevant collective sense of identity, which in turn laid the groundwork—the modes of discourse—upon which the Mothers' goals and expectations could be discussed and developed. Yet new membership, shifting discourses, and altered economic and political contexts all propelled collective identity as a dynamic rather than static creation.

"Alone You Can't Do Anything, Organized You Can"

Through their participation in the revolutionary process, core members came to value solidarity and organization as a means of challenging those in power or receiving recognition and material support. They learned to combine their voices, resources, and efforts in condemning contra atrocities and struggling on behalf of their own members. One Mother, Doña Ana María, spoke of how members accompanied each other to overcome crises arising within the home: "United, one has greater strength. If we have economic problems, or some other problem, we solve them together. For this reason, we live united, always." Such a support group became increasingly valuable as the expense of the contra war and U.S. trade embargo exacerbated the economic crisis and led to cutbacks in social programs and benefits.

Repeatedly in the interviews they explained, "Alone you can't do anything, organized you can." Working together gave members a sense of political efficacy. As Doña Ventura put it: "We have to unite because all united we will accomplish something. Alone you aren't going to do anything. But among everyone, and with each one doing a bit, all together we will get something done."

When asked why they participated in the committee, respondents almost never spoke of the material benefits and showed ambivalence at the political nature of the committee. They struggled on behalf of others, particularly in the name of the fallen, and recognized that united they had greater strength. However, they most readily and comfortably spoke of what could be called the emotional benefits of the committee.

As Elizabeth Jelin wrote, a sector of the population mobilizes "in order to make felt its presence, interests and demands in the public forum of power and in socio-cultural relations. Thus in one sense one is dealing with the theme of *presence*."[25] This notion is similar to that which Alberto Melucci terms the *visibility* of a collectivity—the aspects of a collective identity that are presented outward and directed toward the state and general public.[26] This is the "public face" of a collectivity in its attempt to effect change. It involves public pronouncements, speeches, protests, and interviews with journalists—the effectiveness of which requires a unified, coherent message. This dimension—the unified voice, the public face—along with its observable results (anywhere from the implementation of a barrio water system to takeover of the state) are usually the focus of social movement research.

Yet there is another dimension to movements, less often recognized but vital nonetheless: the "latent" dimension. This dimension is the process of collective identity that is directed inward, its "private face." Melucci suggests that in the latent dimension, emotional ties develop among participants, and through interaction participants gain a measure of confidence, some self-realization, and a sense of community. It is in the latent sphere that actors find the opportunity to live differently, to practice cultural innovation.[27] The collective identity process is propelled through the interactions "behind the scenes," for a sense of "we" that also involves social change requires not just marches and manifestos but also, and more importantly, it requires communication, understandings, shared practices, and the recognition of common goals and emotional bonds.

Therefore, these two dimensions of collective identity are not so much separate as mutually dependent or complementary. Melucci writes: "Latency allows visibility in that it feeds the former with solidarity resources and with a cultural framework for mobilization. Visibility reinforces submerged networks. It provides energies to renew solidarity, facilitates creation of new groups, and recruitment of new militants."[28] As such, the latent dimension is no less important for being less empirically detectable.

Earlier I addressed the Mothers' construction of their specificity from fathers of the fallen. But collective identity also involves the "development of emotional investments which enable individuals to recognize themselves in each other."[29] Analysis that fails to look at the latent dimension of a group such as the Mothers fails to grasp the basis for solidarity, the bonds that hold the group together, the distinctly maternal quality of their collectivity, and the personal developments in terms of empowerment and self-realization. After all, individuals do not simply or suddenly unite in a single voice and body to make demands. They interact with each other to develop a collectivity based upon a common understanding of goals and strategies. Furthermore, political collectivities do not just influence society, they influence (as they are influenced by) their members.

"I Joined Because I Felt Alone": The Latent Maternal Community

The Mothers of Matagalpa were largely poor, single, middle-age or elderly, unemployed women with very limited means of support. Many were illiterate, relatively unskilled for urban work, and/or "too old to work." Combined with the economic loss entailed by the death of an adult son or daughter, the average Mother was in desperate need of the material support offered in the Mothers' Committee. As such, it might seem a relatively straightforward hypothesis that the average member joined for material aid.

However, the messages of the Mothers that reached the national press and international NGOs during this period largely involved the political ideals of carrying on the revolutionary struggle described previously. If we were to rely only on the speeches, published communiqués, and pamphlets of the Mothers of Matagalpa, the explanation for why Mothers joined the organization would seem clear: to carry on the struggle of their children and, to a lesser extent, to provide economic support for its members.

Because they do not problematize members' motives for participation, studies on the Mothers of the Plaza de Mayo (Argentina) and other maternal organizations in Latin America tend to present members' reasons for activism as clear and univocal.[30] Women joined to demand the whereabouts of their disappeared loved ones, and over time they took up vigilance against state violence. However, in maternal groups that existed for over a decade after the disappearance or death of loved ones, can the official goal of vigilance over human rights or carrying on the revolutionary struggle alone account for why these women joined and continued to participate on an almost daily basis? The answers provided by core members of the Mothers of Matagalpa suggest that they do not. When I asked these members why they participated, they pointedly denied that it was for economic benefit and often spoke of their political goals. But they most often and most eloquently spoke about the latent but powerful emotional bonds and the fulfillment they found through their sense of maternal community.

Some Mothers who were better off economically expressed their desire to help others. This help was directed at poorer Mothers, people in their community, ex-soldiers, war orphans, and war disabled. These Mothers described their participation as motivated through the desperate conditions of many members. More than an abstract notion of rights or even the "higher cause" of the revolution, they spoke as if they were being pulled into the committee through the increasing sense of obligation they felt toward other members. In helping others, they also helped themselves. Committee work was not simply a matter of self-abnegation—it gave members a sense of purpose in their lives. They felt useful, needed—feelings that had been threatened or lost upon the death of their child. As Doña Ernestina put it: "My strength came from participating, helping." Often they spoke of how they felt compelled to help other Mothers because they personally knew the emotional and economic strain the loss of a child entailed, as Doña María L. explained: "We had to look after them, to accompany them in their suffering . . . because when you lose your child, you become depressed, you suffer greatly."

This "mothering" of others was also directed beyond members of the committee. Doña María L. remembered the work they did during the contra war with mobilized and wounded soldiers and their families: "It was great work, very beautiful, because we were looking after the war wounded. It was a joy to share with them something that we all worked to get. . . . The family would feel better knowing that, 'Good, my son is not alone—the Mothers of fallen combatants are there. . . . Mothers that bring joy to our children.'"

The emotional bonds among the Mothers were reinforced by their concern to accompany other women in their grief. But the emotional support clearly went beyond accompaniment and concern. Committee members wanted to know about one another's feelings in order to better understand their own. Both informally and in group discussions, they spoke with other women who understood the pain of losing a child. As Doña Olga said: "When you lose a child, you are left sad and you want to be able to talk with someone who has felt the same loss. . . . Almost all of us have suffered the same, so there is a bit of comfort [in the committee]. . . . [We go] to talk, to share our ideas, our feelings about the loss of our children."

Discussion of their losses readily extended into conversations about other problems as well. Mothers came to the committee for a respite from domestic problems and for emotional help in dealing with the daily crises in the home. Committee activities provided a temporary escape from problems they confronted within the household—money shortages, unemployment, health problems, domestic violence, and alcoholism, to name but a few. The following comment by Doña Paquita was typical: "You're distracted there, meeting, listening to them talk. For a little while you aren't thinking about your poverty or your suffering."

Over and over again, the Mothers used the word "alone" to describe how they felt before joining the committee. Doña Juana recalled: "I joined because I felt alone. [I said to myself], 'There are more mothers that have had happen to them what happened to me, so I'm going to seek out this organization so that I'm not alone.' I felt a kind of selfishness—that I cannot only feel this pain alone, I have to feel it along with another." In contrast to "alone," with striking consistency they used the word "same" or "equal" (*igual*) to describe the relationship they developed with others in the committee. Doña Antonia: "It was the same pain. We all carried the same thoughts, the same words. There is mutual support." Doña Haidee: "We help each other. There we understand each other's pain, which is the same because we are all mothers—we are all the same." This sense of sameness was based upon both their daily experiences as poor mothers and the singular pain of losing a child.

The Mothers' Committee offered its members a forum, a rare group of people who would hear them, understand them, and comfort them. It would be difficult to overstate the importance of the attention and affection many found in the committee: they listened to each other, encouraged each other to speak, and provided a relatively safe environment in which to discuss the details of their lives. In the words of Doña Jesus, "You can tell anything to your companions [in the committee]. When we're sad, we talk." And Doña Petrona explained, "We work united. I feel happy to arrive at a meeting. One feels better, closer to people, happier."

In learning about and confiding in one another, they arrived at the understanding that they were not alone in their problems and that only through collective efforts could they overcome them. This development within the latent dimension reinforced the visible aspects of the collectivity. The emphasis they placed on establishing a sense of unity and support echoes closely the processes of the mothers of the disappeared in Argentina and El Salvador.[31] They too emphasized to other mothers that they were not alone. The similarity suggests that such latent aspects of organizations, so often glossed over in analysis, are vital to the development and success of a collectivity.

Through years of work and interaction, many of the Mothers developed a deep sense of responsibility and affection for one another. They helped each other with problems, they trusted each other, and they found comfort, love, and belonging that they did not find in other social or political organizations or perhaps even within their own family. This bond was an important factor in the growth of the Mothers' Committee, and Mothers such as Doña María Elsa emphasized it to explain their dedication to committee activities: "That was another thing I gained from the committee—having a friendship with each one, making intimate friends. I felt happy. I felt peaceful. I felt trusted because I love them, all of them."

Some mentioned their difficulty in meeting new people and making new friends before joining the committee. Belonging to an organization meant new social outlets and a relief from the monotony and extreme pressures of poverty and unemployment within the home. Doña Leonor: "There's no way to work, so we feel like getting out of the house. If you feel like it, you can go to the organization to meet, to see and talk with the other Mothers. . . . Because we don't have things to do in the house. We just think about what we should do, about what to do so that we can give our children something to eat." Doña Esperanza C.: "What happens is that you feel, being in the house hour after hour, that you are closed within yourself. You are doing the same things over and over again. And this, in my experience, does not solve anything because I can solve the problems within my own house, but I cannot solve the problems of others."

This bond of intimate friendship did not just happen, however. The Mothers described it as something they learned about, worked on, and accomplished: "We have learned to love each other, to be united, to see each other's problems. [In the committee] we find love. If we have a problem in the house, we go there and talk with a *compañera* and forget the problem. Being united is very beautiful" (Doña María Elena). "This is the struggle— to have us all united to help each other mutually and see to each other's needs. If one is poorer or sick, we look for the way to help. I feel that we have to give support and not let ourselves fall because we Mothers need each other. . . . I would never say: 'I am going to participate in the committee, and I don't care about the rest of the Mothers, only about myself.' It is for the rest" (Doña Lourdes).

Members visited the committee house to enjoy themselves for a couple of hours, to gossip, celebrate accomplishments, talk to visitors, and even sing and dance. Doña Geronima stressed the opportunities to form new friendships: "Being organized is a beautiful thing because you have support— moral as well as material. You meet people, interact with them, making friends. And if you aren't organized, this doesn't happen because you don't leave the house, don't meet people." The Mothers developed cultural and craft workshops, which Doña Lourdes praised for their therapeutic effects: "As Mothers we live sadly in this situation, but we sometimes feel happy because in the Mothers' Committee we have a dance group that helps us, animates us, and gives us new strength."

As these Mothers attest, women of the Mothers' age and class in Nicaragua often have limited social or political activities outside the home. Unemployment and poverty can make the home a stressful, depressing place. The committee offered women a unique opportunity to leave the home and go where they could both socialize with friends and do socially useful work. Accordingly, I suggest that the ties of affection and the social atmosphere the Mothers created within their committee were vital to the growth and longevity of the organization.

One way of viewing the development of emotional bonds among the Mothers is as an extension of their traditional maternal roles. They nurtured other Mothers, thus filling some of the emotional emptiness they felt upon losing a child. Just as important, they received attention from others—they were listened to, comforted, fussed over. As they recalled the loneliness they felt after the death, they explained that the time spent with other Mothers made them feel accompanied, less alone. They mothered each other and were mothered, forming valuable friendships.

Notes kept of a 1991 workshop for leaders and other core members of the Mothers' Committee organized by a Matagalpa woman's organization, *Grupo Venancia*, support my findings concerning core members' reasons for joining. In the workshop, members reflected upon why people unite and why they themselves joined the committee. The responses, listed below, reflect the interview responses discussed above. They joined for political and relational reasons and for personal growth—the first directed outward with the aim of impacting society, the latter two directed within the group of Mothers with the intent to create a strong web of mutual support:

—*political:* to have strength through uniting; to have the strength to continue fighting; to have strength in order to defend rights; to struggle; to work better; for a better Nicaragua; for the happiness of the people and the dispossessed; to confront the war; to fight for revindications; to defend our rights and make gains; to dialogue, be respected, be taken into account; to have more ideas; to continue the ideas of our children; to solve our problems; to respond to needs.

—*relational:* to unite with the other Mothers, share the pain and not feel alone; to be understood, to have love, moral support; to have care and trust; to have caring relationships with each other; to be in solidarity; to have company (or diversions); to have moral support.

—*personal growth:* to develop ourselves as people; to gain confidence.

Members alluded to the economic benefits of membership with the last two responses in the political category: "to solve our problems" and "to respond to needs." Indeed, the committee developed separately from AMNLAE in 1984 in part to address members' economic needs, and the biggest project the Mothers took on was the construction of houses for homeless members. Yet even though the committee directed much of its efforts to establishing economic benefits for its members, core members very rarely (almost never) spoke of such benefits in their accounts of why they participated in the committee. An untold number of these core members originally joined with material benefits in mind. However, their almost daily participation over the years and their enthusiasm for their work in the committee cannot be explained by material cost-benefit analysis alone. Rather, in attaching meaning to their maternal collective identity, they embraced the nonmaterial goals of upholding their children's political ideals and establishing the latent, relational dynamics of friendship and mutual emotional support. Conversely, they branded economic benefits as an inappropriate motivator. Members gained fulfillment carrying on the struggle of the fallen, belonging to a group, caring for and being cared about. Thus, for many core members, participation was its own reward, and their time put into the committee was not calculated as a cost so much as a benefit alongside the economic benefits they silently enjoyed.

Contradictory Subjectivities and Barriers to Participation

With the committee's move toward autonomy and the greater time commitment required of members, tensions began to arise within some homes. Some Mothers developed their activism to the point that they had to choose between various valued subjectivities. Their participation in the committee at times conflicted with their own interpretation of what it meant to be "good" wives and mothers—drawing into question the definition of what a good wife and mother was. Even more troubling was when their own interpretation of good or proper maternal behavior contradicted their family's interpretation.

Traditional discourse located women within the home—a proper, respectable wife and mother catered to her family and did not venture far beyond the front door. Coordinator Esperanza C. described how committee work caused conflict in many households, including her own: "[Committee activism] has cost us a lot. . . . The women are very conscientious of the work to be developed, but the husband can say, 'How can it be that now this woman is out in the streets more than me?' And they believe that she is not being a woman because they think that women are only for inside the home. Right? And this happened to me also because I was a baker, and taking care of my children inside the home and the flowers in my garden had become part of my life. But I forgot about my garden because I felt it was more important to work for these women."

With some very notable exceptions, there was an impatience, lack of respect, or even ridicule on the part of male companions for women's participation in the committee.[32] Doña Rosa Emilia, though single herself, spoke of men's "*machista*" aversion to organizations such as the Mothers' Committee: "Men don't like [the committee]. Men are very *machista*. They say that it is vagrancy to go to these meetings, but to me it doesn't seem that way. I like to help the other Mothers, and it seems the men don't like this. They say that all these old ladies do is go to meetings." Several respondents spoke of the conflicts they experienced when they became active, conflicts that centered on their positions as a wife and a mother. Doña Esperanza R. recalled the resistance of past male companions and suggested that this resistance was widespread: "You always have problems with the father when you fully involve yourself in an organization. Even if he is the real father of the child [who died] . . . because the man is always accustomed to having the woman in the house from the time he gets up to the time he goes to bed. And when the organization formed, we didn't manage the house, we managed things in the streets. . . . At times the meetings are long, and you get back late at night. So there's always problems. It's that the mother always feels more for a child than the father in all sentiments."

As was common, she explained a mother's activism and a father's resistance in terms of the different levels of emotional attachment and loss. As I have stressed, dedication to the committee was linked to obligation to the fallen. Doña Ventura explained her devotion to the Mothers, despite what others, including her husband, might say: "'Look,' I would say, 'I'm united with them for a cause that my son told me about. If you like it or not, if my husband likes it or not, I have to work with them. Perhaps my old man doesn't like it, but I do.'" Doña Esperanza C. explained the greater difficulty

women had in the revolutionary struggle. During the insurrections, she supported her son, a Sandinista collaborator, while hiding her support not only
from society but also from her own husband:

> It was harder on the mothers. Like in my case, at times you had to involve
> yourself, make more sacrifices because you were farther along [politically]
> than the man. Your husband didn't know that you were involved because you
> were afraid of losing your husband. And perhaps one should not take this in
> a bad way because it was such a hard war with such an imbecile *Guardia,* he
> had reason to fear that something could happen to his woman. . . . And so
> because of this fear, perhaps the same man said, "How could this woman be-
> come involved in this? If they kill men, what are they going to do to women?"
>
> And women, or at least me, I didn't tell my husband that I was involved
> or that Ernesto was a collaborator. So I had to lie. . . . But at times it was so
> lovely when your son says, "You have to be here at 10 AM," and I had to leave
> in a hurry and arrive to have them tell me what I had to do. But also to be
> ready for some man to say, "What were you doing, Esperanza?" or "Where is
> your mamá going?" The man could think badly of me.
>
> And so you accept all of this out of your love of life, love for your child,
> and love for your country. Three things. Love for your child because your
> child is involved, and the mother always looks for ways to protect her child
> so that nothing happens. Love for life because involved in this, you have the
> hope that one day there will be freedom, that the killings of so many young
> people will stop. And love for country because we all care for our country—
> but a free country, a country for everyone.

Doña Esperanza C. went on to discuss the friction within her own household after she joined the committee. Her statement below about earning
less and losing much of her business as her commitment to the Mothers of
Matagalpa grew marks a fundamental change in her life. She gave up the
stability and financial independence of the bakery and she gave up her mar-
riage (though not her family) to dedicate herself to more socially meaningful
work:

> Everyday it was like I was feeling more obligated to [the Mothers]. So I
> worked less in my house and gave more time to the committee. But I came to

have more economic limitations. . . . My children understood, but my husband didn't. He wouldn't accept this. It wasn't that he was against the *Frente*. It was that I had to dedicate myself to the house, or he would leave. "Fine, I'll let you leave because I have a great obligation to these people. I can't leave them." So he left, and I kept working [with the Mothers]. My children understood better. . . . And so [my children] weren't a negative influence on my work. They were a support for me.

Men were not inevitably hindrances on women's political activism. As Esperanza reveals, her sons (and daughters) actively supported, even made possible, her time-consuming participation in the committee. Furthermore, of the twenty most active of the core members I interviewed (those who spent the most time doing committee work), half were living with a male companion compared with 28 percent of members in general. Six of these men were active Sandinistas who supported the Mothers' Committee; another male companion was bedridden and mentally fragile from wounds he received as a guerrilla; and the other three were out of the home most of the day with steady work and were generally supportive of the revolution. These cases reveal that male companions can also promote and facilitate women's activism. Indeed, although single women did not have to deal with the resistance of a male companion, women with actively supportive male companions and adult children participated with the greatest ease.

Concerning barriers to women's political activism, Elizabeth Jelin wrote, "The organization of the family and the sexual division of labor hinders women's public participation because of their domestic responsibilities and the ideological burden of being female. It would seem, therefore, that women more frequently participate in protest movements at critical moments than in long-term, formal, institutionalized organizations that imply taking on responsibilities, dedicating time and effort to the organization and also—why not say it?—the opposition of men."[33] Although she identifies certain obstacles encountered by the Mothers, the Nicaraguan case offers several exceptions to Jelin's analysis. While they formed in 1979, the committee only grew beyond ten or so members once it separated from AMNLAE and began to plan time-consuming, long-range plans and projects. A key difference, I suggest, is that so many Mothers were without male companions to discourage activism. Furthermore, Sandinista discourse, with its image of *Las Continuadoras*, combatant mothers, and patriotic wombs helped counter Sandinista men's objections and lent legitimacy to the group, so that some of the most active members had male companions and adult sons actively supporting the committee.

But perhaps most important in explaining the long-term dedication of core members are the latent aspects of the Mothers collectivity. The Mothers insisted that they bonded through a grief that could only be shared by other Mothers, thus forming a separate maternal community. However, as Doña Elsa A. stressed, they did not seek to establish total separatism but rather in developing women's sense of self-worth they also sought to convince others, including male companions, to value women's work: "Most of the concern is for this—that women are not objects. The fact is that women are equal to men . . . at the level of ability to work. And we look for ways to involve the husbands, the rest of the family so that they see how these women have worked so that they realize, become conscious of what the women are doing. It's hard to raise the husband's consciousness. . . . They have to *see* what you do." Thus, in addition to promoting the image of *Las Continuadoras*, the Mothers set out to nullify the contradictions between mothers as *amas de casa* (housewives) and mothers as activists through demonstrating women's achievements outside the home.

Contradictory Maternal Messages: Peaceloving and Pro-Draft

A peacemaker's hope is a militarist's fear: that the rhetoric and passion of maternity can turn against the military cause that depends on it. Mothers have supported their boys and their leaders, but in the contradiction of maternal and military aims there is a dangerous source of resistance.
—SARA RUDDICK, *Maternal Thinking: Toward a Politics of Peace*

Key to understanding the Mothers of Matagalpa's process of collective identity in this period is a comparison of the committee's official position and individual members' reflections on the *Servicio Militar Patriotico* (SMP). The intersection of the draft, draft-age men, and their mothers was a major focus of FSLN propaganda and organizing during this period. The Mothers of Matagalpa were the objects and the subjects of this campaign, both acting and being acted upon. They were held up as an idealized example for emulation, which in turn pressured them to live up to this invented image of themselves. Their task of wartime "decorative representation," as Doña Esperanza C. termed it, involved potentially contradictory subject positions: Spartan Mothers, Combatant Mothers, the Virgin Mary, and Life-givers. The intense Sandinista effort to sway mothers' opinion of the war testifies to these contradictions and their own difficulty reconciling the popular notion that motherhood and war run in contradictory directions.

The international myth that women are peaceloving was well circulated in Nicaragua. The Mothers of Heroes and Martyrs were portrayed in the Sandinista and international pro-Sandinista media as naturally peaceloving, opposed to Reagan's war, and the ultimate victims of this war. As *Madres Sufridas*, they condemned U.S.-contra aggression from a very powerful moral standpoint. As a *Barricada* editorial put it, the mothers of the fallen "are the ones who have the most moral authority to demand peace and to talk about it."[34] Yet the Mothers were also mobilized to promote the draft and the war effort in general. Despite some creative rewriting to make the discourses meld, these two positions—pro-peace and pro-draft—left many Mothers feeling uneasy about the FSLN. Although no one personally admitted to it, Mothers claimed that other members opted for Violeta Chamorro's 1990 campaign that promised both peace and an end to the draft.

Compulsory military service became law in September 1983 and was implemented in January 1984. Men between the ages of seventeen and twenty-five years old were required to register for a two-year service in the army, and those ages twenty-six to forty were to register for the army reserves. The draft came to be the least popular of Sandinista policies, particularly among *campesinos*. Those who supported the draft referred to it as the Patriotic Military Service (SMP). The opposition called it the Obligatory Military Service (SMO), emphasizing the lack of choice rather than patriotism. The draft forced young men who would rather remain outside of national politics to choose sides and risk their lives. Harsh Sandinista conscription methods, particularly in the draft's first year, drove many young men in the countryside to join the contras. One young man discussed with me his decision to join the contras. Unable to prove to the Sandinista draft authorities that he was underage, he and his three brothers were imprisoned several times for draft evasion:

[My brothers and I] didn't want to be drafted into the *Servicio Militar*, and upon seeing the oppression, we decided to go with the *Resistencia*. . . . When I was only 12, [the FSLN] threw me in jail because I didn't want to go in the *Servicio Militar*. . . . They imprisoned us [3 times], and so we didn't like the Sandinista government. So we had to flee and join the ranks of the *Resistencia*. We did it voluntarily.

Interviewer: So either way you had to fight — in the *Servicio Militar* or with the *Resistencia*? Did you think that the *Servicio Militar* was worse, or more dangerous?

It was all the same. You were just waiting to die. But we went voluntarily because we didn't want to be recruited or go against our will. It's true that the danger was the same in the *Resistencia* and the *Servicio Militar*, but it was with our own will.

Doña Teofila, having spent the war in the countryside, echoed this experience from a Sandinista mother's perspective, saying that the contras kidnapped young men who did not want to join either army: "The young ones they took to Honduras. And they left the mothers crying. That is to say that the contras did it, *La Guardia*, because for those who didn't want to go to either side, they took by force. And the one who suffered was the mother. We decided to go with their mothers [to the Honduran border] to demand that they set our children free."

Charges were also made that the draft was biased against the poor. The sons of the rich and well-connected could find ways to avoid military service if they chose to — scholarships abroad, safe desk jobs, flights to Miami. Doña Chica asserted, "Some boys went willingly because . . . they wanted to serve. Others didn't because they were from the rich, the bourgeoisie and so they were sent to the United States." The poor had few options but to fight.

Mandatory military service represented an economic loss to many families, which also threatened popular support for the draft. Desperately poor families sometimes had their primary means of financial support taken away when a son was drafted. One Mother, Doña Gregoria, explained her opposition to the draft on this basis: "[The draft] is the only thing that I didn't like because, you see, after this first boy left, I had two more that were taken from me into the service. One was in the mountains for two years . . . [and] when he came back, he didn't get his job back, and he was left unemployed. . . . This is what I didn't like. And as a mother, it was very difficult. As a mother, I didn't like the *servicio militar*." Single mothers felt this economic loss the most, and, like Doña Gregoria, many mothers had several sons drafted.

Mothers and their sons were also distressed at the two years of lost education during the son's service. Doña Chepita tried to convince her son to avoid the draft. "And he'd say, 'Mama, what good is that? Either way I'm not going to study. If I don't have an identification card for the *servicio militar*, they aren't going to register me for school.' So that's why he did it—to get his identification card in order to study. . . . At times people don't like to say this out loud, but I'll say it: this is the reason he went."[35]

Of course, the deepest felt complaint against the draft was the danger involved. Many Mothers recounted their panic each time a military vehicle slowed in front of their house for fear that it arrived to deliver bad news. Doña Elba spoke of her anxiety: "I was always afraid. . . . I was imagining the worst. I hardly slept because I thought they were going to come to tell me [that my son was dead]." Her fears were justified when one day the military vehicle did stop in front of her house:

I was frying some rice and . . . a vehicle came up. The children were still young. "Mamá," they say, "Filomena is here." I thought she came to bring some things to [my son in the army]. . . . But when I went outside, I saw that she was coming toward me. I didn't let her say anything to me because my heart told me that she came to tell me bad news. When she came in, she hugged me. And I didn't let her tell me because I had guessed. Then she told me that [his body] was in the hospital. . . . Other people came to be with me, and they confirmed that it was true. And so that's how I found out. That time, seventeen boys fell. It was an ambush.

Sandinista popular discourse claimed that all countries with armed forces had drafts, so some Mothers rhetorically asked, "Why should Nicaragua be an exception?"[36] This encouraged a certain amount of resignation among the Mothers: "Look, the SMP is the law. I think that even in countries at peace there is this law." However, Doña Gregoria spoke for many mothers when she described her feelings about the *servicio militar*: "As a mother, I didn't like the *servicio militar*. They say that every country has it. But not like in those times. After some battle, three or four boys from this neighborhood would come back dead. . . . [For visits] we would have to go see [our sons] where they were—very far away. . . . We went where they were and only saw them for a little while. One time I went to Bocay and there were battles all the time. . . . I only saw him for half an hour, then they took him away. . . . It was dangerous. But we had to go out of our love for them."

Other Mothers expressed certain resistance to the draft. Doña Josefina, for example, urged her son to evade the draft: "I said to my son, 'It's best to leave. You have to flee.' 'No mama, I'm not leaving because if I leave, it's going to be worse because the *servicio* will catch me. And so it's better to go, *mamita*.'" Doña Carmen, with exasperation in her voice, spoke of what she recalled as her underage son's perverse determination to join the army: "It was just that he liked it. It was impossible to keep him from going—he wasn't of draft age or anything, but he wanted to go. In the war he suffered because he went around with the [military] groups, helping them. And so I lived only crying and pleading for him not to go. He would go into military bases, and I would go to take him out. I'd bring him home, and he would be very resentful because why should I take him out if he wanted to go? . . . I would tell him, 'They're going to kill you—you're not even old enough yet.' And he would say, 'I like it.'".

Despite the draft opposition expressed privately by many individual members (at least in terms of their own sons), the publicly held views of the Mothers of Heroes and Martyrs stressed patriotic duty. Indeed, part of the committee's wartime work entailed reinforcing patriotism and the duty to serve. In the interviews, some members stressed the pride they felt in having sons and daughters who voluntarily served. Others stressed the urgency of the situation and the necessity of protecting the revolution. For example, Doña María L. commented: "If there hadn't been a *Servicio Militar*, the contras would have entered the city. We were very clear on this. There were many people who went voluntarily, including us women. Standing vigilance was also necessary because right around the corner [the contras] burned a school and the children were threatened. We didn't take young men and put them in the *Servicio* just because we felt like it. No, it was necessary because there was a war imposed by imperialism. One had to defend, come what may. . . . If there hadn't been this aggression, everyone would have been safely in their own homes." Here Doña María L. is addressing the potential contradiction between bellicosity and motherhood by emphasizing the war as a case of contra aggression, U.S. imperialism, and Sandinista self-defense. Even women had to pick up the gun, she stressed, in order to protect the children.

The following statement by Doña Haidee reveals the contradictory positions posed to a Sandinista mother, namely, the desire to protect her children versus the urgency felt as the contras advanced: "Well, you know that mothers never want anything to happen to their children. . . . So it was painful to say good-bye to my son, but at the same time it was an obligation because they had to put up a human fence so that [the contras] didn't come to kill us." Similarly, Doña Jesus explained her support of the draft through the lack of alternatives: "He went into the *Servicio Militar*. And one has to be very conscious of the situation we were in—what was the reason one's sons went to the mountains? To defend *la patria*. It was also for the struggle of the other brothers who had fallen. And so he presented himself [to the military], and I went with him . . . and signed the papers, and he fulfilled his military duty. . . . I worried. But at the same time it was something in our interest. We had to put up with it."

Doña Elba spoke of the contradictory emotions of mothers concerning the war, her own role in promoting the draft, and her development of political consciousness:

> The CDS [Sandinista defense committees] decided that we would give young men the notice for their appointment to join the *Servicio Militar*. I, as a mother, felt comfortable going to a house to explain to the mother of a boy [about the SMP]. . . . At times we went to mothers who hid their sons and didn't understand. But when we had to give these little appointments out . . . I was becoming conscious that it was a matter of defending the piece of land on which you live, the land on which you were born. It wasn't a matter of going to attack other cities or other people or other countries. Rather it was within our own country. I gave permission for my son, the big one, to join. And I always was afraid.

The ideal, politically conscious Sandinista mother recognized the necessity of the draft. Doña Adela, who lost one son and her husband before 1979 and whose other sons fought in the contra war, painted a detailed portrait of Spartan Motherhood with the following story of herself and two neighboring mothers.

> Their kids left their books at the school, took their guns, and went off to do their patriotic service. And their mothers worried throughout the two years of service. Nothing happened to them and they came back safe, but they lost two years of school. But these mothers weren't resentful. These mothers saw what their sons were doing. They left their books and took up their guns so that others would be free. . . . The contras was going about killing defenseless people. The kids who were studying saw this and left for the mountains by their own free will in order to defend their country. They fought like a Nicaraguan has to fight so that the war didn't bring disaster. So the mothers also had the same goal. . . . They say, "My son went to fight so that so many other people wouldn't die, so that the contras didn't enter the cities." And so these mothers are combatants also, same as their children.
>
> But other mothers were different. They didn't want their sons to go into the army. And for this reason many mothers voted for UNO [United Nicaraguan Opposition]. Me, I never told my sons not to go to war. What I did was help them, tell them it is necessary to fight: "You can't stay here with these contras shedding blood in the haciendas!" I said, "I am going to pray to God so that he helps us . . . because what you are doing is not a bad thing, it is a just thing. It is necessary to fight." . . . The contras was killing defenseless people.

Some studies support Doña Adela's assertion that many who voted for UNO's candidate Violeta Chamorro in 1990 did so to end the draft. According to a Cid-Gallup poll taken in November 1993, 94 percent of those polled felt President Chamorro's most important achievement in office was the elimination of obligatory military service.[37] Despite Sandinista efforts to manufacture consent for the draft, many Mothers of Heroes and Martyrs— one of the FSLN's primary vehicles for promoting the draft—revealed their own ambivalence and discomfort in choosing between protecting their children and protecting the nation, between peaceloving motherhood and Spartan motherhood.

To the extent that dominant Nicaraguan discourse historically positioned mothers as peaceloving, the contra war and the draft were practices that threatened maternal subjectivity. Many women attempted to hide sons from the draft. To counter this maternal resistance, the FSLN tried to insert the complicated twist of peaceloving draft supporters. The ideal Sandinista mothers understood that their sons "had to put up a human fence so that [the contras] didn't come to kill us." As we have seen, the FSLN had only partial success in mobilizing draft support among the Mothers of Matagalpa. The voices of the draft dissenters among the core members of a pro-Sandinista organization reveal the limitations of this campaign and suggest the very severe electoral damage the draft inflicted upon the FSLN.[38]

The undercurrent of ambivalence and antidraft sentiment among the Mothers also demonstrates the importance of listening to the individual voices of an organization, in addition to official policy, in order to understand the key issues at stake in the collective identity process. The war and the draft polarized society and drew the Mothers' public message in tight alignment with official FSLN policy. Officially, the Mothers' Committee was unwavering in its support of the draft, yet amongst its members there was ambivalence. The draft loomed large as a factor explaining the unexpected election of Violeta Chamorro. In the postwar and postelection period, however, pressures for such tight mass organizational alignment on FSLN policy dissipated.

Doña Jesus stands beside a mill used for grinding corn and coffee, which was one of the income-generating projects developed by the Mothers of Heroes and Martyrs of Matagalpa.

FROM A WAR OF BULLETS TO

A WAR OF THE STOMACH

Discursive and Organizational Strategies and

Regime Transition, 1990–1994

In the 1990 presidential elections, UNO candidate Violeta Chamorro un-expectedly defeated Daniel Ortega.[1] It was widely believed by citizens and scholars alike that the vote for Chamorro was in large part a vote against the war and the draft.[2] As one FSLN official put it, "The people, tired of a long, hard war and not being stupid, voted for peace."[3] Yet soon people began to talk of the new war, Violeta's war: "First it was a war of bullets. Now it is a war of the stomach." The neoliberal policies of the Chamorro ad-ministration led to cuts in welfare, education, and health programs, as well as an end to the moral and financial support most popular movements had enjoyed under the Sandinistas. However, as one door closed for mass orga-nizations, another opened when the FSLN shifted from top-down control of organizations to allow for greater organizational autonomy.

This chapter traces the changes in priorities and membership in the Mothers' Committee in relation to competing representations of women and the political and economic contexts. Those contexts include the 1990 elections, the FSLN's transition to a political party out of power, and neo-liberalism combined with conservative social policies. Structural changes heightened economic desperation among the poor, and the Mothers responded by broadening their definition of membership, focusing on members' basic economic needs.

Women's Vote in the 1990 Elections

In trying to comprehend the unexpected Sandinista defeat, many looked to the female vote.[4] The draft, war casualties, inflation, and scarcity of goods negatively affected many women's ability to carry out their domestic role as mothers and caretakers of the household.[5] Despite its work with AMNLAE and the Mothers, the FSLN did not adequately address the majority of women's concerns.[6] Furthermore, most women who worked within the home and in the informal economy remained unmobilized throughout the war. In the Sandinista struggle for hegemony, mass organizations were essential to the spread of ideology and material resources, and so unmobilized women were less exposed to Sandinismo and had less access to government benefits. In light of this, it is not surprising that in a 1988 opinion poll, two of the most disaffected groups from the Sandinistas were the domestic sector (housewives and maids) and the informal sector (predominantly women).[7] Such women were seriously affected by the war, with the drafting and death of their children and wartime scarcity and inflation. Yet if they were not active in the Mothers or neighborhood committees, they generally received little economic or ideological attention.

Surveys conducted before the elections found that homemakers, particularly older, rural women or strongly religious women, were among the weakest supporters of the FSLN and the strongest supporters of Violeta Chamorro.[8] A postelection survey confirmed this trend, finding that 52.4 percent of housewives voted for UNO and 33.2 percent voted for the FSLN.[9] In marked contrast, women twenty-five or younger were among the FSLN's strongest supporters. This was especially the case for professional urban working women—women more readily reached by the FSLN and more likely to have benefited from Sandinista policies.[10]

Nicaragua's María versus the President of Peace: Elections as a Gendered Struggle

Violeta Chamorro effectively capitalized on many women's discontent.[11] Arguably, the 1990 Chamorro campaign was the most obvious and success-ful anti-Sandinista mobilization of maternal imagery for political ends. In gearing up for Chamorro's electoral bid, women's entry into formal poli-tics had to be legitimized within conservative ideology. To do this, anti-Sandinista gendered discourse placed the responsibility for the salvation of humanity in women's hands. On Mother's Day, Cardinal Obando y Bravo, an outspoken opponent of the Sandinista government, told his audience, "The Nicaraguan mother has a big responsibility. . . . Nothing great happens except through women, since God appointed the sacred Mary to act for the salvation of man. . . . Nicaraguan mothers, in your hands you have the salva-tion of Nicaragua. . . . Maternity is the sublime energy that runs the world."[12] Within this discursive strategy, the ideal woman followed Mary's example and did not suffer silently but acted to protect her family and even humanity as a whole. Soon after Cardinal Obando's speech enjoining women to "com-mit themselves to constructing a more humane world," Violeta Chamorro launched her bid for the presidency.

Chamorro, through her family newspaper *La Prensa*, framed herself as the maternal peacemaker capable of uniting the squabbling Nicaraguan family.[13] In her logic, she would make a superior president because she was a "great mother" who had "forged a spirit of limitless self-sacrifice."[14] Cha-morro unequivocally embraced traditional feminine roles, striving to dis-sociate herself from the image of an independent or power-hungry woman. She reassured the public: "I'm not a feminist nor do I want to be one. I am a woman dedicated to my home, as Pedro [her martyred husband] taught me."[15] Rather than seeking power, she represented her goals as selflessly seeking to bring peace and unity to the Nicaraguan family. Neatly pack-aged as Nicaragua's María, she dressed all in white and referred often to her martyred husband, Pedro Joaquín Chamorro.

Chamorro, as the maternal peacemaker, was depicted as the candidate who would put an end to the unpopular draft and finally bring peace to a country that had suffered so under the Sandinistas. *La Prensa* quoted a woman, identified as one of the many mothers and housewives voting for Chamorro, as saying, "Doña Violeta is capable of carrying this country to peace because she, as a woman of the home, knows what we have suffered through in our own homes. . . . The militant women only know about weapons and not about the love of the home."[16] The gendered stakes entailed in the elections were clear. The Sandinista expansion of identities and opportunities for women, however limited in the context of war, was pitted against a return to more strictly defined places and priorities. The anti-Sandinista electoral discourse posed Nicaraguan politics in terms of gendered opposites: women/love/peace/Chamorro versus men/hate/war/Ortega. In contrast to Sandinistas, especially Sandinista "militant women," Chamorro was portrayed as domestic, compassionate, and loving. President Ortega, on the contrary, was depicted in *La Prensa* cartoons as a vulture picking at a skeleton, Dracula pulling out his victim's heart, and an Attila the Hun–style torturer.[17]

In sum, Chamorro's campaign relied on traditional gender identities that involved women's special relationship to peace, family, and God. The UNO platform called for the moral and social recuperation of the family unit and respect for *patria potestad*.[18] *Barricada Internacional* reported that "the common element among the majority of the opposition parties is their reference to women in the role of mother."[19]

The FSLN campaign, however, did not consistently present more progressive alternatives for women.[20] The FSLN and AMNLAE's precampaign focus on mobilized mothers of combatants, fallen combatants, and the disappeared, at the cost of ignoring other women and the gender-specific problems confronting them, was arguably instrumental in the FSLN's electoral defeat. As Dora María Téllez stated in a 1991 interview, "The war prevented us from concentrating on [women's] specific demands; we oriented the women's movement toward being the underpinning of the country's defense, which was essential and a priority: the cost of this was clearly reflected in the 1990 vote."[21]

Daniel Ortega's election strategy was also disconcerting to feminists. In contrast to Chamorro's María image, he was referred to as "the spurred gamecock," donning a macho image as a younger, more stylish man that seemed superficial and was thought by some to serve "no other purpose than to win the greatest number of female votes."[22] A memorable example of the FSLN's campaign was the series of ads calling the public to an election rally on Valentine's Day sponsored by *Juventud Sandinista*, the Sandinista youth organization. One ad featured a young couple embracing, with the heading, "In February, in order to love in peace, we will see you today in the Plaza Park." Less ambiguously, another ad showed just a couple's bare feet amidst tossed-off clothing and a single, long-stemmed rose, with the caption, "The first time is beautiful when it is done with love."[23] The double meaning of "the first time" — as the ad compared teen-age sex and voting — was a clear attempt to appeal to Nicaragua's younger, "hip" voters.

When Ortega was not showing up in jogging outfits at youth rallies, he was photographed embracing *madres sufridas*. Ads declared Ortega "The President of Peace," a title evoking Jesus Christ, "The Prince of Peace," and responding to Violeta's Virgin Mary imagery. Ad copy, placed alongside a photo of Ortega hugging an older woman who symbolized the *madre sufrida*, read, "Everything will be better with a president who accompanies us in the difficult moments, who understands our problems, and with maturity resolves them. A president with a long history of politics and experience in state matters. Daniel is the working man, the only one who can guarantee the well-being of all Nicaraguans."[24] Here, the implicit question posed to voters was "Are you prepared to place your trust in an inexperienced, privileged housewife rather than a politically experienced 'working man' who truly understands the suffering of Nicaraguan mothers?"

Another newspaper ad addressed specifically to housewives read, "Peace is now near. Your child has the right to grow in peace. Your child is the future of Nicaragua. For this reason, Daniel and the *Frente Sandinista* work to give you a dignified and durable peace. Guarantee your family peace and well-being. Give your vote to the FSLN."[25] Appealing to women yet again through the image of the self-abnegating mother, this ad enjoined women to vote with their children's long-term interests in mind.

Sandinista ads featuring women did not universally rely on the housewife/mother imagery. For example, an AMNLAE ad featured photos and short biographies on the eleven female candidates for National Assembly in Region III, Managua. In the copy, the candidates informed readers, "We are with the Frente because it guarantees us the struggle for equality, peace, the right to organize, and because they enact laws that benefit us. We are representatives of the interests of women and the Nicaraguan people."[26]

There are disagreements amongst Sandinista women concerning how heavily the "sexist" imagery weighed on women's votes. Gioconda Belli, who worked on propaganda for Ortega's 1990 campaign, was an outspoken critic of the sexist nature of the campaign.[27] However, she hesitated to argue that women's vote against Ortega had much to do with feminism. Instead, she pointed to women's experiences of war and economic crisis as well as the FSLN's lost ability to identify with what ordinary Nicaraguans were feeling.[28] Dora María Téllez argued that sexist imagery did not keep women—housewives or feminists—from voting for Ortega. As Téllez saw it, the "housewives' vote is a conservative vote" because it is they who confront most immediately the economic crisis and the problems attendant with inflation, scarcity of goods, the black market, and ration cards.[29] There was also, of course, the draft: "Almost every mother was up in arms about that, her sons forced to go to war, and so many of them not coming back."[30] Reflecting upon the electoral loss, Téllez concludes, "We never managed to do adequate ideological work, with women especially. We just didn't."[31] Much more work was needed to establish ideological consensus among the majority of "housewives" that could withstand the twin threats of economic crisis and war. Perhaps this was an impossible task for a new revolution fighting a war with such scarce resources. As Téllez explains, all energies were put into defense and production: "We didn't have time for more."[32]

Despite the varied Sandinista attempts to appeal to women, the anti-Sandinista coalition successfully mobilized traditional maternal roles and images toward its interests. These images competed with Sandinista discourse by consistently appealing to the more traditional and thus more familiar versions of motherhood—those that were already grasped by so many mothers faced with the drafting and death of their children.[33] The Sandinista alternative vision of motherhood required greater leaps from the norm and greater sacrifice. It entailed years of time-consuming volunteer work in Sandinista popular organizations and the willful release of sons to the military. In the context of war and economic crisis, it required women to have faith that with the FSLN, "*Todo será mejor*" (everything will be better). In this light, it comes as little surprise that many women (and men) found solace in the candidacy of a woman emulating the Virgin Mary and claiming peacemaking powers intrinsic to women. As the FSLN returned yet again to the maternal field to harvest symbolic resources, this time for electoral battle, it constricted the political identities available to women even as Sandinista organizations such as AMNLAE attempted to broaden the gendered frontline. But if the FSLN regarded maternal imagery as a bunker and retreated to its safety, Violeta Chamorro wore maternal imagery as a bulletproof vest and successfully worked the crowds.

Mobilized Women and the Chamorro Administration

A new female president for Nicaragua was hardly a guarantee of progress or improved conditions for Nicaraguan women. Rather, government cutbacks on social benefits, such as health care, education, and social security, hit women particularly hard.[34] The "feminization of poverty" rate worsened, as women were often the first to be laid off as a result of the government's anti-inflationary adjustment plan.[35] Furthermore, as structural adjustment cut social services, shifting the burden to the household, women were disproportionately affected as they made increasing sacrifices to ensure the survival of their families.[36]

Organized women participated actively in the two massive strikes during Chamorro's first three months in power. The March Eighth Women's House mobilized a protest outside the presidential offices where, reminiscent of women's anti-Somoza demonstrations of the late 1970s, they banged pots and pans to protest the administration's economic policies.[37]

The cutbacks in benefits and the "feminization of poverty" were accompanied by the rising influence of the most conservative sectors of the Catholic Church. One primary concern of this sector and its UNO allies was the promotion of traditional roles for women as mother and housewife and the prohibition of alternative lifestyles, such as homosexuality.[38] For example, in June 1992, the National Assembly passed Article 205 of the Penal Code stating, "An individual is guilty of the crime of sodomy if he or she induces, promotes, propagandizes, or practices in a scandalous manner, cohabitation between individuals of the same sex."[39] In its final form, Article 205 read, "The concubinage between persons of the same sex or against nature constitutes sodomy and those who practice it in a scandalous manner or offending the public modesty or morality will suffer the punishment of one to three years prison; but if one of those practicing it, even in private, had over the other disciplinary or authoritative power, like a relative, teacher, boss, guardian or in whatever other concept that implies influence of authority of moral direction, the sentence will be for him from two to four years, the same when practiced with a minor of fifteen years or through use of force or intimidation." Thus, homosexuals were legally defined as criminals along the same lines as rapists, pedophiles, and sexual harassers.

In the same legislative reforms it was determined in Article 209 that rapists would be the legally recognized fathers of children resulting from their attacks. The original proposal called for the legalization of abortion for pregnant rape victims. Conservative sectors of the National Assembly opposed this and had the Vatican ambassador speak to the assembly on the Catholic Church's position on abortion. In turn, supporters of the original proposal argued that if the state would not permit abortion in the case of rape, then the state should accept financial responsibility for the child. The socially conservative sector, inspired by neoliberal economic theory, was not willing to place this financial responsibility on the state. Instead, the rapist was held financially responsible, thus establishing a legal and permanent relationship between rapist and victim. Female Sandinistas and emerging gay and lesbian groups led the protests against these two laws.

The Chamorro administration reinforced traditional identities for women through images of feminine domesticity projected in school textbooks, the media, and the traditional Catholic Church. However, the anti-Sandinista organizations of mothers mobilized on behalf of political prisoners and against the draft disintegrated. Unlike the mothers of fallen Sandinistas, the mothers of fallen contras were virtually ignored by the press and the Chamorro government, much less exalted for their sacrifices.

Although organized anti-Sandinista women disbanded and images of mothers in La Prensa clung tightly to traditional Catholic notions, women's roles multiplied in Barricada after the 1990 elections. Barricada became a primary outlet for exploring new identities for women that extended beyond motherhood. Yet motherhood remained a potent Sandinista symbol, and women-as-mothers were more singularly represented as the natural peacemakers for Nicaragua—apolitical, forgiving, loving. For example, after the elections, on International Women's Day, Barricada covered a protest by Mothers of Heroes and Martyrs and Mothers of the Disappeared demanding peace and the immediate demobilization of the contras.[40]

The FSLN's electoral defeat in the 1990 presidential elections also led to changes in AMNLAE and to the growth of a variety of other women's groups. Sandinista feminists who had seen women's interests subordinated to the defense of the revolution viewed the Sandinista electoral loss as a turning point at which women's priorities, not those defined by the FSLN, could be attended to by organized women. As Milú Vargas put it, "Women are no longer going to defend the country as our first priority. We are going to defend women as our first priority. That means fighting for the right to abortion and against violence."[41] One organizer of the March 1991 "Festival of the 52 Percent," celebrating International Women's Day, said, "We no longer want party leadership, structures and orders."[42] Instead, many women activists strove for an independent movement that was truly representative of women's interests and that would enable them to become a political force with which the government and various political parties must reckon. Many within AMNLAE promoted internal debate in order to generate a broader-based, more democratic group in which all sectors of the women's movement would be represented.[43] Despite such attempts, however, AMNLAE ratified its current structure and methods at its National Assembly on 9 March 1991—which took place at the same time as the Festival of the 52 Percent, and in which AMNLAE did not take part. By this time, AMNLAE was no longer the primary women's organization, but another organization within the Nicaraguan women's movement.[44]

In a Mother's Day editorial, Doris Tijerino, as the director of AMNLAE, wrote, "Whenever we think of the word 'mother,' what comes to mind is the image of an older woman, tied to the home and her daily housework. . . . We forget that in every mother there is a woman, a person with her own aspirations and needs."[45] Glorified maternal images in both Sandinista and anti-Sandinista discourse produced and reinforced the expectation that women must act selflessly, making demands only on behalf of others. Under such expectations, childless women implicitly were not full women, and women who pursued careers appeared neglectful of their children. Feminist goals such as affordable birth control, safe and accessible abortions, pay equity with men, and an end to sexual harassment were that much less attainable if women could only legitimately organize on behalf of others. About Sandinista Nicaragua, Maxine Molyneux wrote, "Representations of women acquired new connotations, ones that *politicized* the social roles with which women are conventionally associated, but did not dissolve them."[46] Thus, women's primary role remained motherhood, but they came to have explicit political responsibilities and modes of political action—action on behalf of others.

The primacy of the maternal image was dropped from Sandinista discourse as the contra war ended, the 1990 elections were lost, and *Barricada* established more independence from the Sandinista party. A wider variety of gender images appeared, and feminist issues gained more attention. In *Barricada's* Friday supplement, *Gente*—run by one of Nicaragua's best-known feminists, Sofía Montenegro—many less conventional women's topics, such as feminist theory, women's sexuality, domestic violence, and the feminization of poverty were regularly covered. *La Boletina,* distributed five times a year free of charge to women throughout Nicaragua, focused on the daily problems and priorities of Nicaraguan women. For over two years (seven editions), the Comite Nacional Feminista published *La Feminista,* a magazine that included editorials, humor, poetry, interviews, and articles on feminist meetings around the country.

Seguir Adelante: The Mothers' Postelection

Although the Mothers' Committee as an organization supported the Ortega presidency, some core members suggested that many mothers of the fallen and mothers of drafted sons had voted against him. For example, Doña Juana, although arguing that the draft was necessary, also believed that many Mothers voted for UNO in order to end the draft.[47] Asked her opinion about Chamorro, Doña Ana María replied, "What was good first of all was the end to the *servicio militar.* Everyone was grateful on this point. Mothers don't like their children going off to the mountains and coming back without an arm. So we were all grateful. Everyone recognized this in the Mothers' Committee."

Despite the prospect that the war and draft would end, the FSLN's loss in the 1990 presidential elections shook the ideological foundation of the Mothers of Heroes and Martyrs. Could such a costly revolution so fiercely fought for so long be lost in one day at the voting booths? Was all the blood shed for nothing and the lives of their loved ones given in vain? Although the first reaction of many was shock and despair, by 1992 members expressed cautious optimism through the familiar theme of martyrdom—turning loss into gain. Doña Elsa A.'s voice spoke for many Mothers who came to terms with electoral defeat and still held hope for the future of Sandinismo:

> At first when the Frente lost, I said, "*Caramba* daughter, how we have failed you!" . . . So this day we felt dead, like our [fallen] children were demanding to know why we had allowed this to happen. . . . But later, after analyzing it . . . we felt proud when the world knew that we had had clean and honest elections. . . . [The fallen] have left behind capable men and women who will always uphold the names of the FSLN and the cause for which our children died.
>
> There was a plaque for [my daughter Martina] in the neighborhood, but after UNO won they took it down. . . . I haven't worried about whether it was still there, or stained or dirty because I say that the only place where the signs and names are well recorded is in the hearts of the people who knew them, first of all their mothers. . . . What is important is to always uphold the names of your children.

After the elections, there were attempts on many counter-revolutionary fronts to undermine Sandinismo and alter popular memory through removing plaques, painting over revolutionary murals, and renaming markets and neighborhoods. Because the Mothers of Heroes and Martyrs had been one of the most visible forces behind the creation of memorials to fallen Sandinistas, members often took this as a personal attack. Indeed, it *was* an attack in the struggle over whose version of history would prevail. As names faded from public memory and plaques and murals disappeared, the Mothers positioned themselves as the protectors of a history under discursive siege.

State support of mass organizations such as the Mothers of Heroes and Martyrs also disappeared. The new government refused to acknowledge the existence of the Mothers as a legal organization and resisted, through neglect, economic support for individual members. The Sandinista loss, however, led to new space for grassroots organizations to operate with greater autonomy.[48] The Political Secretary of the FSLN of Estelí, Isais Parrales, claimed, "When the Sandinistas lost the elections . . . the FSLN became less vertically oriented with top-down decisions. Now it is more horizontal, open, and with increased critical discussions at all levels. The organizations have more autonomy. The members are individually Sandinistas, but they make their own decisions without Frente mandates or direct guidance."[49]

Reflections upon their electoral loss led to Sandinista self-criticism over the party's authoritarian tendencies toward the mass organizations. The Mothers of Matagalpa had recognized and acted against this top-down control in 1984, long before such criticisms emerged within larger Sandinista organizations. Nonetheless, they had still made decisions based upon the goal of supporting the Sandinista state and were clearly influenced by FSLN directives and priorities. After the 1990 elections, the Mothers became a pro-FSLN group that now organized against the state, condemning the new administration's policies.

Although many of the poor belatedly recognized the economic benefits of Sandinismo, the electoral loss, along with the end of the contra war, provided an opening for reflection upon and criticism of Sandinista mistakes. Some Mothers, such as Doña Adela, were at times critical of the FSLN, particularly in terms of the self-enrichment of some revolutionaries: "I supported the Revolution, but . . . I, as a humble woman, didn't know anything about politics, and I went back to working. And when the Frente lost the elections, I was only left with this little humble house, but the big politicians, they got a lot from the Revolution, with their big houses and nice cars. And why? Because they were politicians." Referred to as La Piñata, Sandinista leaders took ownership of houses, land, cars, and funds during their last days in office, putting themselves in much better position to weather the neoliberal economic policies than their Sandinista followers.

The Chamorro administration implemented structural adjustment programs promoted by the International Monetary Fund (IMF). It managed to tackle inflation but exacerbated the problem of unemployment. Estimated at 23 percent in 1985, by 1994 unemployment had risen to 54 percent.[50] Roughly 30,000 public sector jobs were eliminated, and by 1993, more than 80,000 military personnel had been demobilized. Government food subsidies also dropped, and the government implemented fees for education and health to the extent that they became inaccessible to many of those falling below the poverty line (50 percent of the population in 1993).

Throughout Latin America, such stabilization policies in the 1990s had a devastating impact on the poor, particularly women and children, as they have increased unemployment and underemployment, decreased real

wages, eliminated state subsidies for food, and cut into government expen-
ditures for social services such as health and education.[51] These factors,
coupled with the already tentative safety net of the growing number of single
mothers, has led to an increased frequency of collective action by women
throughout Latin America.[52] Because in Matagalpa many of the Mothers
were refugees from the rural violence, the traditional informal networks of
mutual support based on family and neighborhood ties were weak. To respond to the declining economic situation of the poorer sectors of society,
the structure of the Mothers' Committee was increasingly geared to address economic needs. Thus, the Mothers of Heroes and Martyrs, formerly
known as the selfless champions of others' causes, made *Barricada* headlines
by making demands more explicitly on their own behalf—demanding from
the Chamorro government an increase in their pensions, health care, and
food subsidies. Their inclusion in the political discussions of the nation,
secured by wartime discourse on motherhood, gave them a footing in the
political sphere that extended beyond the Sandinista regime.

During the intense period of strikes and protests against Chamorro's neoliberal agenda, the Mothers used their position as *Madres Sufridas* to add
moral weight to their demands, as in the following declaration in support of
striking workers: "As Mothers who have suffered, we condemn the imprisonment of people who act within Nicaraguan laws. . . . Señora Violeta, do
not continue committing such injustices."[53] Soon after, some Mothers took
over the Sandinista Workers' Federation offices and began a hunger strike
in support of workers' demands for better salaries. They called on all the
Mothers and the Christian base communities to follow their example: "As
Nicaraguans and as Christians we are under the moral obligation to suffer
the calvary that this malicious government has imposed upon each one of
these humble workers who ask nothing more than the right to survive this
crushing crisis."[54]

Throughout much of the 1980s, the Mothers were a "moral force" struggling on behalf of others. Yet with the crushing effects of the new administration's austerity programs, the Mothers more openly and aggressively
made material demands not only on workers' behalf, but also on their own
behalf. In December 1990 and January 1991, the Mothers of Matagalpa
participated in a strike in Managua by various branches of the Mothers
of Heroes and Martyrs and handicapped war veterans. The strike by these

"victims of war" called for, among other things, increased pensions, exemptions from taxes, the continued delivery of free AFA packages (rice, beans, and sugar), and the protection of historical sites, monuments, and names of places relating to Sandinista heroes. Doña Teofila described the mobilizations: "We went to Managua to demand from Doña Violeta that they can't stop the pensions because *they are a right.* What's more, they need to increase them and give the people of the Resistance pensions and help. . . . We had several strikes. And for this we still have pensions. It is only a little."

As part of the same strike, the Mothers of Matagalpa allied with the laid-off workers of Apoyo al Combatiente when the Chamorro administration terminated this program, "leaving 79,900 victims of war without a government agency to attend to their needs."[55] Although the administration eventually made promises to the Mothers and veterans, they were rarely implemented, and the agency created to replace Apoyo al Combatiente, the Institute of Attention to Victims of War (INAVG), lacked the funding and administrative support to be effective.

"Life Is Harder Now": Postelection Politics

Concerning the post-1990 political situation, one thing the Mothers all agreed on was that life was harder under the Chamorro administration. Many looked back with nostalgia at the FSLN era. Doña Lourdes: "[The FSLN] looked after the poor. . . . [With the current government] we don't have any of its support—most of all us poor. They cast us aside. Now there are more rapes, more hunger, malnutrition. . . . It is a war of the stomach. Many of the people, especially mothers, who voted for Violeta did so to end the draft, but now things are worse than during the war." Doña Bibiana: "With this government, everything stopped. They don't give us anything. Before, they did. We were fine. We received a pension; they gave me provisions—rice, beans, sugar, and they gave us enough. Soap, too. Now we get nothing. Before the elections none of us had to pay for anything. And now we have to pay taxes. We're about broke. It's also possible that they will throw us out of these houses."

Studies in Nicaragua reported an increasing level of dissatisfaction and despair in the 1990s. A study released in June 1995 found that although 41 percent of the population was dissatisfied with their lives in 1990, five years later the percentage jumped to 60 percent.[56] In polls asking, "Do you feel that your interests are represented by the government of Violeta Barrios de Chamorro?" the percentage of negative responses rose from 47 percent in 1991 to 87 percent in 1994.[57]

The Mothers' support network became particularly valuable in weathering the post-1990 economic crisis and austerity program. According to several Mothers, those who were not organized lost many of the material benefits—land, housing, food subsidies, jobs, and pensions—that they had gained while the Sandinistas were in power. Doña Elba argued, "Organized you are able to defend your rights—because if you're not organized, no door will open to you. . . . If we weren't organized, it would be like what's happening to many Mothers who aren't organized. After the triumph of Violeta, many retired from the committee. And now many of them are coming back because they see the hard times they are going through." And Doña Elsa recounted, "Now, people are without work—perhaps the same people who voted for Doña Violeta. They've taken away their homes that the Frente gave them. All the gains so that they would be treated as human beings. Now it is the same as the time of Somoza. Now they think that yes, their children died for something. They are once again organizing themselves."

In Doña Elsa's interpretation, mothers of the fallen who previously had not been active were finally realizing the cause for which their children had died. However, in my interviews with them, new members rarely mentioned their children's ideals as their reason for joining the committee. Instead, as I will discuss in Chapter 6, they spoke almost exclusively of their own economic needs.

Weathering Neoliberal Austerity

It is difficult to estimate the number of active Mothers of Heroes and Martyrs on a national level. The group was rather amorphous—in many regions a woman who lost a child in the violence of the insurrection or the contra war could call herself a Mother of the Heroes and Martyrs without ever having attended a meeting. Membership numbers in the 1980s was largely determined by the number of women registered as having lost a Sandinista son or daughter rather than based upon actual participation and agreement on certain organizational goals. In 1986, the Committee of

Mothers in the Department of Managua reported 8,000 members.[58] In 1991, the membership of the Mothers nationwide was registered by the Nicaraguan Institute of Attention to Victims of War (INAVG) as 15,000.[59] There were tens of thousands more mothers of fallen Sandinistas. The number of 15,000 most likely reflects those who were officially registered as Mothers of Heroes and Martyrs and received a government pension.

The relative success of the Matagalpa Mothers of Heroes and Martyrs' income-generating projects in the late 1980s attracted both more NGO aid and new members once austerity programs were implemented. The Mothers of Matagalpa began to keep detailed records of its membership in the mid-1980s. Between 1989 and 1991, the Mothers of Matagalpa had grown from just over 300 members to 650 members. In this time, they had developed seventeen income-generating projects, including neighborhood corn mills, sewing cooperatives, agricultural cooperatives, and used clothing shops.[60] The committee received used-clothing donations from the United States and loaned it to individual members, enabling them to sell this clothing, repay the loan to the committee, and retain a small profit. The committee also began plans for more educational and social projects, such as a health clinic, a counseling center, a large housing project, and various vocational and craft workshops.

In 1992, a number of projects and individual members of the Mothers of Matagalpa were threatened by wealthy landowners and the conservative mayor of Matagalpa, Frank Lanzas. One member's family was burned out of their home after they refused to leave the land to which they held a title from the Sandinista government.[61] In the same year, the mayor announced his plans to build a motorcycle racetrack on the land on which the Mothers of Matagalpa had planned to build 150 homes for homeless "victims of war," including mothers of fallen Sandinistas and contras, those from both sides disabled in the war, and war orphans. This land had been granted to the Mothers in 1989 by the Sandinista government.[62] Punitively high rent hikes on the Mothers' income-generating projects located on city-owned property, eviction threats to two agricultural cooperatives and a popular eatery run by Mothers, and a plan to replace the Mothers' monument to their fallen children with a new "Government Palace" were further instances of political threats to the Mothers' projects. In response to such threats by the reempowered right wing, the Mothers organized protest marches, launched a media campaign, and asked international supporters to write to Mayor Lanzas.

The Mothers still received foreign delegations, though the size and frequency of such delegations had diminished after the war. These were opportunities to spread their political message, keep alive the memories of the fallen, and generate international interest in their projects. In their testimonies, members emphasized that even though the war was officially over, the Nicaraguan people, contrary to UNO rhetoric, still suffered immensely. Doña Haidee was one of those who regularly met with delegations: "It was very hard, but you have to [give your testimony] so that the people know all the bad. Because UNO only presents the good things, but they don't talk about all the suffering that we are going through. Like we say, we speak with our hearts in our hands." The Mothers also continued to be voices for the poor and the fallen, a task that members such as Doña Haidee saw as all the more important in light of the new administration's attempts to turn back Sandinista gains.

The committee assigned each Matagalpa barrio at least one *responsable* to keep track of members, inform them of upcoming events and new projects, recruit new members, and report to the committee the members' concerns and problems. Increasingly, *responsables* mobilized their barrios to gain services—water, electricity, or a school. These mobilizations were not official Mothers' projects, yet they had the active support of the Mothers' Committee, the Sandinista community movements, the popular church, and various international NGOs. Doña Adela, the Mothers' *responsable* for Barrio Apoyo al Combatiente, successfully mobilized Mothers to obtain running water for her barrio: "Tule [the neighboring barrio] has been there for a hundred years, and they never fought for water. Only the Mothers of this barrio worked to get water. The Communal Movement helps us in organizing the barrio, for the people to work to get water. We always struggle to raise the consciousness of the barrio because the barrio is very hard. It doesn't want to work. [Water is] a necessity not only for ourselves but also for our children. Life was so hard without water, but now, it isn't."

Through organizing such as this, the strategy and style of the Mothers increasingly resembled a community movement. The committee acted as a broad umbrella organization for struggle initiated by its members in individual barrios. With such a rapidly growing membership and the broader goal of helping all victims of war, the committee increasingly relied on the work of *responsables* in the barrios for membership information and the initiation of projects.

By 1994, the Mothers of Matagalpa reached a membership of 2,100. This included many women living in the countryside, some of them a five- to seven-hour bus ride outside the city. The committee described itself as "a broad-based, democratic organization that joins together all those widows and mothers of children who died during this terrible war of more than thirteen years, without distinction to political beliefs, religion, or other identity."[63] Coordinator Esperanza explained that although originally the committee focused on supporting Mothers through their grief, in the 1990s the focus turned toward helping members to survive the economic crisis. "There is desperation," she said. "Mothers keep coming, looking for help." The committee claimed that by 1994 its projects had directly benefited 457 people in an economic sense and indirectly benefited many more due to its services for Matagalpa's poor. The following is a list of the projects implemented between 1990 and 1994:

- Completion of the housing project in Barrio Juan XXIII (1991)
- Five neighborhood grain/coffee mills (1991–92)
- Seven communal gardens in rural communities
- Distribution of roofing materials (zinc) to sixty families (1989–93)
- Medical clinic and psychological counseling (1993)
- Promotion of natural medicine, agriculture, and cultural programs (1992–94)
- Expansion of craft and skill workshops (1990–94)
- Opening of building for workshops (1993)
- Beginning of housing project: 150 houses for Mothers of Heroes and Martyrs, Mothers of the Resistance, and other victims of war (1993)
- Artisan project for Mothers of the Resistance in Waslala (1994)

Increased loans and donations, whether from the FSLN or NGOs, had generated their own problems within the committee. Committee leaders, barrio *responsables*, and others familiar with the Mothers expressed concern that less active members had become too accustomed to having things given to them. Members would say "Daniel [Ortega] gave the Mothers land" or

"The Frente gave the Mothers housing materials." The consensus was that these donations nurtured a learned helplessness and sense of dependency upon the FSLN and NGOs. To resolve this, beneficiaries were increasingly expected to work, to the best of their ability, directly in the housing projects. The committee, with the aid of Instituto Juan XXIII and the Quixote Center, researched brick-making and began carpentry workshops for victims of war and their family members. In a meeting concerning eligibility for housing, coordinator Esperanza C. clarified to members that this was going to be an "honest process" to determine who most needed housing, and families would be expected to help in the construction of their houses. Esperanza closed the meeting with a reminder that members could not solicit "Daniel" for a house because it was the committee, an "independent group," and not the *Frente* that would decide.

A leader of the Rancho Grande Mothers (who affiliated with the Mothers of Matagalpa in the early 1990s) complained in another meeting of how too many Mothers thought of committee loan projects (such as for building corn mills, planting crops, and raising livestock) as donations and thus did not feel obligated to pay back the loans. The leaders agreed that this was partly because in the 1980s, "the *Frente* gave and gave and the people didn't have to pay anything back." In response, in 1992 the Mothers had workshops in which loan recipients were taught bookkeeping skills and shown the committee's accounting figures to demonstrate how unrepaid loans compromised future projects.

The problem of learned helplessness was not the only one that faced the Mothers of Heroes and Martyrs. In December 1992, coordinator Esperanza C. was invited to visit the Mothers of Estelí (a city of roughly the same size as Matagalpa and less than one hour away by car). The Mothers of Estelí had split into two groups due to disagreements over distribution of finances, yet they came together to solicit advice and support from the Mothers of Matagalpa. For much of the meeting, the Estelí Mothers complained about the slights, rumors, and jealousy that had torn their group apart. Doña Esperanza responded, "We've all had the same pain. No organization is perfect, but you must work through these problems. Personal differences should not enter into the work of the Mothers of Heroes and Martyrs. When you're separate, you're weaker. Here, the only thing to do is work. Those who say you're going to be given things, it's a lie. Money from where? With this government? No. But meeting with the Mothers can give you more life. When you sit home all day you feel sad. But when you come to a meeting and see all the Mothers and talk with them, you lighten your load."[64]

Coordinator Esperanza stressed sameness, shared experience, and the latent benefits of membership as well as Sandinista ideals to these Estelí Mothers who were arguing over distribution of their very limited funding. However, the Mothers of Matagalpa themselves during this same period, behind closed doors and in hushed voices, strayed from the priority they claimed to place upon latent benefits.

Over its lifetime, the political essence and style of the Committee of Mothers of Matagalpa evolved, adapting to political and economic changes at the national and international levels. In this period, it still worked in solidarity with and received occasional material aid from the FSLN. It developed its projects and programs independently, yet with the aim of promoting Sandinista ideals. But by 1994, the committee was no longer a political symbol with little public voice other than FSLN-orchestrated testimonies. It was an independent pro-Sandinista organization that made demands on the state for members' own perceived rights as Mothers and broader political rights for the poor and all victims of war. They mobilized against threats to members and other FSLN organizations, solicited nongovernmental aid, and conducted counseling, cultural, vocational, and health workshops. By the neoliberal era of the early 1990s, the committee was a women's community organization in which their community was defined by identity and experience, in addition to neighborhood boundaries. Yet the organization was hampered by an expectation among the general membership of receiving without giving. Coordinator Esperanza publicly claimed, "We don't wait to be given things, nor do we ask for them," yet leaders privately recognized this as still an unrealized goal.[65]

"She's Not a Woman Who Has Struggled"

Even though President Chamorro shared with the Mothers the tragedy of losing a loved one to political violence, both sides worked to maintain a wide political and symbolic space between them. Chamorro did not publicly recognize the Mothers and even refused to meet with them in private.

Doña María Elena claimed, "[Chamorro] is more with capitalism, the bourgeoisie. She doesn't like us. She won't receive us or anything. We have sent letters, we have called her, and she doesn't want anything to do with us."

For their part, the Mothers positioned Chamorro as the epitome of "other." In terms of loss, she occupied a similar position to the Mothers (her husband's assassination was attributed to Somoza), yet her behavior was interpreted to reveal an emotional, moral, or political inferiority. In a typical anti-Chamorro narrative, Doña Bibiana criticized Chamorro's lack of empathy: "She doesn't have a conscience, that's what I say, because if she had a conscience, she would say, 'Pobrecita, she is a widow just like me.' I think that she didn't feel much for her husband." The Mothers often criticized Chamorro's self-image as the consummate griever, Nicaragua's María who knew suffering and loss.

They also positioned Chamorro as allied with the wealthy and detached from the rest of the population. As Doña Nacha put it: "[Chamorro] is the president of the bourgeoisie and not of the poor. She has never bothered to say, 'We are going to send a commission to Matagalpa—only for those who have needs, who don't have work.' Nothing. She is only on the TV and in Managua. . . . She doesn't remember the poor, or the other cities." Echoing Ortega's campaign rhetoric, Doña Lourdes called into question Chamorro's legitimacy by describing her as a leader who had never struggled for anything: "She's not a woman who has struggled, so she hasn't done anything. Daniel did. For how many years was he imprisoned? He was persecuted, tortured. . . . But Violeta didn't fight for anything."

In 1991, some Mothers, together with disabled veterans, camped across from the presidential offices for over a month, demanding that the government maintain the social benefits provided by the previous Sandinista government. In a 1991 letter to Chamorro, the Mothers of Estelí and Matagalpa explained their demands:

> We come representing the calls of thousands of mothers all over the country who, the same as us, are suffering a difficult situation in their homes. . . .
> Currently, the pension we receive does not even cover the costs of food for a week, not including the other costs that come up. . . . We believe that your good sense, sincerity and spirit of justice will lead you to understand that our request is not a response to a whim or a political position because we

are also asking that you help the mothers of dead children who were in the Resistance. Even though their struggle was wrong and they were clearly manipulated, these mothers also suffered the same pain that we experienced in losing our children.

Demands:

1. Revaluation of the pension to the *cordoba oro* [the new monetary unit].
2. Exoneration from paying taxes for small businesses that are the property of mothers of fallen children.
3. Respect and fulfillment of the housing law . . . which will assure the stability of our residences.
4. Exoneration of taxes for cemetery rights.
5. Free education for our grandchildren who are direct descendants of our fallen children.
6. Free medicine for us and the grandchildren of our fallen children.
7. Respect for the memory of our children, preserving the historical sites, monuments, names of institutions, and the rest of the places that carry their names with dignity.

This last point, Señora Violeta, you should know hurts everyone since there is not a house in Nicaragua without a victim of these decades of pain, including yourself and your children. . . .

We believe, Madame President, that what we ask is not so much compared to the suffering, pain, and anguish that we have lived through because for us, even though the war has ended, in our hearts we will continue feeling its effects until the day the Lord calls us home.[66]

These demands express both a concern for others—their children, grandchildren, and even mothers of contras—and the individual long-term economic crises mothers experience at the loss of an adult son or daughter. The Mothers stressed that their protests were on behalf of all eligible for benefits, whether Mothers of Sandinistas or former contras.[67] This added moral ammunition to their mission by presenting themselves to be above politics and thus more truly deserving of the state's assistance.

Although it appears the Chamorro administration was not swayed by such demands, such letters were also directed at the larger Nicaraguan audience. In the realm of discursive struggle, the Mothers undermined Chamorro's legitimacy through three common narratives: her lack of love for her husband, which inhibited her sympathy for the Mothers; her alliance with the bourgeoisie at the expense of the poor; and her lack of experience because "she's not a woman who has struggled." All these questioned Chamorro's legitimacy by comparing her to their own dominant identity — poor mothers who had struggled and grieved for lost loved ones. Through their maternally informed discursive strategy, the Mothers undermined the political mileage Chamorro gained from presenting herself as a nurturing, self-abnegating widow and maternal figure. As the Mothers positioned the issue, the government that ignored such maternal suffering, particularly as it extended across traditional political lines, was heartless, and Chamorro was a woman unmoved by the suffering of others — the very antithesis of a Nicaraguan Virgin Mary.

"They Are Mothers, Just Like Us": Mothers of the Resistance

The terms *revanchismo* and *reconciliacion* referred to two dominant themes in post-1990 political discourse. *Revanchismo*, or revenge, was often used in referring to one's despair at the politically motivated hatred, discrimination, and violence. *Reconciliacion* was the light of hope that many looked toward in this despair, referring to the process of coming to terms between the warring parties, learning to coexist, to live in peace. Genera, a nurse and radio technician during the war, lost a brother in the war and regularly attended the committee's meetings and events with her mother. Her account describes the sense of loss and fear of many who benefited under Sandinismo:

Now with Violeta everything costs money. . . . When the Frente was in government, there was medicine. We had enough food. [Now] everyone is asking for help because in this country you can't survive. I need work, but because I was working with the Frente, they don't give it to me. . . . This *revanchismo* in Nicaragua never ends because it is hate for someone who was with the Frente, or with the Resistance, or with UNO. And this *revanchismo* is never going to end, the hate, because in the *montaña* . . . there are troops going about killing. And I think that if things continue this way . . . there's going to be war, and none of us are going to be left.

Coordinator Esperanza C., in a 1994 speech to supporters in the United States, spoke of the Mothers' search for an end to this cycle of *revanchismo*, for a *reconciliacion*:

[In the contra war,] poor people were fooled because of their ignorance into taking up the gun to assassinate their brothers. . . . Now they have realized that this government also ignores them. . . . We have committed ourselves to share with them the little that we have because they . . . return like the prodigal son returned to his father when he realized that he had failed. Now we want to resolve some of their problems because they are human beings, they are victims of war, just as we are.

We have a great obligation to them because our own children taught us to give love, to work for our fellow human beings, even though some of them are found to be wrong. The *reconciliacion* is for us the best expression of humanism, of sincerity, and above all the best way to give our love to God.[68]

In this spirit of *reconciliacion*, mothers of fallen contras—known as the Mothers of the Resistance—became eligible to join the committee. Individual mothers of contras joined within the city of Matagalpa, invited by neighbors and barrio *responsables*. In rural areas in which there was a Mothers of Heroes and Martyrs group affiliated with the Mothers of Matagalpa, small groups of mothers of contras joined. The Mothers of the Resistance who joined tended to be women from rural areas on the edge of subsistence who lost more than one child in the war.

Because their children died at the hands of the contras, some Mothers were upset by the inclusion of mothers of contras. However, others felt that they could not turn their backs on mothers suffering in ways so similar to their own. In public statements, the Sandinista mothers often stressed the similarities between the two groups, thus muting the internal disagreements. Both groups of mothers lost their children to war and experienced similarly the emotional trauma and economic losses. However, due to the Sandinista ideology projected in the 1980s, mothers of Sandinistas were more likely to take pride in and support the ideals for which their children died. According to the Mothers of Sandinistas, the Mothers of the Resistance did not have the same understanding of or commitment to the ideals for which their children fought.

Although the Mothers of Matagalpa's solidarity with Mothers of the Resistance purportedly arose out of the bond created by their losses, the FSLN's embrace of these same Mothers of the Resistance was motivated at least partially out of its desire to incorporate disaffected groups under its own banner. In comparison to the Mothers of Heroes and Martyrs, the Mothers of the Resistance previously had received almost no recognition or support from any source. Although at times their existence was displayed prominently by the anti-Sandinistas during the contra war, this did not translate into policy in the post-Sandinista era. In many ways, these were politically abandoned women. The UNO government ignored them, as they were largely ignored by contra supporters during the war. Given that these women were not on the winning side of Chamorro's public policy and that their position as mothers afforded them great symbolic power, some Sandinista leaders publicly embraced them. As a political strategy, this also made sense since poorer housewives and mothers were thought to be the largest group disaffected with the Sandinista government during the 1990 elections.[69]

Daniel Ortega attended the 1992 Mother's Day celebration for Mothers of Heroes and Martyrs in Matagalpa, which attracted thousands of Mothers from all over Nicaragua. Mothers of the Resistance were present for the first time at this annual event, and Ortega sought them out, posing with them for photographers and addressing them in his speech with promises to struggle on their behalf. In his speech, Ortega positioned mothers as apolitical peacemakers: "Between mothers there are no different ideologies or politics—they are mothers." He also claimed, "The mothers, with their love, can spread love to all parts of the country."[70] Appearing apolitical may have added credibility and moral force to the Mothers' cause; however, after years of struggle to instill a Sandinista ideology amongst the Mothers of Heroes and Martyrs, many members were strongly pro-Sandinista and resisted the idea that they were apolitical or without ideology.

In the Mothers' own statements for this national gathering, they discussed the need to continue struggling for their political beliefs. For example, in a letter submitted in the same week to the *Barricada* by the Mothers of Chichigalpa, these women encouraged other Mothers to "continue struggling for our ideals, our principles, and for peace."[71] Ortega's representation of mothers as apolitical also contrasted with the speech given at the same gathering by coordinator Esperanza Cruz de Cabrera, in which she maintained that both the mothers of fallen Sandinistas and the mothers of fallen contras should unite despite political differences: "Today we meet with some Mothers of the Resistance who also suffer the pain of losing their children. We have perhaps different ideas, but a singular heart. They should feel themselves to be the same women as us, with the same rights and with the same love of life that essentially is the love of peace."[72] Notably, although they differed on the Mothers' political identity, Ortega and Cabrera agreed on the vision of mothers as peacemakers capable of spreading love throughout a war-torn nation.

The acceptance of contra mothers also played well to the international solidarity groups on whom the mothers were increasingly reliant for funding in the neoliberal era. In the Mothers' meetings with international delegations, "Maternal love overcomes political enmity" was a story that the latter seemed anxious to hear. But it was also a story many Sandinista Mothers were not ready to accept. So the decision to include contra mothers was quietly made by the leaders at the urging of several international NGOs. In 1992, international fact-finding delegations were enthusiastically told what many Mothers themselves still did not know—that contra mothers had joined the group. For the leaders, neoliberalism necessitated the prioritization of material aid over democratic decision-making. Thus, the limited autonomy the Mothers established in 1984 was partially forfeited in the early 1990s to a distant yet intensely well meaning leftist international public.

The Mothers of Heroes and Martyrs of Estelí arrive at the annual Mother's Day gathering in Matagalpa in 1992. National political figures, including ex-president Daniel Ortega, spoke at the event. On this day, the Mothers of Matagalpa began to publicly discuss the inclusion of Mothers of the Resistance in their organization.

❧ 6 ❧

TESTING THE LIMITS OF

MATERNAL IDENTITY

Regime Change and Expanded Membership,

1990–1994

The differences between entities . . . are shown to be based on a repression of
differences within entities, ways in which an entity differs from itself.
—BARBARA JOHNSON, "Opening Remarks," *The Critical Difference:*
Essays in the Contemporary Rhetoric of Reading

After the 1990 elections, the FSLN was less able to back up its ideology with economic benefits and force. The new Chamorro administration was decidedly neoliberal, building off the ideas of limited state economic intervention and expanded civil liberties. It was unwilling (and unable, if it wanted to maintain IMF support) to mobilize mass support through carefully channeled social programs.

Why, then, when Sandinista combatants were no longer dying, was the Mothers of Heroes and Martyrs of Matagalpa growing so quickly? And how did this rapid influx of new members affect the committee's collective identity and goals? Further, how did the shift from a mobilizing revolutionary regime to a neoliberal one impact the Mothers' collective identity and membership profiles? These questions provide the foundation for my analysis of the Mothers of Matagalpa in the post-Sandinista era, 1990–94.

In previous chapters, I made a case for the importance of a sense of maternal sameness, cooperation, and friendship, as well as the shared maternal identity of *Las Continuadoras* in understanding why members joined and remained active in the 1980s. Yet social movement literature, the older cohort's sense of collective identity, and the committee's public self-representation in the early 1990s do not prepare us for the gossip, resentment, and even anger generated by the influx of the new, post-1990 cohort. In comparing membership profiles and listening as newer members discussed their motivations for joining, I found that regime change led to a large cohort of new members with identities and interests that fundamentally differed from those expressed by older cohorts. As in the 1980s, the committee supplied an environment for members to develop an emotional-support network and to mobilize politically. However, in sharp contrast to the reasons core members gave for their participation, the women joining or returning to the committee after the 1990 elections rarely recognized the emotional or ideological benefits. Rather, after a devastating war and then neoliberal austerity, these women organized to receive the increasing economic benefits the committee generated and distributed. This flood of new members with strong economic motives and a weak sense of collective identity disrupted the collective identity so carefully nourished during the Sandinista period, compelling many members of the older cohort to define their identity in selective, even exclusionary terms.

I examine these distinctions between older and newer cohorts as linked to the social, political, and economic context in which they became active, arguing that those active in the 1980s were active because of political, ideological, and emotional reasons (more accurately, the intersection of these three). In the 1990s, however, members were drawn into the committee primarily out of economic circumstances—they needed material support. But the matter is never that simple. On the one hand, this is a matter of how members (especially the older cohort) described their reasons for participating—how they framed them to me and to the broader public, rather than their "true" reasons for joining. Are there really "true" reasons? As I discuss in this chapter, the older cohort, though they officially denied it, also seemed to feel an economic stake in the committee. This is striking and important because everything about the Mothers' visible collective identity had so consistently stressed the self-abnegating, maternal Sandinista motivations rather than self-interested, material ones.

On the other hand, I do not know how older members would have described their reasons for participating to me if I had asked them soon after they had joined in the 1980s. Perhaps many members joined in hopes of acquiring economic benefits, and only over time both became familiar with (and embedded in) the Sandinista maternal ideology that supported it and developed friendships and a sense of personal empowerment through activism. Even so, interviews of the Mothers conducted by academics, activists, and journalists in the 1980s, as well as speeches and public pronouncements made by Mothers of Matagalpa, jibed with what the core members told me in 1992–94—namely, they stressed ideological and relational motivations for activism.

In the end, I am not arguing that either economics or ideology is more conclusive or the more fundamental motivator for the Mothers' collective action. Rather, I hope to show how intertwined and even inseparable they are, even though sometimes one appears more salient than another, depending on the always-shifting structural contexts. Economic interests and "needs" are mediated by cultural constructs. Even the hunger and homelessness experienced by many members was given meaning through various political practices. In other words, meaning-making practices shape how people recognize, interpret, and respond to threats to their survival. A core group of members was attracted to the committee through maternal mobilizing identities in the Sandinista struggle for hegemony. But over a thousand mothers arrived at the committee's doorstep as it gained new access to donations in the context of the Chamorro administration's economic austerity programs. Comparison of these two groups provides rich context through which to understand the strengths and limits of hegemony in relation to collective organizing, economic scarcity, and (post)war.

The Pull of Ideology and the Push of Economic Desperation

In criticizing the Chamorro government, the Mothers of Matagalpa mobilized images such as the *Madres Sufridas* and the Virgin Mary. Yet with such high, uncompromising ideals, the Mothers had difficulty living up to their own collective image. Veiled behind the proper images and actions according to the Mothers' public identity—selfless concern for others and the duty to carry on the struggle—were the growing economic benefits to be had through the committee. In public statements, leaders increasingly described the committee as addressing the material needs of the poorest of the poor and war victims, and these material benefits attracted new members. Strictly speaking, the end of the war meant that new Mothers were no longer being "created." Yet counterintuitively, membership in the Mothers' Committee grew quickly as it retained active members, as women whose children died years before joined the committee, and as Mothers in other communities and even mothers of fallen contras were accepted as members.

These newer members—desperately poor and less immersed in the Mothers' ideology—readily spoke of the financial "favors" they sought. Although cultural, political, and economic motivations all contributed to participation in the Mothers' Committee, these new members did not situate economic benefits within an identity of selfless, loving, patriotic motherhood. In other words, newer members did not participate because of who they were, but because of what they might receive.

Newer members' statements about their participation were in marked contrast to those made by women who joined during the Sandinista era, the latter emphasizing the duty they felt to their dead children, emotional support, and political empowerment. For example, Doña Antonia—a *campesina*, a refugee, and a widow—joined in 1985, soon after the death of her son, a long-term Sandinista combatant. She described the limited financial options open to her once her son, who had been supporting the family, died. If it were not for the war, she stressed, she could have returned to her farm. Instead, she had to remain in the city and supplement the small income she earned selling tortillas by collecting a government pension and whatever donations came through the committee. Yet despite her precarious economic situation, she focused on the emotional support to explain why she decided to join the committee: "[I joined] in order to feel consoled . . . so that I wouldn't think so much about the death of my son. . . . [In the committee] we all carried the same thoughts, the same words. There is a *conjunto de consuelo*. You don't carry inside what you have in your head. We talk about how to solve our problems. And you enjoy the work. You come home from work and fall fast asleep. Your problems fade away."

Doña Rosaura was also a refugee from the countryside and a core member who joined in the mid-1980s. Her husband, a disabled revolutionary veteran, was unable to work, and so her son had been the primary provider for the household. When he died, she not only lost his economic support but also gained the financial burden of raising his daughter. To help Doña Rosaura get by, the committee gave her a small salary for her work in its used clothing store ($40 per month). She recognized the economic benefits the committee offered, but like Doña Antonia, she stressed the emotional, latent benefits: "Life is very hard for me. And so we feel, or I do in particular, very grateful to the committee because I feel the support, I feel it very closely. And it's not the monetary support, because at times some say that the help is in the form of my work. But I feel content because at least in the meetings you forget your problems."

In contrast, the newer members and those now returning after years of inactivity rarely expressed (in informal discussion or formal interviews) a political obligation to their fallen children or to the FSLN. Nor did they place much emphasis on the latent benefits of belonging—friendship, emotional support, self-realization. Rather, newer members were openly attracted to the committee by the material benefits. Many of these members arrived at the committee in a state of economic desperation. As one such woman, Doña Julia, replied when I asked why she had joined the committee, "What else can I do? Tell me, Lorena, what else is left?"

Rather than seeing themselves as *Las Continuadoras*, newer members spoke of their individual and family's material needs—food, medicine, a new roof—and their hopes of meeting some of these needs through soliciting the Chamorro government and perhaps gaining some "favors" from the Mothers' Committee. As Doña Gregoria explained when asked why she joined the committee in 1990, "I don't have any work. I'm looking for work—that is to say, in the committee I'm looking for help, or support, because when one is alone without the support of the children who died, one feels helpless." More specifically, she was hoping for committee support in the form of a new sewing machine.

Thus, members who joined in the early 1990s expressed economic motives for activism and had a less defined sense of collective maternal identity than did longer-term members. In speaking to these more recent members, it became apparent that despite an outward, visible appearance of homogeneity and strong solidarity, the Mothers' Committee was heterogeneous, fraught with contradictions and competing interests.

The philosopher Heraclitus counsels us that we can never step into the same river twice, for other waters are forever flowing past us. Indeed, all the world is in flux, including social organizations and collective identity. The Mothers' collective identity was shaped by the changing current of membership, which in turn was shaped by cultural, political, and economic circumstances.[1] As new individuals arrived in the committee, driven by economic crisis, they challenged the group's dominant self-understanding. The divergent views on the raison d'être of the committee (emotional and political emphases versus material benefits) were based upon the different and continually shifting discursive realities, economic situations, and political experiences of older and newer members.

Although many studies portray poor women as being "pushed" into movements by their inability to fulfill domestic obligations in times of economic crisis, Joann Martin writes that the Mexican women of her study emphasized the "pull" that crisis exerted on them because of their gendered roles as mothers.[2] This distinction is helpful in understanding the Mothers of Matagalpa. Members who had joined in the 1980s stressed the pull of the committee—the obligations they felt both to their martyred children and to the other Mothers. This pull relied on a discourse of maternal care, responsibility, and self-abnegation. More recent members, those especially who joined or returned to the committee after the 1990 elections, expressed their participation through a metaphor of being pushed—it was a last resort in a time when unemployment was increasing while social programs were slashed. The crisis had them backed against a collapsing wall, and their motivation to join was economic desperation less obviously mediated by Sandinista discourse.

Women were propelled to join the Mothers' Committee based on several factors: neoliberal economic policies (including fewer government programs and subsidies, an increase in unemployment due to government downsizing, and an end to special exemptions from taxes); threats to those who held Sandinista-era land titles; urbanization; and the perceived preference of many employers to hire UNO supporters. These factors also pressured the committee to increase its focus on income-generating projects, health services, and material donations. Coordinator Esperanza C. told me,

"The Mothers in our meetings tell us that they don't have anything to eat, they can't pay to go to the hospital—before, in the hospital everything was free. So we see a difference, because I have spoken with many people, not only with the Mothers of Heroes and Martyrs but also with the Mothers of the Resistance, and they are desperate."

The "pull" of the committee reflects the success and limitations of Sandinista attempts at establishing a gendered hegemony. Gramsci posed hegemony as a social order in which a certain way of life and thought is dominant, so that the predominance of a social group is based primarily on consent rather than coercion.[3] As Marx and Engels put it, the dominant class must "represent its interest as the common interest of all the members of society, that is, expressed in ideal form: it has to give its ideas the form of universality, and represent them as the only rational, universally valid ones."[4] At an organizational level, Mothers in the older cohort tended to see the FSLN and the committee's interests as complementary to their own individual interests. This was not so with the newer cohort. Their expression of their interests was relatively untouched by Sandinista ideology, leaving them more clearly focused solely on their own (and their family's) interests, uncomplicated by the needs of the committee or the FSLN. So, in a sense, these newer members were coerced, out of economic desperation, to join the committee. Thus, their discourse reflected a sense of being pushed into the committee—economic force rather than hegemony.

It is questionable whether this new cohort can really be said to have a sense of collective identity. They knew the requirement for membership (a child who died in the revolution or war) and in a sense perhaps adopted this identity. However, they knew little about the public goals, interests, priorities, and history of the Mothers' Committee. Furthermore, in terms of a latent sense of collective identity, I found little evidence to suggest a sense of "we"—unlike many of the older cohort, when they looked at another member, they did not seem to see themselves.

Las Interesadas: "Those Who Are in It for Profit"

In social movements, Nancy Whittier found, "the collective identity of an activist cohort remains consistent over time"; however, "cohorts construct different collective identities based on the external contexts and internal conditions of the movement at the time they enter."[5] This, she claims, contributes to the changing character of a movement over time. The Mothers' Committee is comprised of two distinct cohorts easily distinguished depending on whether they became active in the Sandinista era or the Chamorro era.

By the early 1990s, the older cohort had retained a sense of collective identity over time that was markedly different from that of the newer cohort. The overwhelming number of the "pushed" (new cohort) strained the collective identity of the "pulled" (old cohort). The tension between the "pushed" and the "pulled" is illustrated by Mancur Olson's classic problem of "free-riders"—or as they are called here, *Las Interesadas*.[6] In the 1990s, the committee generally did not selectively distribute material benefits based upon members' participation in committee work and attendance at meetings. Rather, they were distributed either to all members (donated food, for example) or according to need (such as housing). This created a problem of *Las Interesadas*, members who benefited materially without contributing.

Several core members of the older cohort identified this problem in their interviews. Doña Juana asserted, "The Mothers who are in it for their own interests don't have principles. I notice that, for example, when it's said that there are going to be presents given out, you're going to see many Mothers. When it's said that we are going to work, only some Mothers come. So this is where I see the difference—a difference that shouldn't exist. We have to be accustomed to things like we were in the beginning, like in '84-'85. There weren't presents, donations of clothing didn't come. . . . But now I see selfishness because if one gets more than another, the other complains. For this reason I say that the committee could fall apart or become commercialized." Similarly, Doña Paquita claimed, "There are some members who are *interesadas*. They don't behave well. When there are donations to be given out, they come. But when there are meetings, when the priest comes, they aren't there. . . . The mothers behave this way, and it embarrasses me. They don't take it upon themselves to change, to better themselves. And this is what our children died for. . . . They wanted a better country, progress so that one day things would be better."

These long-standing members who based their identity on Sandinista political ideals and maternal self-abnegation mobilized these ideals against *Las Interesadas* through gossip. This gossip often included the axiom that she who participated for personal gain did not really love her fallen child and did not honor her child's memory and ideals. Doña Elsa, one of the earliest members, criticized certain Mothers in these terms: "Our children gave their lives for the country, and not for us to take advantage for our own selves. In my work with the organization here, I don't earn a cent. And I work here all the time, more than the time I spend in my job. And I have never asked for anything on behalf of the memory of my daughter. I am not going to dirty her memory. Even though I don't do it, many mothers do dirty their children's memories, but they shouldn't be deceptive or opportunistic."

Within their discourse of love and obligation, a Mother's unselfish commitment to political struggle was taken as proof of her love for her fallen child, as Doña Ventura expressed in her moral equation: "If you don't feel love for your children, you don't feel anything. But I have seen—if you feel very hurt, you always continue forward in the struggle."

This strong current of opinion served as a moral deterrent against self-interested behavior. Members who came to the committee meetings only when there were donations to be handed out risked the charge of not only being greedy, but also of dishonoring the memory of their fallen loved ones. The ideal Mother thought only of others and brought home her share of the material benefits only after spending an acceptable amount of time in committee work. Those who strayed from this image were positioned as the "others," outside the circle of "we," deviants from the Mothers' collective identity. Although formally they were members, symbolically they were not. Thus, in a twist to Olson's selective incentive solution to the free-rider problem, new members were selectively excluded from the latent benefits of membership.

According to core members, activism was not simply a means to another end—for example, clothing donations or loans. Support, cooperation, and a sense of belonging, all components in the process of collective identity, were ends in themselves.[7] These women enjoyed the very act of participation. Recall the explanation Doña Antonia gave for her participation: "[In the committee] we talk about how to solve our problems. And you enjoy the work. You come home from work and fall fast asleep. Your problems fade away." Core members framed their activism in terms of maternal solidarity and obligation to both the fallen and each other, rather than self-interest.[8]

When the subject of conversation turned to these new *Interesadas*, how-

ever, many old members shifted their portrayal of participation from a benefit to a heavy burden. New members who did not recognize the latent benefits, and who took without giving, lowered old members' return on their
invested time and reminded them that activism took time away from other
things—the family, housework, remunerated work. The strain of increased
competition for material benefits and declining state support, in addition to
a rapidly growing and changing membership, jeopardized nonmaterial benefits and inflated the "cost" of membership. As some older members alleged,
in the neoliberal era it was becoming increasingly difficult to find personal
fulfillment in participation.

Of course, for Mothers who did not recognize obligation to the fallen or
the nonmaterial benefits of solidarity, active participation was not costless.
Attendance at meetings was seen as simply the means to material ends, and
activism was instrumental, not expressive of an identity. The difference in
motives for participation involved the clash of two contradictory discourses
on motherhood and economic relations. Mothers who were not mobilized
soon after the death of a child—through lack of opportunity or ideology
—were often unaware of the larger moral issues at stake in the Mothers'
Committee. They rather innocently saw the committee as little more than a
resource or charity. These members operated more completely within a traditional gender discourse, in which suffering equaled status for middle-age
and elderly women. Within this discourse, the most victimized and helpless—those least capable of active political participation—were the most
deserving of charity. This discourse encouraged a competitive identity of
suffering (the most victimized victim) among many new members.

Confusion surfaced over the conflicting maternal identities. Were Mothers suffering victims of war who deserved to be taken care of? Or were they
agents of change, struggling to improve both their own situation and that
of the nation? The committee leaders set out to promote the latter identity. Yet with the committee's growing number of projects for the members
in greatest need, it made economic sense for individual members who did
not recognize nonmaterial benefits to present themselves as helpless, needy
victims.[9]

Mother versus Other: Struggles over the Definition of Membership

The challenge to identity posed by the mothers of fallen contras is in-structive in terms of discourse and power relations within a collectivity. The impetus to accept Mothers of the Resistance did not arise from the rank-and-file members. As groups of mothers of contras approached the commit-tee, they were rather discretely accepted by the leaders with the support of international organizations and the FSLN. The issue was not put in front of the membership for a vote. Rather, in committee meetings the leaders set out to convince and prepare the older cohort through mobilizing vari-ous images and key themes. Although most core members came to uneasily accept the broadening of membership as the right thing to do, a significant minority did not.

In encouraging acceptance of these contra mothers, committee leaders, as well as priests, Catholic activists, and religiously based NGOs working closely with the group, stressed Christian forgiveness and shared maternal grief. In turn, Mothers' comments concerning the Mothers of the Resis-tance often included the familiar notions of loving one's enemies and the common bond of maternal suffering. Note Doña Antonia's statement: "As [coordinator] Esperanza says, 'If you are mothers, you have to have felt the same pain as they felt.' And so we should have love for these mothers also. I, as a Christian, accept them. They are made by the same hands of the Lord."

In the following, Doña Nacha also showed empathy toward contra moth-ers on the basis of shared pain. Yet in contrast to the mobilizing identities of La Continuadora and the Spartan Mother, she denied that mothers have responsibility for the ideals and actions of their children: "It's like my boy killed somebody somewhere, and some mother is also with this same pain of losing her son, just as we here lost. So her pain is the same as ours. . . . I am not against encouraging these mothers to join. What blame does the mother have if her son goes and joins the contras and sheds people's blood? We aren't to blame that [our sons] had to go defend . . . the country while the others were destroying it." Many Mothers approached the subject in this way, arguing as Doña Josefina did that the mother was not accountable for the actions of her children: "They aren't to blame, nor are we. [Our sons] went because they wanted to. We didn't send them." In framing maternal responsibility this way, she contradicts the mobilizing identity of Sandinista

Spartan motherhood, in which women "sent" their sons and daughters to war and "offered" their children's lives for the good of the nation.

Mothers often added a claim that the contras were deceived, and in a time of *reconciliacion* it was necessary to forgive in order to achieve peace. In her welcoming speech at the 1991 national Mothers of Heroes and Martyrs celebration, coordinator Esperanza C. drew from both a discourse of Christian forgiveness and one of innocence rooted in ignorance: "We as Christians make use of the pardon. . . . We pardon those who were used to kill, even though they killed a part of our happiness. Because as Christ said, 'Forgive them Father, for they know not what they do.'"[10] A statement by Doña Geronima, punctuated by an urgent desire to end the cycle of hate, echoed this notion of forgiveness for misled mothers: "They are mothers the same as we are. What happened is that they are deceived mothers—their children went off to fight for a cause that wasn't just, and our children fought for a just cause. We all have to reconcile and be equal because we are the same. We must be careful, or we're never going to have peace, and we'll continue in war because if we hate and our children continue hating, that's how it will be."

The Mothers of Heroes and Martyrs stressed often in interviews and speeches that although the Mothers of contras shared the same pain, they could not take the same pride in the cause for which their children died. Contras died without honor. The Sandinista Mothers asserted that many Mothers of the Resistance were embarrassed to say their sons died as contras and did not even understand the contra's cause. In this way, some Sandinista Mothers distinguished themselves in terms of purpose, status, and experience. As coordinator Esperanza C. spoke about the inclusion of Mothers of the Resistance, she pointed to this difference: "The mother isn't at fault for what her son did. Of course we're here to continue on with what our children were doing. But for them and this war, it was very difficult because the contras would come, take them away, and give them a gun. Sometimes a Mother of the Resistance is embarrassed to say what her son did."

The arguments of maternal "sameness" relied on a contradiction in the maternal discourse. On the one hand, so many long-term Mothers of Heroes and Martyrs related their own activism to their children's politics and struggled to carry out their children's ideals—a struggle that depended upon obligation and a deep involvement in their children's lives. On the

other hand, Mothers of the Resistance were presented as deceived or innocent of the "sins" of their children, thus denying the same sense of involvement and obligation of a mother toward her fallen child. Were the mothers
of contras sullying their children's memory by turning their backs on contra
ideals? No, many members seemed to say, because these mothers and their
contra children were deceived, tricked into fighting against their Sandinista
"brothers." Indeed, the contra rank and file generally did not have a strong
ideological framework beyond being anti-Sandinista.[11] Yet the contradictory distinction within the Mothers' Committee remained, and with the increasing membership of Mothers of the Resistance, it challenged the foundation of the Mothers' collective identity.

The older cohort of Mothers invariably agreed that the pain of the
Mothers of the Resistance was the same as theirs, and many felt this meant
that both groups had the same rights to material benefits. For example,
Doña Esperanza R. spoke of equal rights derived from suffering based on
their common identity as *Madres Sufridas*: "They aren't to blame that some
bad men got their children involved in this. I think they have the same
rights we do because they are *Madres Sufridas*. . . . If we are given something,
they have the same right to receive it." Yet although Doña Esperanza R.
often spoke of the latent benefits to be found in the committee—friendship,
accompaniment, personal fulfillment—she did not speak of sharing these
with the Mothers of contras.

Although at the time of my main fieldwork (1992–94) there was no overt
hostility toward the Mothers of the Resistance, there was a definite undercurrent of discomfort. A minority of active members clearly disagreed with
the decision to include Mothers of the Resistance. For example, Doña Berta
held them indirectly accountable for the acts of their children: "I, for one,
wouldn't work with them. I respect them because they are also mothers and
because they suffer like we do, because they have the same heart as we do. . . .
The pain is the same, except that their children died attacking our children.
For this we can't be united with them. At least I can't."

Doña Chepita, whose son's body was never recovered, replied that she
felt too much pain to forgive and offered an amendment to the notion of
Christian forgiveness: "It could be because I never buried my son that I feel
so much pain. But I'm going to say that I'm not going to work even one day
with the Mothers of the Resistance because I imagine that the son of some

mother that's next to me, how do I know that he didn't torture my son, or kill my son, or disappear him? It's ugly. I can't forgive them. God says to forgive, but God also gives us hatred."

Interestingly, Doña Juana was the sole Mother to explicitly assert maternal responsibility for the actions of contra sons and daughters. But in making such an assertion she, like Doña Chepita, felt compelled to address the notion of Christian forgiveness:

> They are mothers. I know that they suffer, but they suffered with an ideal— they know that their children were fighting against other people. But what is the ideal they fought for? All those who were fighting were poor people, marginalized people. And so why were they fighting? They fought because they were financed by Reagan. The way I see it, to fight because one is financed is not an ideal. And so I say that in terms of pain we suffer the same; but the knowledge of why our children fought, in this we are different. If for this I am not a Christian, well, OK. I'll ask God to give me this moment of repentance in order to be able to accept it. But I would not feel comfortable working with a Mother of the Resistance because they are never going to accept that we are Sandinistas. Nor are we going to accept that we are with contras because I would know that I am with some mother of the one who assassinated my child.

Although all identified with the pain of the Mothers of contras, many members (including those not opposed to giving contra mothers membership) refused to shift the identity of Mothers of contras from "other" to "we." A number of Mothers interviewed were not even sure whether mothers of contras were official members and attended meetings. The notions of forgiving enemies and accepting the Mothers of the Resistance as fellow *Madres Sufridas* were common themes in meetings; however, actual Mothers of the Resistance attending meetings were not introduced to the group as such. Leaders felt more time was needed before the identity of individual Mothers of the Resistance could be formally revealed. This perhaps hindered the process of collective identity by impeding discussion and negotiation over such a drastic alteration in membership. It perhaps also prevented the group from fracturing or dissolving over the issue.

Inclusion of the Mothers of the Resistance threatened the collective identity of the Mothers of Matagalpa in several ways. Due to the manner in which the decision was made, members' inclusion undermined the committee's internal democracy and created conflict over their identity as *Las Continuadoras*. Leaders argued that by accepting the Mothers of the Resistance, the Mothers of fallen Sandinistas were continuing their children's struggle on behalf of the poor and oppressed. However, for other members, the inclusion of mothers of their children's enemies presented an irreconcilable conflict with their own political ideals. Also, their inclusion secured a tendency among the leadership to view the committee more in terms of the economic aid to war victims than in terms of the friendship, emotional support, and sense of maternal community that many core members valued. Indeed, as the leaders realized, their success in attracting NGO aid was based upon the former, not the latter.

Identity and Exclusion

New Social Movement (NSM) theory tends to focus on the construction of community without delving into the process of exclusion that this entails.[12] However, in neoliberal Nicaragua, exclusionary practices within the Mothers' Committee became difficult to ignore. In the context of disappearing social programs, the Mothers were increasingly reliant on international NGO support. Poor people's shrinking access to basic goods and the increasingly material aspect of the committee's goals motivated members to constrict access to an identity linked to rare material aid. Despite the ideal of the self-abnegating mother and many of the Mothers' own comments on the love and cooperation that they found within their committee, competition, jealousy, and even greed coexisted with maternal love and compassion. Contrary to what dominant gendered revolutionary discourse, as well as "women's difference" theories suggesting women's self-abnegation, might lead us to expect, many Mothers under the stress of extreme poverty and eroding government benefits prioritized their own material interests.[13]

As such, the feelings the Mothers' attached to their identity were marked by ambivalence. They spoke so often of the love they found within the committee, but they also reacted harshly to members who appeared to threaten their material interests. In an extreme case, one member had another thrown in jail over a dispute concerning their neighboring plots of land that both had obtained through the committee.

In another example, several members who rarely attended committee activities appeared at one meeting to complain that the coordinator and the *responsables* were not visiting all the members in their homes.[14] Although the idea of regular visits was generally recognized as valid within the committee, by the early 1990s there were more than five hundred members living within the city. With so many members, *responsables* considered frequent visits to those who rarely attended meetings to be a draining and rather thankless task. Visits exposed the *responsables* to complaints and the overwhelming number of domestic crises, which were especially frustrating coming from members who refused to actively participate in committee work. Several of the most active Mothers privately expressed their desire to quit after this meeting—that "it is not worth it." This meeting revealed the strain of a growing organization that, due to leaders' concern to address members' financial crises, had increasingly less time to attend to the latent aspects of collective identity.

As this implies, although the Mothers of the older cohort so often stressed the sense of sameness within the committee, and even extended this sameness to mothers of fallen contras, a number of those I interviewed also deployed a discourse of exclusion. Several volunteered that only "true" Mothers—whom they defined as those having at least one child who died as a Sandinista in combat—should be members of the Mothers' Committee. This definition excluded many members of the committee: mothers of noncombatants who died in the revolution or war, women whose husbands or siblings died, mothers of soldiers who died in an accident rather than in battle, mothers of disabled veterans, and of course, Mothers of the Resistance. In the following, Doña Paquita and Doña Chepita defined the "true" Mothers and spoke of why they were different and more deserving:

Doña Paquita: The true Mother who is in mourning, who has the pain of having her child killed in the search for a better country . . . these legitimate Mothers are the ones that should be organized. Not wives [of fallen Sandinistas] because they . . . have other men, they've already remarried, and they still have children. These women don't understand anything. They're only [in the committee] because things are given to them — in order to profit. And so it would be good if it were only mothers, not sisters, fathers, or wives. We hurt very much for our children, and the legitimate Mothers deserve something very special, not to be mixed in with others who haven't felt the same pain. Nor with the contra. . . . And almost all of us Mothers have this resentment.

Doña Chepita: I don't accept [the claims of suffering by] a sister or a wife of a fallen person because a wife or a sister is never going to feel what the Mothers feel. Perhaps they feel the same for a little while, but after two or three months they forget. Perhaps the husband was *machista,* offensive . . . so when one has suffered through all of this and then the husband dies, it is more like a relief. For me that's how it was. And so when the widows [claim to suffer], I don't believe them. If my husband was drunk, he got very angry with me. So I say it is a relief [when a husband dies]. It is true that I have to work more [since my husband died], but it is a relief. I don't have this torment.

Doña Adelia explicitly addressed material gain, arguing that only true Mothers deserve compensation: "We say that if there is something, it should only be for the Mothers, because in the committee there are many who are not truly Mothers. . . . Our pain should be respected, because you can't compare one who hasn't suffered the pain of losing a child with one who has." My conversations with members yielded several such comments: "true" Mothers suffered more emotionally, and so they should be organized separately. Since others did not feel a mother's pain, and thus could not understand it, their motive for joining must be for personal gain, or so the argument went. Only women who felt the incomparable grief of losing a child in revolutionary struggle should belong to the Mothers' Committee. Yet it was also implicit, and sometimes explicit, that they were the only ones who deserved the material benefits.

The argument for exclusion was precariously balanced upon a contradictory language of compensation (for pain and grief) and self-abnegation (true Mothers were not in it for material gain). The ironic bottom line was that only the truly self-abnegating deserved material benefits. Those Mothers' discourse of compensation and self-abnegation based upon their specificity painted a thin veneer over the matter of the distribution of scarce goods—they were speaking a moral language that also protected their economic interest.

I attended meetings in which Mothers pointed angry fingers of blame at various people in the room and even made bitter statements about the division of resources and expressed suspicions about how much money came in and where it went. I listened to leaders attempt spin control in which they mobilized notions of Christian forgiveness and charity and revolutionary sacrifice for the common good. And I had the feeling that I was witnessing an interaction that had been played over and over again throughout the life of this revolution. People came with individual complaints, questions, and concerns, and these were addressed by leaders with reminders of the higher goals and noble beliefs they, as Mothers of Heroes and Martyrs, profess to share. The war was over and the FSLN was voted out of office, but the struggle for hegemony continued, waged so often on such microlevels as lectures in a hot meeting room, gossip on the doorstep, the choreography of a dance, the design of a parade float. This was everyday spin control not directly orchestrated from above but diffused throughout society—symbolic guerrilla warfare, if you will.

The public discourse of the self-abnegating Mothers implied the unanimous acceptance of all mothers who had suffered. However, the discourse circulating amongst long-term members involved exclusion on the basis of different levels of emotional suffering. In the context of economic crisis and declining social programs, the ideals of Christian charity and self-abnegation were shifted aside as unaffordable luxuries rather than viable options for many members. The redefinition of membership did not occur through spontaneous empathy or democratic decision-making on the part of the general membership. Rather, in reaction to declining economic conditions and in the spirit of maternal self-abnegation, the leadership created broader definitions for membership in order to address the material problems of more women. The leaders not only clung more tightly to a Sandinista ideology of selfless struggle, they were also in a slightly better financial position to weather the government's austerity programs. Not coincidentally, they were more inclined to broaden the definition of membership even if it meant current members would receive less.

To summarize, decreasing access to government-supplied material goods and greater dependence on non-FSLN organizations led to two contradictory strategies within the Mothers' Committee. First, the leadership followed a strategy of inclusion and broadened the definition of a Mother of Heroes and Martyrs to include a wider variety of women and establish alliances with other "victims of war." Leaders saw this as the best way to implement the political goals attached to their identity, which involved both self-abnegation and struggle on behalf of the poorest of the poor. This strategy had two benefits for the Mothers' Committee as a whole. It attracted international funding by representing the Mothers as a group of all-forgiving mothers—a viable, peaceful alternative to war and violence. Also, by increasing membership it increased its strength as a political organization in its ability to make demands on the government and attract more NGO attention.

The second strategy was that of exclusion of certain members, which would allow benefits to be divided among fewer people, leaving more for the "real" Mothers. Several core members also could not resolve the ideological differences they had with mothers of fallen contras. Although the first strategy was practiced by the leadership and was publicly upheld as the official policy, the second was a submerged strategy operating amongst the general membership. Ultimately, it was an internal struggle over the availability and distribution of resources.

But how do the economic priorities and the strategy of exclusion jibe with the latent dimension of collective identity involving, as the Mothers described it, love, trust, and sharing? After scratching the surface of public identity, rather than a unified, fixed organization, we find a fragmented, shifting collectivity with conflicting interests and visions of identity being worked out discursively. It is a false dichotomy to oppose instrumental (material) and ideal (expressive) meanings of actions: "Just as an adequate material life is an essential means of preserving normative relations, so cultural and symbolic relations provide material resources for livelihood."[15] The long-term Mothers had an arsenal of cultural meanings to apply to their actions. They did not necessarily cover up their "true" material meanings of action. Rather, their identities were embedded in certain cultural ideals (*Las Continuadoras* and maternal self-abnegation), and economic meanings were filtered through these. By the same token, their physical survival was embedded in certain material needs around which cultural meanings were framed.

The meanings applied to the appropriation of material benefits varied across space and time. Members of the older cohort viewed themselves as deserving because they worked more and/or were "true" mothers who had suffered. They situated material matters deeply in political/cultural meaning. New members, conversely, saw the committee as a source of material aid shorn of political meaning or a sense of community.

Time and selection play a role, as many new members either eventually develop and value bonds with other members or leave the committee. Although there was certain conflict in the committee, and newer members often did not see beyond the material benefits the committee had to offer, some committee leaders recognized that empowerment, politicization, self-development, and feelings of care and responsibility took time. Doña Elba allowed that members sometimes acted out of self-interest, which caused tension in the committee; however, she added that activism not only meant mutual economic and emotional support but also led one to become a better person:

> It's true that there are some difficulties, but they pass with patience. I've had moments in which I've said, "No more. I'm not going back to the committee." But then I start to think that I like being organized. One of the wonderful things about the Revolution was this—that we learned to organize and to share the little that we had. . . . Because before the people didn't know what it was to clean the barrio. Before they only knew to hide a little piece of something for themselves. And now I think that . . . there are many people who have forgotten what the Revolution taught us. We are back in the time of Somoza [when] it was, "I am me and only me." . . . See that woman over there? [She points to a neighbor.] She hasn't been to a meeting in two years. Now she wants to go because she knows there is food. But this woman is going through some hard times. . . . It's necessary to understand people.

During the moments of infighting and exclusion, there was still hope among core members that new members attracted by material benefits would with time recognize the latent, intangible benefits and learn the value of sharing and helping others.

Goal Transformation

In the literature on Latin American women's movements, it is sometimes noted that although women organized in the face of a crisis, the movement disintegrated once the crisis subsided.[16] Feijoo wondered whether the "political discourse about women that was constructed by Argentine women themselves led the women's movement down a dead-end street."[17] She was concerned that mothers of the disappeared continued to use a confrontational discourse that was more suitable to opposing a dictatorship than working within a fledgling democracy. Their refusal to shift to tactics of negotiation and bargaining was not only detrimental to their own cause, but also seen as harmful to democratic stability.[18]

It must be noted, first, that the groups of mothers of disappeared were in a fundamentally different position from the Nicaraguan Mothers of Heroes and Martyrs. The former spent much of their organized lives opposed to the state, whereas the latter was originally constructed by a revolutionary alliance that was soon institutionalized. Furthermore, in such countries as Argentina and Chile, the fates of relatively few of the disappeared were ever known and the murderers remained largely unpunished. Conversely, the Nicaraguan Sandinista mothers often knew the details of their children's last moments and the bodies were usually recovered.

David Sills, in his classic sociological text, *The Volunteers*, described the organizational dilemma of finite goals, such as the alleviation of polio in his March of Dimes study.[19] As the realization of a goal becomes assured, organizations are faced with the prospect of dissolving—unless, of course, they re-create themselves through a new set of goals. In 1990, the Mothers were faced with the prospect of dissolution—not through the achievement of their goals, but through the apparent obsolescence of their goals. What use did society have for Mothers of Heroes and Martyrs once the war was over and the revolution had been electorally defeated?

As testimony to their creative agency, the Mothers reinterpreted their raison d'être amidst changing political and economic circumstances. They shifted to goals, strategies, and membership requirements more appropriate to postwar democracy and neoliberalism, showing more flexibility than Feijoo credits to the Argentine Madres. The leaders of the Mothers of Matagalpa decided that the ideals of economic justice and struggle on behalf of the poor were all more urgent in this new economic context. The Mothers as an organization sometimes deployed confrontational tactics against the Chamorro government, yet they also were flexible enough to be willing to form new alliances and forgive old enemies. Still, as the Mothers demonstrate, such flexibility of goals and priorities engenders a different set of dilemmas and conflicts.

The Fetishization of the Mothers of Matagalpa

For many core members, the committee remained a community of mothers. Yet in its organizational form, it was an increasingly impersonal and bureaucratized umbrella organization that prioritized distribution of goods and services to all victims of war. The committee's success in attracting members and NGO support jeopardized the tight-knit maternal community. By 1994, the Mothers' membership and goals were bifurcated. There were those members, *Las Continuadoras*, who participated because of both Sandinista ideals and their sense of maternal community but who also received economic benefits from membership. And there were those newer members, *Las Interesadas*, who participated almost strictly for material benefits.

In reaction to the sharp increase in new members, long-term members reported a decline in unity and input from the average member and lamented the confusion over the committee's reason for being. They noted an increasing number of members who expected to be given things without working for them and who attended meetings for donations but not for work projects. Gramsci referred to this dilemma in social organization as fetishism: "A collective organism is made up of single individuals. . . . If each of the single components thinks of the collective organism as an entity extraneous to himself, it is evident that this organism no longer exists in reality, but becomes a phantasm of the intellect, a fetish. . . . The individual expects the organism to act, even though he himself does not act." [20] The committee's growth and diversification of membership and its decline in inner democracy and active construction of collective identity led to its fetishization. New members saw the committee not as their own construction, but as a preexisting "thing" to which they may appeal for aid. As Gramsci described, they expected the committee to act even though they did not.

The arguments, gossip, and complaints within the committee were, in part, an attempt by long-term members (now a decreasing percentage of total membership) to assert control over collective identity and benefits. The economic crisis and government cutbacks affected all members, both old and new. But as some old members saw it, just when they most needed the committee's material support, a steady flow of "others" was also given access.

By 1994, the Mothers' Committee was poised between either becoming a bureaucratic vehicle for aid distribution, or splitting up after too many contentious meetings and ideological disagreements. Ironically, both tendencies sought to improve the collectivity: the leadership promising to extend benefits to a broader spectrum; the old members striving to retain ideological integrity, community, and limited access to material benefits.

Sandinista ideology and the latent, emotional bonds—the nonmaterial benefits—were the glue that held the core of the committee together and accounted for its relative longevity. Perhaps members first came out of a sense of duty to their fallen child or, later, for the donations of oatmeal, but a core group remained because they also developed meaningful relationships and came to see themselves in a new light.

At the same time, a subtext of the Mothers was that they were different, unique, and more deserving than others. For instance, fathers of war victims were thought to grieve less intensely and were less able and willing to organize over grief and loss. There was also a submerged effort to exclude women who wanted to join but did not fit their image of a "true" Mother. As such, although the construction of collective identity provides a foundation for collective action, it must also be recognized as a definition of who will and will not benefit from the collective action.

Finally, according to the images presented by and through the Mothers of Matagalpa, women are more self-abnegating, more other-oriented, and less individualistic than men, and therefore they unite more readily in order to protect their families, console themselves, and form emotional relationships. The Mothers' voices in this sense echo those of mobilized mothers elsewhere in Latin America. Yet women in this study also clearly mobilized on their own behalf. However much they emphasized the emotional benefits and political goals, the economic incentives were present as well. These older women, often single and with fewer adult children to support them, could ill-afford to be fully self-abnegating. Members found emotional support and a vehicle for their political ideals in the committee, but they also found access to food, clothing, and sometimes even housing.

With the theories of women's difference, we may find an academic hook on which to hang our sympathies. It is enticing to accept the public image of organizations such as the Mothers of Matagalpa—that they as *Madres Sufridas* know the value of life better than men, that they are self-abnegating, that they are unwavering FSLN loyalists, and that their activism is motivated purely out of political ideals and maternal love. But public identities can mask the latent dimension of identity that involves multivocality and contradictions. Although the visible aspects of a collectivity suggest unity, agreement, and understanding, analysis of its latent side reveals the fissures as well as the bonds.

Scholars of social movements do not speak enough of struggles within a collectivity. Those seeking to explain the success of a movement (especially a much-admired movement) are perhaps reluctant to muddy the waters with details about how much name-calling, gossip, and hurt feelings can go on behind the façade of a seemingly close-knit movement based on respect, shared purpose, and love or friendship. More specifically, why go out of your way to dredge up negative details on an admired social movement that has improved the lives of its members and made a positive impact on society? But as a result, we are suddenly at a loss to explain the implosion or split of what had externally appeared to be such a cohesive group. It also means that we still have little theoretical understanding of the day-to-day interactions or micropolitics of collectivities, much less how these micropolitics accumulate to affect "bigger" changes.

Doña Esperanza cuts the ribbon to formally open the Mothers of Matagalpa's new workshop. There, members and their families learned and taught various skills, including sewing, dancing, nutritional cooking, and piñata-making. Sale of the products of this workshop generated income for individual members and the Mothers' committee.

VOICE, AGENCY, AND IDENTITY

Counting the Mixed Blessings of Revolution and

Maternal Identity Politics

The changes engendered by the Mothers of Matagalpa have not shaken the foundations of the state or halted the feminization of poverty. As mothers of the fallen with an ambivalent position on the military, they neither won a war nor put an end to wars. Nor did they overturn the gender balance of power, much less set out to do so. For many Mothers, and increasingly so during the Chamorro administration, the goal of collective action involved simple existence more so than grand forms of resistance against collective enemies or systems.[1]

But in theorizing change in relation to collective action, we need not look only for significant structural shifts. We also find change at the individual level in the lives of those directly involved. Lilia Rodriguez described this notion of change in terms of women's collective action when she wrote, "These soundless processes are perhaps not changing the world, but they certainly have changed *their* world."[2] Committee coordinator Esperanza C. also had the microscopic notion of change in mind when she described her goals of collective action:

The goal for me is to fundamentally change these women's ways of learning, at least so that they feel they are people. So that they feel they can develop themselves, have conversations with people from other places, and so that they have a fundamental change in their lives. So that they have the security as women to say what they feel; so that they don't have this fear they had in the past. So they have work given to them so that women can feel useful to humanity and not feel exploited. And this is what we can do here. Perhaps a *campesina* can be a seamstress. An illiterate woman can learn to read. A woman who has taken many orders every day—ironing and washing—can take a class.

Using the categories of voice, agency, and identity, this chapter probes the consequences of maternal mobilization in terms of such small-scale goals.

Some of the committee's accomplishments are easily identified. The Mothers' Committee developed income-generating projects, held workshops for members to gain new skills, and provided an avenue for older women and women outside of the formal economy to mobilize politically. Although the Mothers of Matagalpa commonly stressed maternal images in gaining access to the national political arena, their activism carved out new space for older women in the political sphere. In addition, the new lives and positive self-images attained by some of these women demonstrate that maternal images do not necessarily restrict the development of women's capacities.

Still, the mobilization of women-as-mothers within the institutionalized revolutionary arena is best seen as a mixed blessing: it prioritized the role of mother for women while at the same time expanding the notions of what mothers could and should do.[3] In revolutionary Nicaragua, death coexisted with new life, hierarchy with empowerment, and dreams deferred with vigilant optimism. In this atmosphere of apparent contradictions, the challenge in analyzing women and revolution is not to explain why revolution failed to liberate women, but rather to understand the changing locations of control as well as sites of struggle.

Conflict and Contradiction

Economic and political shifts in Nicaragua engendered changes in both dominant images of women and the collective identity of the Mothers of Heroes and Martyrs. Initially, the Sandinista mobilizing regime produced a very small group of dedicated Sandinista mothers of the fallen who, in sync with the Sandinista mobilizing identity of *Las Continuadoras*, set out to continue symbolically their martyred children's ideals. With the onset of the contra war, and its subsequent increase in combat deaths (and thus an increase in mothers of the fallen), the implementation of the draft, and the tighter state control over ideology, identities, and mass organizations, the Mothers of Matagalpa grew. They remained symbolic representations of their children's revolutionary hopes, yet in 1984 they took over from the FSLN direct control of their organization in order to more actively carry out their children's struggle, as well as to address their own economic needs. Like the members of the earlier period, women who joined in this period (1984–90) prioritized Sandinista ideology, emotional support, friendship, and sense of usefulness they found in the committee. Finally, with the 1990 election of Chamorro and implementation of neoliberal economic austerity programs, the Mothers' committee paradoxically saw a rapid increase in its membership, despite the decline in war-related deaths. This was largely an economic response within a context of shrinking government social programs and continued economic crisis. Accordingly, the meaning many new members attributed to the committee had little to do with ideology or homage to the fallen, and much to do with economic desperation.

Particularly in relation to this latter group, I at first wondered, "Why won't these members follow their own committee's discourse on maternal selflessness and Sandinismo?" In response, I have presented the politics of maternal identity in terms of fragmentation rather than synthesis and complexity rather than parsimony. The Mothers refused to be simplified, and they would not be held in by their own discourse. Their self-sacrificing representations did not always inhibit them from recognizing and acting upon their own economic interests. Their constant stress on their maternal sameness did not preclude their differences. Most were not overdetermined by the discourse that they promoted, by the self-images that they upheld, or by the material relations of production and consumption. Rather, their subjectivities were flexible and members were forever ready to shift the discourse and adjust the social lenses so that others would see things their way.

It is simplistic and even counterproductive to explain the mobilization of mothers of the fallen only through references to Sandinista ideals and "natural" maternal traits without exploring the possibility of broader political motives, political tensions within the group, outside influence, or economic benefits. Recognition of such "political" or self-centered motives might be viewed as undermining the moral strength of the movement or stripping away its romantic veil. Yet refusing to acknowledge them leads to an inadequate analysis of resistance and a very shallow understanding of a wonderfully complicated group.[4]

Agency, Identity, and Voice: Categories through Which to Consider Change

Agency, identity, and voice are not mutually exclusive categories. They are theoretical constructs that complement and overlap, yet each provides different insights into nontraditional modes of doing politics. Together, they illuminate the gendered politics of this specific women's organization and also stimulate new modes of considering "politics" that capture, appreciate, and explain a more diverse array of women's collective action and individual accomplishments.

Agency is often the focus in considering collective action's ability to generate change. Agency as it is employed here recognizes politics as power relations operating at a microlevel. We as agents are neither overdetermined by structural constraints nor free to do as we please. As William Sewell, building on the work of Anthony Giddens, argues, agency is constitutive of, rather than opposed to, structure.[5] Agents struggle to assert control over social relations, implying the ability to transform those social relations to some degree.[6] This degree of control over social relations is found in agents' "capacity to transpose and extend schemas to new contexts."[7] Agency is also exercised when actors find and work out contradictions and gaps in structures.

Collective identity—involving the individual's recognition of self in others and the construction of "we"—is a continual process fluctuating in relation to economic, political, and social change.[8] Collective identity is political because it is influenced by structural change but also because it has a social impact. Collective identities can present an alternative mode of "being" to society. In the Mothers' case, it demonstrated to Nicaraguan society a wider range of women's capabilities and interests. An important aspect of the process of collective identity for the Mothers was the negotiation of conflicting gender identities. The working out of these conflicts was a political process that impacted and was impacted by social structures.

Finally, research suggests that listening to how women talk about voice can be an analytical focal point for learning about women's development of confidence, self-worth, and connection with others.[9] Indeed, the most common way core members expressed empowerment was in terms of voice— learning to communicate, to speak to strangers, and to express themselves. Daniel Levine, in his examination of voices of the poor in Latin American Catholicism, asks us to "reflect for a moment on how difficult it must be for people to find an authentic voice when they have long been given to understand that their opinions have no value or—to be more precise—*that they have no opinions*. Voices are found only through a long process compounded of discovery, conscious self-invention, and struggle."[10] This struggle is especially arduous for poor, older, and semiliterate women. But many developed their voices, or developed opportunities to speak, through their work within the Mothers' committee.

Collective and Individual Agency

In the Nicaraguan case, collective agency was a dominant theme in FSLN discourse—"together, we will get something done." In this discourse, collective struggle promised to free Nicaraguans from oppression. The most active members of the Mothers expressed this notion of agency as a key reason for their activism, and the efficacy of Sandinista-style collective action was an assumption they rarely questioned. Doña Ana María spoke of how members accompanied each other to overcome crises: "United, one has greater strength. If we have economic problems, or some other problem, we solve them together." As Doña Ventura put it: "We have to unite because all united we will accomplish something. Alone you aren't going to do anything. But among everyone, and with each one doing a bit, all together we will get something done."

At the collective level of the Mothers' committee, there were also instances of agency as attempts to control and alter the social relations in which the Mothers were immersed. In this sense, collective agency is not singularly a mobilization outside of and against social structures but rather it is also (and at the same time) struggle within structures. The latter sense does not involve questioning the "rules of the game" (that is, challenging the structure itself) so much as attempting to resolve gaps and contradictions within the structure. For example, in 1984, the committee established some autonomy from the FSLN. This occurred through members' reevaluation of their own goals as Mothers of Heroes and Martyrs in relation to Sandinista ideology. They found contradictions between their interpretation of Sandinista ideology and the role encouraged by the FSLN. Sandinista discourse supported people taking an active role in the construction of society, yet the FSLN and AMNLAE placed the Mothers in a very passive role, planning the Mothers' protests for them and defining their interests. The Mothers grew concerned that the state mobilized them for their symbolic power as *Madres Sufridas* rather than to empower them or address their problems. The Mothers came to interpret and critique their position as animate symbolic tools used *by* the revolution, preferring instead to assert themselves as active participants *in* the revolution. In response, although still working within Sandinista discourse, they repositioned themselves in order to more effectively carry out the ideals of the fallen and address their own economic problems.

In another case of agency asserted within rather than against social structures, throughout the 1980s Mothers criticized the Catholic Church hierarchy through interpretations of biblical passages and figures. As the right wing accused Sandinistas of being antireligious, the Mothers reversed this discourse to pose the right wing, including members of the church hierarchy, as motivated by political rather than religious interests. For example, they charged the cardinal and many bishops as being politicized by the right and out of touch with the problems of the people: "We say to them that no one has manipulated us but rather imperialism has manipulated some bishops." [11]

Members of the Mothers of Matagalpa were conscious of the symbolic power of *Madres Sufridas*. It was in this role that the Mothers portrayed themselves in public demonstrations, news interviews, and visits with foreign delegations. Members implicitly recognized that the loss of a child could be translated into social capital that could produce material goods from the FSLN, local politicians, and especially international organizations. This use of maternal identity is another example of the exercise of agency within structural parameters. The *Madre Sufrida* imagery portrayed through Sandinista channels to garner support for the war effort was creatively reinterpreted by some members hoping to gain in a more direct, material manner.[12]

The Mothers of Matagalpa altered dominant social ideas as they altered their own about what women can and should do. Safa argues that women's community movements, although they do not set out to challenge gender relations per se, transform the dominant discourse on gender: "In moving their domestic concerns into the public arena, they are redefining the meaning associated with domesticity to include participation and struggle rather than obedience and passivity."[13] She adds, "They may also lead to a greater consciousness of gender subordination and the transformation of practical into strategic gender interests."[14] This is an example of finding agency working within structures, and over time such struggles might actually alter social structures. Through their activism, the Mothers of Matagalpa were exposed to different experiences and ideas—to alternative structures. Also, they realized that others had similar experiences and problems, which made the contradictions and gaps in various social structures easier to detect. Thus, women began to exercise more control over the structures in which they were immersed.

As such, a construction of a strict dichotomy between feminine and feminist organizations, or practical and strategic gender interests, is misleading.[15] Organizing over practical gender interests, such as food, electricity, and shelter for the families of a community, can lead women to question certain aspects of traditional gender relations. It can lead to a gender consciousness in which women recognize, question, and attempt to change the everyday dimension of gendered power relations. But women's agency is not always in the guise of what are commonly considered feminist demands. Furthermore, there is never a complete emancipation from structural constraints, and creative control in one context does not necessarily translate into other contexts. Yet because of the incompleteness of and contradictions within and between social structures, agents can maneuver, fill in gaps, reconcile contradictions, and reinterpret rules.

Identity: Natural, Fixed, or Fragmented

Building upon this analysis of agency, politicized gender identities are a related site for discovery of change initiated by and impacting women. Through politicized identities, women generate structural change not only through conscious, deliberate, collective acts; change is also generated as their everyday practices and experiences in collective organizing comprise messages to society that challenge dominant representations of women's abilities and proper place in society. The Mothers individually and collectively adopted, constructed, and altered identity in several ways.

The Mothers of Matagalpa faced a variety of potentially conflicting gender identities, each of which had different implications for women's social roles. Portrayals of women as natural peacemakers and protectors of children—incarnated by those women who hid sons from the draft—contradicted the images of Patriotic Wombs and Spartan Mothers who bore future combatants and proudly sent sons off to war. Traditional representations of the Virgin Mary—a passive, mournful, maternal figure—conflicted with those of the revolutionary "New Woman" who could fire an AK-47 and stood watch over the neighborhood. The "good" wife and mother, inhabitant of the domestic sphere whose life revolved around home and family, contrasted with the political woman who went to meetings and protests. Many active Mothers had to negotiate competing identities of the ideal wife/mother: the wife/mother who followed the footsteps of her martyred loved ones, thus participating in time-consuming meetings, trips, and protests; and the wife/mother existing only for the home, readily available to feed and nurture her family.

How were these contradictions in maternal identity reconciled? Members reported that some quit because their male companions objected to their political work. Others solved conflicting interpretations of the "good" wife and mother through separation from or gradual mediation with their partners. The committee supported its members by providing women with an emotional support network, a sense of higher maternal and political purpose, and some self-confidence to withstand male objections. Furthermore, the Sandinista mobilizing identity of *Las Continuadoras* provided women with ideological support for their activism in political organizations and a sense of equal rights. Indeed, some male companions explained that because of their own adherence to *Sandinismo*, they actively supported women's political work.

Another power negotiation with men that employed gender identity relied on essentialized gender differences. The Mothers of Matagalpa mobilized a biologically based maternal identity to differentiate their experiences from those of men, thus constructing a power relationship through definitions of what constitutes knowledge. They asserted knowledge based on their experiences of bearing and raising children. Because fathers were excluded from the embodied experience of childbirth, they were ignorant of the unique knowledge, pain, emotions, and bonding that arose out of this experience. Without this knowledge, fathers were said to experience the death of a child less profoundly. Mothers of the fallen, therefore, were special and more deserving of state recognition and support, and thus had a higher sociopolitical status than did fathers of the fallen. Furthermore, because fathers were excluded from this experience, the Mothers' knowledge claims were beyond male dispute.

Collective identities based upon "natural" or "innate" qualities are common in political discourse, yet they are problematic because they ignore history and deny the possibility of change.[16] When some characteristic or response is defined as "maternal instinct" or a mother's "natural reaction," it is posed as beyond politics, change, and dispute. The support members gave to mothers' greater attachment to, obligation toward, and suffering for their children reinforced a dominant gendered discourse promoting paternal detachment and irresponsibility. This, in turn, might be found to promote single-female-headed households, the feminization of poverty, and, in women's old age, a greater economic dependence on sons and daughters. As structures are enabling and constraining, these mothers' expression of shared maternal identity and appeals to the natural were articulations of power, but they might also estrange men from the family and in that sense limit women's options.

Furthermore, discourse based upon maternal identity excludes some women and establishes hierarchies amongst others. Mothers of the fallen who did not mobilize as Sandinistas were portrayed as uncaring and selfish and even accused of not really loving their fallen child. Mothers who had not lost a child to political violence and especially childless women had less status and symbolic resources to exploit. Unless their lack of the identity "mother of the fallen" was offset through some other Sandinista identity, these women had less access to official and unofficial material benefits. In terms of large-scale structural implications, maternal mobilizing identities reliant upon "natural" traits can narrow the avenues of political participation for women and further reinforce childbearing as an essential characteristic to being a woman.

Yet as already suggested, the maternal identity promoted change. The notion of shared pain that only mothers can experience, combined with the Sandinista concern to carry on where martyrs left off, provided the ideological foundation upon which the Mothers of Matagalpa constructed their collective identity—their sense of "we." Members' reinterpretation of women's capabilities and their relations with men were encouraged both by this appeal to the natural as well as the contradictions in gendered discourse highlighted by the ideology and experiences of political activism. Through her committee work, Doña Elsa discovered that women's capacities were far greater than dominant gender discourse portrayed them to be, and thus she came to challenge gender power relations:

> We were learning how to develop ourselves, learning to recognize our rights, to know that we women, we mothers aren't only some object, that we serve not only for working in the house making tortillas, washing, ironing, or for our husbands telling us when we could come and go, if they think well of us, if we can organize ourselves or not. . . . While you are organized, you [figure out] how we are going to work, how we are going to teach so that others learn some trade, so they learn sewing, carpentry, ceramics so that a woman won't be so dependent on her husband. . . . We help [members] so that they understand how to trust, so that they understand that they are important, so that they understand that they are human beings, that we are equal to men, that we can struggle with our heads held high so that some man doesn't tell us what we should do.

As several women observed, a fundamental outcome of their activism was relief from men's monitoring and control over when and where women went. Doña María Elena credits the FSLN for this change within her home: "Before we only lived in the house under the man's hand. The man would say, 'Don't go outside that door.' But now it isn't like that. . . . Because now I say to [my husband], 'I'm going out,' and I grab my purse and go. He doesn't say, 'Don't go' or 'Stay inside.'" Doña María Elena's husband was a loyal Sandinista, a member of one of the first FSLN brigades. In my conversations with him, he explained how his thoughts on gender relations and women's capabilities had been altered through his adherence to Sandinista identity and his experiences in the revolution.

Doña Esperanza spoke of how women, especially rural women, were doubly oppressed during the dictatorship—at the hands of the dictator's National Guard and by their own spouses. The FSLN successfully attacked the first oppression, yet the Mothers over time recognized the importance of addressing problems contributing to women's oppression in the home: "It was due to your own husband . . . that you were cut off from society, as if you didn't have rights. Only the man left the home. *La Guardia* came to where these women lived and raped them. Then the husband kept his woman pregnant, living only for having children. Space is given to women here [in the committee]. . . . Perhaps in her house, the one that represents the family and deals with everything is the man. And it's like the woman wants some escape. . . . Women are more advanced than their husbands . . . because this space hasn't been given to us, but rather we have had to create it."

Doña Esperanza believed that in their struggle to create space for themselves, members developed a collective identity supporting maternal solidarity and sacrifice for the common good. She thought that, as a result of this process, members' political consciousness was sometimes more advanced than that of their male companions. This effort also clarified the contradictions between what traditional gender identities had constructed as women's natural capacities and what women were actually achieving. Control over income was also important in Doña Esperanza's testimony of gendered relations of power. Men, according to Doña Esperanza (and many mothers), often wasted income on alcohol and "other women." A gender identity that included a sense of agency often developed when women earned money apart from men and could spend it based on their own priorities.

La Continuadora was core members' primary political identity.[17] During the war, the FSLN strove to harmonize all voices in support of the war effort, so discourses were simplified into pro- or anti-Sandinista as they were reinforced ideologically through Sandinista institutions and backed by the military. In contrast, after the war and the 1990 elections, political space opened for discourses to multiply and identities to fragment and flourish. This opening, combined with new economic austerity programs, encouraged committee leaders to increase their attention to the growing economic needs of members and to embrace former enemies—mothers of fallen contras. But this also meant a loosening of their Sandinista maternal identity and a broadening of the definition of membership. Whereas their identity as Sandinista mothers had previously obscured other politicized identities and thus the differences among them, after 1990 their collective identity had fragmented enough to allow not only the differences to become more pronounced, but also for confusion over their organization's goals.

Analyzing collective identity over time allows us to see through the static, unified appearance of a collectivity. For many of the less active Mothers, and especially new members, the political goal of carrying on their children's struggle was overshadowed as the FSLN lost political power, the economy deteriorated, and the welfare safety net disintegrated. They became increasingly concerned with their identity as poor, elderly women suffering deteriorating living conditions. Conflicts arose within the committee from the effect these political and economic changes had on collective identity and interests, which in turn challenged members' sense of solidarity. Although they relied for their collective efficacy and internal coherence on their "sameness" as Las Continuadoras and Madres Sufridas, they also pointed out (and in a sense created) each others' differences. For example, active members accused other Mothers of being interesadas, participating out of self-interest rather than on behalf of their fallen children. Thus, Las Interesadas became a contrasting identity to distinguish who was or was not a "true" Mother.

Several studies of the Madres de Plaza de Mayo—Argentine mothers of the disappeared—have argued that changes in political context accompanied by change in identity and consciousness can present a fundamental dilemma for maternal organizations.[18] As members who originally made appeals based on conservative images of motherhood gain more self-confidence and experience and make more forceful demands, thus appearing less "motherlike" and more "political," they lose the political power of moral resources. Traditional maternal identity that projects images of "apolitical" grieving mothers is effective in capturing public sympathy, yet this image also holds women back from developing new political identities and demands that arise out of a heightened sense of agency. This problem was magnified for the Argentine Madres as the political system shifted from military rule to democracy. The Madres' use of their newly developed dissenting voices during "democratization" was seen by many as improper and threatening to a fragile democracy.

The Mothers of Matagalpa were constrained by a similar dilemma throughout their history. Although they retained the sympathy and support of loyal Sandinistas, the unaligned were more suspicious of the Mothers' political intentions and the right wing presented them as either unwitting puppets of FSLN dogma or conniving politicians. Aware of this dilemma, the Mothers at the individual level often expressed their identity as grieving mothers more so than politicized actors, even as the committee as a whole attempted to move beyond the image of passive victimization.

New Social Movement literature often poses collective action in terms of a dichotomy between instrumental and expressive goals. The former might be described as "I act in order to receive"—for example, higher wages, food, lower taxes, or land. In the case of the latter, "I act because of who I am." Here, identity is being expressed and demanding to be recognized. In light of the case of the Mothers of Matagalpa, this dichotomy is misleading. If we study collective action as a process as opposed to a discrete event, we see that collective identities are not cemented into one or the other form. In the 1980s, as a small, cohesive group in the midst of the contra war, the Mothers acted out the La Continuadora identity and saw themselves in each other because "you lost as I lost." In other words, these women acted because of who they had become—mothers of martyred Sandinistas. But the Mothers also crafted their collective identity into a moral instrument to make demands on the national and international community, as in: "As madres sufridas, we demand an end to U.S. aggression." Thus, their collective identity was both expressive and instrumental.

Yet after 1990, in the context of the Sandinista electoral loss, relative peace, and neoliberal austerity, expression of maternal identity at the organizational level became less powerful. In another version, asserted at the individual level with increasing frequency after 1990, identity was more clearly an instrument used to elicit material benefits, as in "I am a poor *madre sufrida*, won't you help me?"

But as instrumental, individualized goals were becoming more apparent, the leaders and core members continued to defend spaces for the expansion of gender identities and solidarities. They focused on self-help and personal change, as well as demanding a greater political voice for women. The meaning of political action did not become entirely instrumental, and the committee was never simply an interest group, as the coming together and forming of a sense of shared community remained for leaders and core members an end in and of itself.

Discovering, Exercising, and Harmonizing Women's Voices

To conclude this chapter's exploration of women's political organizations and change, I consider in greater detail how the Mothers, in the course of collective action, came to see themselves and their place in the world through analysis of their discussions of "voice." Members' experiences varied based on their economic position, their family life, their original reasons for joining, when they joined, and the frequency with which they participated. Some women—the leaders and core members—were profoundly empowered by their activism and expressed this influence most often through notions of voice. But others who did not value latent benefits of collective action, such as a sense of accompaniment and support, and had a loose grasp of the committee's political goals viewed collective organizing as a series of meetings suffered through in order to gain access to material benefits. Some, the most desperately poor, viewed it as their last tiny safety net.

In considering maternal collective organizing and change, we must consider whether members, through their participation, experienced new cultural models that were distinct from, even opposed to, dominant representations of women.[19] What new cultural models, if any, did the Mothers experience within the committee? I found that active members gained a sense of themselves as political beings and agents capable of promoting social change—subjectivities that contradicted the traditional conception of women as passive and apolitical.

In the 1992 national gathering of Mothers of Heroes and Martyrs, co-ordinator Esperanza C. told the 1,500 or so Mothers in attendance, "We have known how to give life, and life in abundance, but not only to give life, but to transform it."[20] Indeed, many women described their participation in the committee as an empowering, educational experience, speaking passionately about the manner in which they had personally developed.[21] Doña Elsa spoke of the sacrifices and the rewards of work with the Mothers:

> I think that if I wasn't organized, I would have free time in my house to do things that I don't do now—cleaning the house, bringing coffee to my husband, having dinner on time. . . . But that is a very empty, very sad life because at times it exhausts me. *Dios mio*, there is so much work to do in the house! But then again, I'm not the person I used to be. I can remember so many times when I felt so proud solving some problem for a Mother. . . . We look out for the poor, see what their needs are, learning more. To learn is a very beautiful thing because I see the empty lives of many people. They don't know about the needs of other people. They don't know anything. . . . We want to work, to learn more in order to make ourselves useful to society and to come to something in this world—not only to pass the time but also to *do* something. You feel good this way.

Coordinator Esperanza C. also spoke of her personal growth through activism in the committee: "[Before joining the committee] all I could say about my house was, 'This house is clean. This house has gardens.' But that's it—a clean house. I had to leave this house in order to do something else more important. The best thing is that I feel very good in this work because I also feel that I have done, or at least I have tried to do things very honestly because . . . [I want] to do a job and look for the way to do it better." Both Doña Esperanza C. and Doña Elsa, two of the most active members, referred to a relatively empty and less meaningful domestic life before the committee. Change, awareness, and fulfillment came through looking beyond domestic responsibilities to address the problems of others.

The Mothers' projects, though they were increasingly geared toward income-generation, were also developed with the expansion of women's horizons in mind. The quickly growing Mothers' Committee prioritized the empowerment of its members, as evidenced in a 1987 report by the Mothers'

Committee: "The participation of the Mothers increases every day, and they are more enthusiastic and confident in the committee. Due to the activities of the committee, they are discovering and developing the role of women in this new society . . . developing the worth that each and every mother has and that for reasons of the past have been kept hidden and undeveloped." [22]

In discussing their process of empowerment, the Mothers most commonly used the metaphors of silence and voice. In a large group discussion, one Mother explained: "Even though we have little education, the committee has shown us that we as women are capable human beings. We can speak out, do things, write poems, sing." Another insisted, "We have learned our rights and how to demand them." [23] Doña Elsa described how she developed her voice through participating in the revolutionary process as a Mother: "Today with the Mothers' Committee we feel that we can speak very well with any person, even though we are lacking a bit in our ability to speak. We feel that we have grown and grown and grown in everything, in expressing ourselves with other people. . . . And so I feel good." Doña María Elena felt empowered when she was able to crack through the code of political language: "[With the Mothers' Committee] we went to political workshops. We began to learn the [Sandinista] party language. . . . You can talk about [political] parties, or whatever, not only with unsophisticated words; there is another vocabulary with which to discuss it, to have conversations, and to argue. And so in this way you learn."

Doña Nacha described her pre-revolution life as a poor, illiterate woman, isolated from society outside her own class and, more particularly, from people outside of Nicaragua. For her, the revolution meant a government that prioritized education for the illiterate and international delegations that wanted to hear from the Mothers: "The committee has served us well, preparing us to meet with people whom we have never seen before, to speak with people. . . . [Before the revolution] we were very marginalized because the aristocracy distanced themselves from the poor. People came from other parts of the world, and the poor person was only alienated—without permission to speak with them, without interacting with them." Doña Nacha's expression of voice was less one of discovery than of opportunity. She did not find her voice so much as she found opportunities to exercise it in a wider arena. During the war, the Mothers traveled to other communities, sometimes to meet with other Sandinista groups, sometimes to give a family the news about the death of a child. The protests and projects of the Mothers' Committee drew women out of their homes and immediate community and into the streets and the public eye, bringing them into contact with other popular organizations and activists, government bureaucracies, political parties, and people from other places. Their consciousness and voice developed as a consequence of such contacts, in addition to the many opportunities for consciousness-raising within their own organization. Oral histories and testimonies, individual and group counseling, Bible readings, cooperative work, and self-empowerment workshops were all collective activities in which women exercised their voices, discussed issues, and even deconstructed and reinterpreted old ideas in new ways.

Women who before rarely ventured beyond the nearest market were now traveling to bigger cities and remote villages hours from home, speaking to strangers and even to large audiences. Also, international delegations met with the Mothers to hear their testimonies. Through such experiences, members gained a new sense of self-worth in their ability to express themselves. Doña Antonia spoke with confidence and conviction about this process: "I was a *campesina* who never interacted with other people . . . while now I have known many places, many people. [Before,] what did I know about interacting with other people or going to other towns? I had never done it. But now I have. I can go to other places with no problems. . . . Before, someone asked me a question, and I didn't know how to express myself. Now, I do. Now, whatever the question, I'm going to express myself. I'm going to talk. I'm going to answer whatever question I'm asked." Doña Elsa emphasized "doing what one can" and "not holding yourself back because you don't know, because you're embarrassed, because you don't speak well," in order to develop one's own internal resources: a voice, knowledge, confidence.

Joann Martin, studying women's collective action in Mexico, contends, "By creating a place where their voices could not be silenced, Buena Vistan women began to have an impact on cultural conceptions of gender relations even as they used those conceptions to modify their position in the community."[24] Much of the literature on women and popular organizing in Latin America applauds these organizations' success in giving voice to the voiceless, or their members' success in learning to speak "in their own voice." However, this implies that these women's "true" voices were uninfluenced by social, economic, and political structures. We must wonder—does anyone really have one's own true or pure voice? Are not "voices" socially constructed and also consciously altered by the speakers according to the audience and in terms of how best to achieve one's interests? I suggest, along the lines of my earlier discussion of agency, that speakers shape their voices strategically within structural parameters according to audience context. Once "found," the voice of the so-called voiceless is not a pure, essential, nonpolitical voice.

Indeed, each person's own voice is complex and ever changing. If we view voice as a process, not a thing, we see that voices are not given so much as listened to, engaged, and recorded. This process of speaking to people who will listen and perhaps even learn from or repeat a version of one's story can be an empowering process. Learning to "speak in one's own voice" is perhaps better thought of as learning to articulate and explore one's various and perhaps contradictory interests, needs, desires, and experiences somewhat independently from what others (father, mother, husband, neighborhood leader, politician, priest, or "society") say they should be. It is also the agent saying, "People have not listened to me before, but now my thoughts will be heard." As such, learning to speak in "one's own voice" is not an individual but rather a communal process. Furthermore, the Mothers' intergroup dynamics and the voices of the members when networking with other groups and the general public were also a message to society: poor, undereducated, middle-age and elderly women can speak out about state policies and international relations and also express their own needs.[25]

The Mothers' Committee aimed to give women a space of their own, away from the domestic pressures, so that they could develop their own capabilities and self-confidence. However, "a place where their voices could not be silenced" proved to be difficult, if not impossible, to attain.[26] In the committee's meetings and group projects, women were able to speak more freely and develop knowledge in an atmosphere dominated by women. But power differentials circulated and interests collided so that the committee did not function as a pure free-speech zone. Arguments intended to silence others were not unusual in meetings. More articulate women were able to present their views more forcefully, and certain discourses were prioritized. Doña Chepita spoke of times when she felt silenced in the committee:

At times you are disillusioned. You have some need and perhaps a *compañera* doesn't believe you. At such times you think about leaving the organization. It's beautiful when the *compañeras* listen to you. You lighten your load, like you've died and been reborn. But when the doors close on you. . . . [She pauses and shakes her head.] Some become resentful and don't come back to the meetings. I have come to this point. When I feel humiliated, I remember the day before [my son] left [for the army], he told me, "If I fall someday, don't let yourself be humiliated by anyone." And so for this, sometimes I start to cry because there are always disagreements [in the committee, and] I think, "I'm not doing what my son asked me to do. I'm doing the opposite." But I have reempowered myself, and I am organized.

Despite the arguments and the slights, one of the strengths of the committee was that, as part of the committee's official policy, members were encouraged to develop their capacities, to speak, and to learn. Indeed, part of the members' lesson in learning to express themselves was to overcome their intimidation, to develop the self-confidence that one's ideas were interesting and one's problems were important. For the strength to develop her voice, Doña Chepita drew on her identity as *La Continuadora* and the discourse prizing martyred children's ideals. Other Mothers, such as Doña Nacha quoted earlier, were emboldened by Sandinista discourse that stressed the historical marginalization of the poor and the revolutionary goal that the poor make their own history. Political meetings that taught members new terminology and foreign delegations that hung on the Mothers' every word also empowered these women to exercise their voice.

There are two notions of voice in collective action that lend depth to the concepts of collective identity and agency. On the one hand, a collectivity is a pooling of resources. These resources are in part bodies that aggregate to make for a louder voice, one that is harder to ignore. There is strength and audibility in numbers. As the Mothers repeatedly expressed their sense of collective agency, "Alone you can't do anything; organized, you can." On the other hand, there is the latent aspect of collective action that promotes personal development through interaction with others of a shared identity, a haven where personal growth may be nourished.[27] Here, the individual voice is developed, and with constructive interaction, collective identity is strengthened, needs are clarified, structural contradictions are addressed, and the voice comes forth more easily. The Mothers, through telling each other the story of their lives, came to see that "you lost as I lost." They also gained a better understanding of the ways in which structures both held them back and gave them greater range. They learned new interpretations and practices from each other and broke through some assumptions about human nature, motherhood, and politics. These two dimensions of voice are not mutually exclusive. They feed into each other rather than exist independently. Exercising voices within the group both eases the strain of speaking to the world for individuals and unifies the many voices to appear as one strong, confident voice when it is directed outward.[28]

By constructing a forum for people to discuss their everyday problems and anxieties, to discover that others have similar problems, and then to place these problems within a context of social structures, this practice raised awareness and demonstrated the many ways in which "the personal is political." Power relationships upon which the "private sphere" is based become visible or audible, questioned, and resisted.

The practice of collective action not only amplifies voices and provides opportunity for practice of voice; it might also bring new voices into earshot. Although poor themselves, urban members were exposed through their work to levels of rural poverty, violence, and despair many had not known existed. Working with war refugees from the countryside, urban members learned about conditions in other parts of the country and established friendships with people from different class and cultural backgrounds. Speaking with indigenous people from the deep countryside and Atlantic coast, members experienced new "ways of knowing" and established friendships that social prejudices as much as geographic distance had previously denied. In this way, they began to unravel stereotypes, gaining new respect and solidarity with the poorest of the poor and closing ethnic and class chasms. Doña Elsa spoke as an urban middle-class woman of her discovery of others' voices—the poor, the marginalized—and how they became, to her, an important source of knowledge: "You see humble people who don't even know how to read, but if you talk to one of them, they express themselves very well, and you learn from them. I have learned so many things, and this serves me well. They are giving this to me in order to help me. . . .

This is a great thing, and only after years of work have we learned this. . . .
I learned to know and value [those who have so many needs]. . . . For my
part, I feel satisfaction, I feel fulfilled that I can do something on behalf of
these needs. . . . When you are eating, it is necessary to know that there are
thousands of people who don't have enough to eat." For Doña Elsa, learning
occurred through a broadening of her sense of community and obligation.
Coming to know about the needs of others put a human face on the formerly faceless and amplified the voices, making them harder to ignore. This
demonstrates how the development of an internalized collective voice that
expresses shared identity and the collectivized voice that makes demands
on society are processes of social organizations that reinforce one another.

Macroimplications of Women's Micropolitics

One of the most eloquent champions of research on small-scale resistance — the "weapons of the weak" — is James Scott. His memorable analogy
of the tiny polyps that gradually develop into a coral reef capable of sinking
the ship of state inspires attempts to better understand incremental political
change and celebrate the accomplishments of those too often overlooked
in political science research.[29] In that spirit, rather than deeming microscale
struggles as "apolitical" and thus further condemning its practitioners to the
forgotten corners of history, I have suggested some tools for directing and
fine-tuning our analysis toward their politics.

The study of organizations such as the Mothers of Matagalpa presents
us with a fuller understanding of the broad spectrum of women who are
political agents of change. Examining the microlevel modes of sociopolitical change as generated by women through analytical categories such as
agency, identity, and voice highlights the formerly unrecognized successes
and the unanticipated consequences of women's politics. Mothers' groups,
though not explicitly feminist, do sometimes challenge the status quo of
gender relations — for example, as a product of political learning and empowerment of participants (thus, members could come to express a feminist
consciousness). This can also occur as a not fully intended consequence of
women's activism. That is, women's collective action, even through a political mobilizing identity based on essentialized notions of motherhood, could

incrementally challenge patriarchy. For example, organizations such as the Mothers send a message to society about alternative modes of politics as well as such women's abilities and interests.

Through their collective action, core members of the Mothers expressed individual change, empowerment, and struggle through the concepts of agency, identity, and voice. These women clearly found ways to change their own worlds, and were also low-key generators of change in gender relations. Political research would benefit from the recognition of such women's micropolitics, which potentially accumulate into structural shifts that eventually might prove to be patriarchy's undoing.

A statue celebrating mothers' abnegation and love was erected in the Somoza era in the center of Granada. Many cities in Nicaragua have a similar monument.

CONCLUSION

Few visitors to Nicaragua in the 1980s could fail to note the maternal emphasis in representations of women on the part of both the Sandinistas and the opposition. Yet studies of Nicaraguan women and politics have spent little time analyzing the mobilization of mothers and maternal imagery. The preceding chapters examined the manner in which large political processes such as revolution, war, neoliberalism, and democratization are gendered and in turn how women collectively respond to and influence such processes. Women positioned as "mothers" were key sites of hegemonic struggle across various political contexts. Maternal identity politics is not unique to Nicaragua, and this study adds to the body of literature on women, war, and the state. Moreover, the power dynamics of collective action as articulated throughout the history of the Committee of Mothers of Matagalpa highlights processes and relationships that we might find in other cases in Latin America and elsewhere.

As a number of studies suggest, in the context of war, women as mothers are a crucial site of discursive attempts to establish hegemonic consent for, or at least acquiescence to, the war effort.[1] Such studies tend to focus on large industrialized societies, leaving countries such as Nicaragua unexamined. The Nicaraguan revolutionary interregnum presents a special opportunity to view and analyze such gendered hegemonic struggles in a poor, agrarian-based society. States in such societies are generally thought to rely on overt forms of force more so than the construction of hegemonic consent. In Nicaragua, however, the ideological battle during the contra war in the 1980s was fierce. As counterrevolutionary war raged in the mountains, anti-Sandinista ideology, though muted at times, had powerful outlets for institutional expression in the conservative press, the Catholic Church, and opposition parties, all backed by U.S. funds and advice. Analysis of the ideological struggle between Sandinistas and anti-Sandinistas, rich in gendered representations of patriotism, grief, duty, and sacrifice, yields a better understanding of hegemony as well as women's politics and collective action.

Women and War

Maternal imagery is not a necessary condition for the ideological battles of warfare. Then again, the Sandinistas were not the first to mobilize mothers for the war effort. Countries at war with a variety of ideological foundations have relied on maternal imagery to stir up patriotism and facilitate the drafting of young men. Vietnam had its own version of the Mothers of Heroes and Martyrs in its war against the United States. The Soviet Union relied upon maternal imagery in World War II. Indeed, the United States in the Civil War and in World Wars I and II mobilized both mothers and maternal imagery in order to capture citizens' hearts and minds.[2]

As such, it is important to move beyond the common "Rosie the Riveter," "guerrilla girl," and "GI Jane" approaches to women in war that focus too exclusively on women's successful entry into the "male sphere." As one Nicaraguan study argued, "What has been given less attention is that the way the war was fought on an ideological plane encouraged and actually reproduced many traditional roles for women on a daily basis."[3] War is not necessarily an opportunity for women to take on roles and identities that contradict traditional notions of femininity. In that sense, war is not necessarily a feminist political opportunity. One way to improve our understanding of the impact that war has on postwar gender relations is to analyze wartime mobilization of women and women's images in the ongoing construction of hegemony.

Neither should it be assumed that the mobilization of women as mothers is a disempowering experience for women.[4] The women of this study, particularly the active members of the Mothers of Heroes and Martyrs of Matagalpa, were insistent in their interviews that they had grown significantly in their feelings of self-worth and empowerment through participating in this

Sandinista maternal organization during the war and postwar democratization. They located their source of empowerment less in the accomplishment of large-scale change than through the daily process of constructing and participating in a community.

Gendered Resources, Strategies, and Demands

Throughout the period covered by this study, women's collective demands were gendered, arising out of a recognition of the cultural expectations of women and an accompanying sense of rights that spurred them into action.[5] In making their demands, they often appealed to images rich in maternal symbolism. Their protest strategies were also suited to women's daily lives. Out of a logic internal to the social construction of motherhood came maternal collective action involving a "woman's way of protesting."

Women mobilized perhaps most readily when they perceived their children to be threatened, and they framed their demands in terms of protection of their children.[6] Threats to their children came in a variety of forms: government-sanctioned violence, imprisonment, inflation, high taxes, scarcity, a military draft, and counterrevolution. Threats were even perceived postmortem, as mothers rallied against ideologies or policies that challenged the ideals of their fallen children.

Mobilized Nicaraguan women also used gendered resources and strategies. For example, in Somoza's final years in power, urban women protested with everyday household implements, banging empty pots and stringing milk containers and aprons along the roads. These handy items drew attention to women's inability to adequately feed their families. One of the most significant resources at women's disposal was the dominant discourse of mothers' moral superiority and selflessness that allowed (and compelled) mobilized mothers to make demands from moral standpoints. For example, mobilized women in the Somoza era employed a moral resource —their social position as the politically innocent weaker sex deserving of male protection—to protect themselves against government brutality.[7] Women's groups' morally based appeals were particularly powerful to the extent that they appeared to be unstaged and above politics and self-interest. Mothers' organizations called for wives of Somocistas and contras to use

their moral persuasiveness to convince their husbands to change their politics. The Sandinista mothers of the kidnap victims in the 1980s challenged
the conservative church hierarchy to behave as "true Christians" by stressing mothers' moral spirituality and apolitical nature. By the same token,
the women prominent in anti-Sandinista protests deployed similar maternal
rhetoric, posing themselves as *Madres Sufridas*, victims of FSLN civil rights
abuses. Violeta Chamorro based her own presidential campaign on maternal
imagery, appealing to mothers hurt by the war that took away their children and caused the scarcity of goods. And when the Matagalpa Mothers'
Committee made demands on members' behalf after the 1990 elections, it
used morally based *Madres Sufridas* language, insisting that all mothers of
the fallen, not just Sandinista mothers, deserved financial support from the
state.

However, the mothers' organizations were not fully autonomous, and
their mobilizations were rarely spontaneous. Rather, pro-Sandinistas were
mobilized by the FSLN through AMPRONAC and AMNLAE, and anti-
Sandinistas were mobilized through U.S.-funded Nicaraguan political parties in the ideological struggle to establish hegemony. Both sides recognized not only the political capital to be gained from images of mothers
weeping for lost children, but also the likelihood that middle age or older
women would be a large bloc of war dissenters. As the Sandinistas struggled
to win the loyalty of mothers of draftees and fallen soldiers, the U.S.-
supported counterrevolution helped organize mothers of political prisoners
and mothers of draft-age sons.

Despite their discourse of self-abnegation and lack of full autonomy, we
see that Sandinista mothers of the war dead began to make demands on
their own behalf, calling for monthly food supplies, medication, a pension,
and even annual Christmas presents. They turned to the state for support
because a right of motherhood—the right to be taken care of by their adult
children—had been denied them. Thus, these women reversed the discourse of care to flow to their own advantage. As the Sandinista discourse
suggested, in addition to nurturing their own children, the Mothers had
nurtured the revolution itself. The Mothers extended the discourse to argue
that the state was thus obligated to care for them also.

The Meaning of Popular Participation

Collective identity is fragmented, contradictory, and continually evolving. New members arrive with varying resources, experiences, and interests. They join as cohorts at different times, under different economic, political, and ideological contexts. With these points in mind, I have argued that the identity a collectivity presents of itself is not complete or uncontested but rather the temporary result of an ongoing process of becoming. In the case of the Mothers of Matagalpa, collective identity developed in relation to political, economic, and ideological shifts, yet not in an automatic or direct way. The evolution of identity was not a smooth, uncomplicated process. Rather, it involved conflict—conflict not publicly displayed (until 1995) but essential nonetheless to the analysis of collective identity as a process.

This study suggests that collective action should not be viewed in dichotomous terms as either for or against the state. If we view collective action as a process over time, we find varying relations to the state and other social actors in relation to varying political, economic, and social contexts. Similarly, we should also be skeptical of dichotomous definitions of collective action as either materially oriented (old social movements) or symbolically oriented (new social movements). In the case of the Mothers of Matagalpa, this collectivity altered the way it presented itself to the world and in a sense reversed from a "new" social movement expressing identity to an "old" social movement focused on material needs. More importantly, this shift was never complete—the Mothers of Matagalpa pursued both expressive and material objectives.

An analytical focus on the meaning of popular participation for individual members highlights the centrality of production and distribution of material goods in Nicaraguan women's movements and contrasts these with the purportedly nonclass nature and largely symbolic stakes identified with the "new social movements" of Europe.[8] The meaning of "popular participation" for the Mothers of Matagalpa shifted from highly symbolic in the early 1980s to also become materially based by the early 1990s. The organization began as the embodiment of idealized, revolutionary motherhood, carrying on the revolution in the name of the martyred. It became also an economic mutual support network that constructed a safety net for the

poorest members in the face of economic crisis, a fall from political favorit-
ism, and disappearing social programs. Yet throughout their history, the glue
that held together the core members was a sense of community and shared
affection. Such findings disrupt the simple dichotomy of "old" versus "new"
social movements.

Social movements must not only be analyzed as a process over time but
also across several social levels, with recognition that members' expectations, understandings, and reasons for participation may vary significantly
from official social movement discourse. Through this multilevel approach,
we gain better understanding of collective identity as a process that is fractured and dynamic. Indeed, we cannot help but note that internal conflict
is a central ingredient. Recognition of this, in turn, comes through an attempt to see contradictions within a collectivity as well as its confrontations
with the state or other institutions.

Studies of social movements often recognize that collective identities
are constructed, but rarely have they systematically examined how they are
constructed. I explored the construction of maternal identity, contextual-
izing it in terms of hegemonic struggle in the revolutionary interregnum, as
well as resistance on the part of the mothers who were mobilized. Far from
a static version of revolutionary, patriotic motherhood, projections of the
ideal woman changed over time. These, in turn, were adopted, rejected, and
altered by organized women.

As should be clear by now, there is never one commonly held, uncontra-
dicted, and uncontradictory identity. The temporary "fixing" of a maternal identity is inevitably constraining to parts of the whole, and this fixing of an identity can become problematic. In part, it is a problem because
these identities are not entirely "freely chosen" but rather arise out of the
social/political/economic conditions of the time. As external conditions
march on with time, a fixed identity becomes counterproductive. In the case
of the Mothers, the political goals of carrying on their children's struggle became overshadowed as the FSLN lost political power, the economy deteriorated, and the welfare safety net disintegrated. New members were more
concerned about their identity as poor (often single) suffering women experiencing deteriorating living conditions. The conflict that arose from the
effect of these changes on identity and interests challenged members' sense
of community. So even though, as NSM theorists argue, establishing and

maintaining a common identity may be a goal of a collectivity, that does not mean that the identity is static or unfragmented.[9]

Meaning attached to collective identity changes — this cannot be helped. But references to versions of the past, to the "true" identity, to "the way things used to be," can be powerful political tools employed by older cohorts of a collectivity. While in certain contexts Mothers relied on their "sameness" as Madres Sufridas, in others they pointed out each others' differences — accusing some of being Interesadas or not "true" mothers. These shifts in discourse can be read as articulations of power. In this case, power was exercised through redefinitions of identity such that certain women would be denied access to resources. Since identities such as "mother" do not have any fixed or intrinsic meaning, the task for a diagnostics of power is to focus intently on the manners in which gendered meanings are attached and altered and how they emerge as "normal" or become eclipsed.

The Limits of Maternal Identity Politics

With respect to women, politics, and change in Latin America, several questions arise repeatedly in the literature. First, are women more pro-peace and other-oriented than men? The Mothers of Matagalpa themselves, in attaching meaning to their collective identity, often affirmed that the experience of birth led them to view war and its casualties differently from men. But we must also search for the politics behind the meaning. There were many instances in revolutionary Nicaragua in which women, contrary to popular maternal representations of pacifism and selflessness, promoted war and their own self-interests. Supposedly "natural" maternal traits — both pacific and bellicose — must be viewed in terms of cultural politics in the context of hegemonic struggle in revolutionary Nicaragua. Furthermore, too much analytical weight on the public discourse of a collectivity — for example, the goals of pacifism and selflessness as articulated by the committee's public documents — renders invisible the power, self-interest, and conflict internal to a group. It also obscures the power of social structures to shape both the public discourse and the internal struggles of a collectivity.

Another question in the study of Latin American women's collective action is whether such organizing necessarily changes the gendered division of labor or alters women's responsibility for family maintenance.[10] Does it just lead to a triple workload (wage labor, domestic labor, and political labor)? Generally, the answers are cautiously optimistic, stressing the small, incremental nature of big structural change.[11]

In addressing this question, authors tend to assume that women activists are young or middle-age. But my observations suggest that political action does not necessarily increase the workload of older women, those who live with daughters and daughters-in-laws who have taken over many domestic responsibilities. It may even increase an older woman's standing within the home if, for example, she becomes a primary provider bringing home the material benefits of collective organizing. Furthermore, the issue of the triple workload assumes that the women have remunerated work. Of course, even though labor may be redistributed within the household to accommodate older women's political activism, this still generally means that the extra housework is redistributed to other women of the household rather than to men. My point, based upon my observations in Nicaragua, is that this burden is not necessarily borne by the activist herself.

Jane Jaquette points to another central concern in the literature when she writes, "The feminist perception of the family as an arena of conflict between men and women directly contradicts how women in urban poor neighborhoods understand and justify their politicization—*for* the family."[12] But does the struggle for the family necessarily mean struggle on behalf of a male-headed household? Several Matagalpan Mothers spoke of home life and husbands as limiting, holding them back, and yet these women were politicized through certain aspects of traditional domestic motherhood. In other words, they criticized male companions while valuing the family. Furthermore, schemas of traditional motherhood and gender relations—for example, prioritizing work within the home—were amended by those women who fought for their family and then the larger Nicaraguan family "in the streets." Through such reinterpretations, fighting on behalf of family survival and criticizing male domination were not mutually exclusive acts. Many Mothers had been abandoned by the fathers of their children, and although several spoke fondly of their supportive husbands, more spoke of the pervasiveness of men's "sins"—domestic violence, alcoholism, and adultery. Recall Doña Chepita's claim that because of domestic violence, some women felt relieved when their husbands died. In the experience of many Mothers struggling on behalf of their families, the family had at some time also been "an arena of conflict between men and women." Simply put, because of the high number of female-headed households, as well as many women's open recognition of gender conflicts, Nicaraguan women's struggle for the family had less to do with male companions than Jaquette found in other Latin American contexts.

The Paradox of Women's Organizing: The Postwar Feminist *Apertura*

An important finding on women's organizing in Latin America has been posed as a paradox because such organizing tends to be more successful in times of political repression and transitions to democracy rather than under regime consolidation and democratization.[13] Nicaragua adds another context for this theory. As I have argued, in the struggle for ideological hegemony during the contra war, both Sandinistas and the opposition channeled women's collective action through politicized versions of maternal collective identities and away from versions of feminism. The immediacy of the war further undermined autonomous women's organizing—feminist or otherwise—as these were viewed as detracting from the war effort. A counterintuitive finding in the Nicaraguan case, however, is that the election of an antifeminist female president in the postwar consolidation of democracy coincided with a feminist *apertura* (opening). Once the Sandinistas lost the elections and the war was over, many Sandinista feminists were freed from the pressure they had previously felt to toe the party line. In response, they created feminist organizations independent from the state and Sandinista party. With greater autonomy to set their own agendas, they focused on issues of domestic violence, rape, incest, family planning, sexual orientation, and the feminization of poverty.

Yet the notion of "autonomy" in the neoliberal context should be used with caution. As the FSLN's power to influence women's collectivities has lessened, the power of international NGOs, through increased funding to Nicaraguan groups, has increased significantly. Although more definitive conclusions await future research, in my interviews with various women's organizations in 1998–99, leaders were quite clear that the survival of their various projects were reliant upon international support. As such, women's organizations often framed their own interests, strategies, and goals to suit the interests of international funding organizations. As one Nicaraguan activist responded in 1998 when I asked her how her organization came to focus on family planning, "Well, truthfully, that is where the funding is." This neither implies that such goals go against these women's own ideals nor that they are completely subservient to the priorities and ideologies of foreign institutions. But it does point to the increased importance of such international organizations in current theorizing about women's collective action in Latin America. Power relations by no means disappear once state funding is replaced by feminist NGO funding.

The Great Divide: The Mothers of Matagalpa, 1995–1999

In 1995, the Mothers of Heroes and Martyrs of Matagalpa split into two groups, one strictly Sandinista and the other open to mothers of the fallen of all political persuasions. This split was not entirely unforeseeable, yet the specific manner in which it unfolded was surprising and distressing.

The split paralleled similar struggles within the FSLN in the mid-1990s. Following a turbulent FSLN party congress and the subsequent departure of several powerful members, Sandinistas split into two political groups in January 1995.[14] The conflict leading to the split had been brewing for years, revolving around ideological tendencies as well as personal power struggles. Some of the attacks by the orthodox Ortega faction were surprisingly harsh as they targeted people's personal lives and families. Among those who left the FSLN were former vice president Sergio Ramírez and FSLN National Directorate member Dora María Téllez. Many of those who left created a new organization, the Sandinista Renovation Movement (MRS), which formally debuted as a political party in May 1995. The MRS was primarily composed of Sandinista intellectuals and others leaning toward social democracy. With the 1996 elections nearing, the MRS called for a shift toward the political center.[15] In contrast, the FSLN both courted the popular sectors and formed alliances with the conservative Antonio Lacayo. In the end, the Liberal Alliance candidate and Managua mayor Arnoldo Alemán won the presidency with 51 percent of the vote compared to the FSLN's 38 percent.[16] The MRS only won a single seat in the National Assembly.

Ramírez, the MRS presidential candidate, asked the Mothers' coordinator Esperanza Cruz de Cabrera to run as the Matagalpa MRS candidate for the National Assembly in the 1996 elections. This is testimony to the power, symbolic and otherwise, that the Mothers of Matagalpa had come to wield politically. Doña Esperanza, in particular, was credited with being a successful organizer and well-respected political figure in the region. Yet her candidacy generated insurmountable tensions within the committee.

A question that had been latent yet troubling by 1992 erupted to the surface once Doña Esperanza agreed to run on the MRS ticket: Was the Mothers' Committee still an FSLN organization? The Mothers had established a limited autonomy in 1984, preferring to set their own agenda while remaining loyal to the revolution. By 1992, in the spirit of postwar national reconciliation, shared grief, and maternal love, the Mothers' Committee began to accept mothers of fallen contras as members. Daniel Ortega himself, according to his own discourse in the early 1990s, was not clear on whether the Mothers' of Matagalpa was a Sandinista organization or an apolitical group acting solely out of maternal love.

This issue was far from resolved in 1995. Once Doña Esperanza announced her MRS candidacy, the FSLN stepped in to prevent the loss of this important organization to the MRS. The resulting conflict was surprisingly ferocious. In a July 1995 meeting presided over by the departmental political secretary of the FSLN, José González, several hundred Mothers met to replace Esperanza with a new coordinator. They elected Genny Herrera Cruz (whom I had never encountered in my year of fieldwork) and named their organization "Mother of Heroes and Martyrs, Camilo Ortega," after Daniel and Humberto Ortega's fallen brother, thus establishing unambiguously their allegiance to the FSLN.[17] In a meeting with journalists in the FSLN offices, several Mothers made a series of accusations against Doña Esperanza, many of which were printed in the Barricada.[18] Emotions ran high, and comments degenerated into unsubstantiated personal attacks. They accused Doña Esperanza of having been a comadre of the dictator Anastasio Somoza Debayle, distributing international donations only to her friends and personally profiting from committee projects. During this period, Doña Esperanza received threatening phone calls and other forms of harassment (for which the Camilo Ortega Mothers' Committee denied responsibility). The large group of Mothers backing Doña Esperanza, in turn, responded to the accusations in *Barricada* by explaining that profits and rents collected from income-generating projects paid salaries and utilities and funded future projects.[19]

In the midst of this conflict, the Quixote Center's Quest for Peace, the Mothers' primary source of financial aid and international solidarity, withdrew all support. This international organization had brought numerous delegations to Nicaragua to hear the Mothers' stories of loss in war and neoliberalism and had used photos of the Mothers in its newsletters and fundraising. Yet rather than attempt to navigate the tumultuous split in allocating its material aid, Quest for Peace withdrew. A further, though not unexpected, blow came when Doña Esperanza's candidacy was unsuccessful.

In 1998, the Mothers were attempting to survive despite the split. The two groups of Mothers each claimed to be the true Mothers of Heroes and Martyrs of Matagalpa. Those core members who remained with Doña Esperanza (though not necessarily with the MRS) retained control of the Mothers' office and other buildings and projects and continued to interact regularly. In 1999 they were busy developing their health clinic, which targeted the poor by offering reduced rates. Though their numbers were reduced, core members continued to value their participation in the committee as a source of personal empowerment as well as an opportunity to carry out their political ideals.

The orthodox Sandinista Mothers had led a land "takeover" soon after the split to gain control of a large housing project that Quest for Peace had promised to fund. As Quest for Peace withdrew its support, the neighborhood developed in a piecemeal, haphazard fashion. By 1999, many Mothers had sold their land or relatives had taken it over, and most of the new houses were unsturdy dwellings put together with scrap as opposed to the dignified, sturdy houses that had been constructed for over forty Mothers in the late 1980s.

Literature on Latin American women's movements notes that while women organize in the face of a crisis, they tend to disintegrate once the crisis subsides and the members return to their homes.[20] There is also concern that women continue to employ a confrontational discourse even once the crisis or dictatorship has passed. During Argentina's democratization process, many deemed the Mothers of Plaza de Mayo's calls for justice on behalf of their disappeared children inappropriate, even destabilizing, for democratic politics, which they said "calls for negotiation and compromise."[21]

Rather than returning to their homes after the war, the Mothers of Matagalpa clearly evolved in relation to changes in political and economic circumstances. They shifted goals, strategies, and membership requirements to those more appropriate to postwar democracy and neoliberalism. From 1990 to 1994, the Mothers as an organization deployed confrontational tactics against the government, yet they were also flexible enough to form new alliances and forgive old enemies. So, unlike the problems some scholars have identified in women's movements based on traditional gender identities, the Mothers of Matagalpa as an organization neither quickly disintegrated under democratization nor maintained confrontational, uncompromising positions. Their successful navigation through extreme political and economic shifts up through 1994 was rather remarkable.

Their crisis came, instead, through the general crisis of the FSLN-MRS split. Despite the committee rhetoric of semiautonomy from the party, the FSLN clearly retained a conception of the Mothers of Matagalpa as its own mass organization—one that continued to supply the valuable symbolic resource of revolutionary sacrifice. This crisis caused a split, as a number of members continued to articulate a strategy of confrontation rather than reconciliation. The group opting for reconciliation survived, though in the new millennium this group now faces the more formidable enemy of failing health due to poverty and aging.

The Future of Women's Politics in Nicaragua

What does this study of gender politics suggest about the future of women's organizing in Nicaragua? An important lesson of the Violeta Chamorro administration is that the election of women to high political office is not synonymous with the representation of women's interests. The Chamorro administration adopted policies that accelerated the feminization of poverty in Nicaragua. Furthermore, although she was somewhat restrained by the burgeoning women's movement and the Sandinista party, she promoted conservative social policies aimed to restrict women's choices, particularly in relation to sexuality and reproduction.

The FSLN is the only powerful party that is also committed to increasing the presence of women in political office. In the 1996 elections, eight of the ten females to gain seats in the National Assembly were FSLN candidates. This was a step back compared to the 1990 elections, in which more women were elected to the assembly, and they represented a wider variety of political parties. The FSLN women's success was guaranteed through the party's new quota system, in which women candidates must represent 30 percent of the party's candidate list.

The MRS only gained one seat in the National Assembly in 1996, despite the high profile and popularity of many in its leadership. In contrast to the "orthodox Sandinistas," leaders of this new party represented the more idealistic, progressive Sandinistas who were profoundly disturbed by the more authoritarian tendencies within the FSLN. Not surprisingly, key Sandinista feminists have aligned themselves with this party, including Gioconda Belli and Sofía Montenegro. The MRS ran as its vice-presidential candidate Dora María Téllez, and Téllez is now the principal director of the MRS. The MRS is the party most committed to feminism; however, as Nicaragua's political parties align and realign themselves into various pacts, the effect of the MRS's feminist ideology will in part depend upon its coalition members.

As suggested above, international NGOs are increasingly important to Nicaraguan politics, and they carry with them gendered implications. Not only did a foreign NGO significantly impact the Mothers of Matagalpa by its decision to withdraw support, but the actions and tactics of hundreds of other international organizations will certainly be instrumental in charting the course of Nicaraguan women's popular organizing. Some of these organizations have overt feminist goals of improving women's lives and have committed themselves to funding Nicaraguan organizations to meet such goals. However, through setting their own agendas and priorities, backed by relatively large amounts of money (especially by Nicaraguan standards), such foreign NGOs exercise undeniable power in terms of women's organizing.

This power is articulated not only through their decisions to support certain groups and projects and ignore others, but also through the "micropolitics" of surveillance techniques. Their common insistence on certain bookkeeping practices (such as receipts, monthly financial reports, and the setting of budgets) and on regular on-site visits by NGO staff are seen as essential in ensuring the efficiency, long-term survival, and eventual self-sufficiency of the women's organizations. However, they also represent newer forms of power relations aimed at disciplining women activists. In my interviews and observations, such techniques were generally new to Nicaraguan women activists, especially those women who were poorer and less educated. Such women tended to experience these politics of surveillance as intrusive and controlling. So, in addition to the more obvious modes of gender politics—namely, the political representation of women through elected office—as well as the gendered struggles for hegemony, I suggest we must increasingly focus on the expanding presence of international NGOs in the everyday lives and power relationships of women in Nicaragua.

Perhaps the clearest window through which to glimpse the future of women's politics in Nicaragua is the political crisis that surrounded the accusation by Zoilamérica Narváez, the stepdaughter of ex-president Daniel Ortega, that he had sexually assaulted her since she was eleven years old. It is easier to detect the ways in which large political processes and state policies have gendered implications than instances in which distinctly gendered power relations and discourse fundamentally impact national politics. But Narváez's testimony of sexualized abuse of power exemplifies the latter. It pressured Sandinistas to not only question the extent to which male members rely upon and exploit the system of machismo and the power relations exercised through attempts to separate "private" issues from public scrutiny. It also, in a more general sense, led Sandinistas to revisit the issue of internal democracy. By placing the abuse of power within a family under a public microscope, it called people to question male abuses of power against women more generally and develop a consciousness about how politics and power are so fundamentally gendered. This questioning of power was due to Narváez's willingness to testify, but also and more fundamentally to the strength of the post-1990 women's movement as it succeeded in coalescing a variety of women's groups around an antiviolence campaign.

Narváez made public her accusation in March 1998 and published her testimony two months later. Party militants quickly attacked her credibility with the claim that the right and even the CIA were attempting to sully the FSLN's most powerful figure, and the sadly familiar suggestion that Narváez was simply a "woman scorned."[22] The FSLN's second ordinary congress was held in the midst of this crisis. Reportedly, it was marked by an unprecedented lack of debate.[23] As Orlando Nuñez argued, this was in part due to the contradictions internal to the FSLN that were generating an identity crisis.[24] How can a party remain revolutionary and support neoliberalism? How can a revolutionary party protect an accused sexual predator from the legal system? But the FSLN elite led by Ortega, rather than questioning its machista foundations, was more prepared to turn its back on its previous revolutionary positions (while still representing itself as the revolutionary party).

This can be seen most clearly through the FSLN pact with Alemán's Partido Liberal Constitucionalista (PLC). The changes generated through this pact work to encourage a two-party system in Nicaragua, thus squeezing out all parties but the FSLN and Alemán's Liberals.[25] The pact was formed in the midst of scandals confronting both parties. As Ortega was accused of incest, Alemán was confronting his own crisis—the "narcojet" scandal in which a Lear jet stolen in Florida turned up as a Nicaraguan "presidential plane" that, when searched several months later, was found to have cocaine particles throughout.[26]

The FSLN has far outdone the PLC in the electoral arena in terms of its progressive policies on the election of women. Yet despite its gender quota system and placement of women high on its candidate lists, its handling of Narváez's accusations confirm the FSLN to be a very hierarchical party, the leadership of which is not open to internal democracy much less feminist critical analysis of gendered power relations. It has not extended itself far beyond its position during the contra war, when it refused to consider feminist policies that might cause it to lose political support from more conservative sectors. Judging from its policies, the FSLN elite never viewed the elimination of patriarchy as fundamental to its democratic agenda. To the extent that it made gains along the lines of women's emancipation, they are best understood as steps toward the larger goal of maintaining power. Indeed, democracy itself seems to be an endangered aspect of the FSLN agenda, in no small part because women's emancipation is not seen as an integral aspect of democracy.

In this new political context of "pacted democracy" between such strange bedfellows, the autonomous women's movement is the motor force behind any real progress toward expanded horizons of opportunities for women and the questioning of politics based on violence. At this point, there is cause only for muted optimism for feminism through political institutions and the party structure of the FSLN, yet the Sandinista party is not, of course, the only organized remnant of revolutionaries or revolutionary ideals. As the Envio editorial team of the University of Central America in Managua put it, "A revolutionary process always goes beyond those who are leading it, or who, even with the passage of years, still say they represent it. The fact is that a revolutionary process scatters the seed of transformations all around, and often harvests what it didn't even sow."[27] It remains to be seen whether the gendered fields of Nicaragua are now prepared to bear the fruits of change. But if Nicaragua does reap a "gender revolution," the autonomous network of women's organizations will have helped to cultivate it, ensuring that this time the revolutionary harvest is also a feminist one.

APPENDIX

The following members of the Mothers of Heroes and Martyrs gave interviews for this project:

Elsa Alemán
María Lourdes Blandón
Adela Blandón Espinoza
Ana María Blandón Sánchez
Ernestina Caballero
Esperanza Cruz de Cabrera
Olga Calderón
Elba Julia Cano
Berta Méndez de Castellón
Adelia Castro López
Juana Centeno García
Antonia Centeno González
Dominga Cordoba
María Eugenia Vargas de Espinosa
Julia Espinoza Sevilla
Estebana García González
María González
Francisca González Castro
Josefa "Chepita" González Chavaria
Ventura González Torres
Juana Granados López

Carmen Guerrero
Rosaura Hernández
Genera Herrera
Ignacia "Nacha" Herrera
Melida Herrera Rizo
María Lanza
Francisca "Chica" López Castellón
Gregoria López Pineda de Granados
Teofila Méndez
Petrona Mendoza Castro
Gregoria Mendoza Hernández
Paquita Francisca Montenegro
Leonor Palacios de Montenegro
Gladys Morales
Geronima Muñoz
Domitilia Murillo López
María Ochoa
María Elena Ortega Cruz
Jesús Ortiz Pérez
Paulina Palacios
Rosa Pérez
Malvina Pérez Rodríguez
Josefina Picado Rizo
Rafael Rayo Díaz
Bibiana Rios Calderón
Valentina Rivera
Esperanza Rodríguez Rivera ·
Santo Salgado Pineda
Rosa Emilia Sánchez
María Elsa Torres
Claudia Torrez Martínez
Angela Urbina Rostrán
Haidee Zeledón

NOTES

Preface

1. Otherwise known by its acronym, COMAHEMA. I will refer to this group also as the Mothers of Matagalpa and the Mothers' Committee.

2. This research was primarily conducted at the Hoover Institute at Stanford University, the U.S. Library of Congress, and the University of Kansas's Watson Library.

3. I did not record, for example, the death of a woman in a car accident or articles in which various men and women were asked about their holiday plans.

4. Power differentials between interviewer and subject in such instances are rather obvious. I do not intend to downplay or deny the privileges attached to my identity as a relatively wealthy, white, U.S. citizen; however, I also see power articulated as the Mothers defined events in their own terms and told their own versions of their history.

5. Many Mothers' testimonials were published in the mid-1980s with their real names in Sola and Pau Trayner, *Ser Madre en Nicaragua*.

6. There are instances in which I do not mention names—particularly regarding personal disputes within the committee.

7. Randall, *Sandino's Daughters Revisited*; Randall, *Gathering Rage*.

8. Two sources were particularly valuable: Randall's *Sandino's Daughters*, which contains interviews of politically active women taken soon after the fall of Somoza, and Sola and Pau Trayner's *Ser Madre en Nicaragua*, a collection of testimonies given by the Mothers of Heroes and Martyrs of Matagalpa at the height of the contra war. I conducted interviews not only with members of the Mothers of Matagalpa, but also with members of the Mothers of Heroes and Martyrs in several other areas (the cities of Managua, Estelí, Jinotega, and the rural areas of Rio Blanco and Rancho Grande), and anti-Sandinista organized mothers (M22, and the Mothers of the *Resistencia*). I also interviewed people who had worked closely with these organizations, such as employees or members of Apoyo al Combatiente, AMNLAE, and FSLN regional offices. Finally, I interviewed several ex-contras, and the director of the anti-Sandinista human rights group *Comision Permanente de Derechos Humanos*.

9. Jones, "Beyond the Barricades," 62–63. See also Valdivia, "The U.S. Intervention," 357.

10. Valdivia, "The U.S. Intervention," 359–60. Accused of endangering national security during the contra war, *La Prensa* was regularly censored by the FSLN throughout the 1980s and was closed down several times, including one fifteen-month period from 26 June 1986 through 30 September 1987. The paper was permitted to reopen without censorship provided it published within the laws of the state of emergency. *La Prensa* reopened with $98,000 in aid from the U.S. National Endowment for Democracy (NED), bringing the total amount of aid *La Prensa* received from the NED since 1980 to $254 million. Kinzer, *Blood of Brothers*, 353–54. See also Edmisten, *Nicaragua Divided*, 98.

Introduction

1. O'Kane, "The New World Order," 28–29; Kampwirth, "The Mother of the Nicaraguans."

2. *La Prensa*, 4 September 1989.

3. Ibid., 1 February 1990.

4. Gramsci, *Selections*, 57.

5. Roseberry, "Hegemony and the Language of Contention."

6. Alvarez, Dagnino, and Escobar, "Introduction," 10.

7. Roseberry, "Hegemony and the Language of Contention," 357.

8. Gould, *To Lead as Equals*.

9. However, despite dominant counterhegemonic discourses based on free-market economics, anticommunism, and conservative Catholic teachings, the anti-Sandinista forces did not pose a unitary counterhegemony. Its eventual electoral success in 1990 relied upon a very fragmented and diverse popular counterhegemony that resisted and evaded in myriad forms. These forms included black market transactions, attendance at conservative Catholic or evangelical services, and draft evasion—resistance in which middle-age and older women figured prominently. See Scott, "Foreword."

10. AMNLAE, "Women's Participation," 125.

11. Scott, "Foreword," ix.

12. See Gaventa, *Power and Powerlessness*; Stokes, *Cultures in Conflict*.

13. Somers and Gibson, "Reclaiming the Epistemological 'Other,'" 53.

14. Cohen, "Strategy or Identity"; Melucci, *Nomads of the Present*.

15. Escobar and Alvarez, "Introduction," 3.

16. See, for example, Alvarez, *Engendering Democracy*, and Escobar and Alvarez, *The Making of Social Movements*.

17. Stephen, "Women in Mexico's Popular Movements."

18. Neuhouser, "'Worse Than Men,'" 39; Safa, "Women's Social Movements"; Corcoran-Nantes, "Women and Popular Urban Social Movements," 249; Rodriguez, "Barrio Women"; Fisher, *Mothers of the Disappeared*; Alvarez, *Engendering Democracy*.

19. Corcoran-Nantes, "Women and Popular Urban Social Movements"; Jelin, "Introduction."

20. Anderson, "Post-Materialism."

21. Hellman, "The Study of New Social Movements," 53.

22. Nash, "The Reassertion of Indigenous Identity," 9.

23. Ibid.

24. Melucci, *Nomads of the Present,* 26.

25. Ibid., 35.

26. Ibid., 30.

27. Scott, "Deconstructing Equality-versus-Difference," 134–35.

28. Ibid., 144–45.

29. Somers and Gibson, "Reclaiming the Epistemological 'Other,'" 73–74.

30. See Scott, "Deconstructing Equality-versus-Difference," 144; Somers and Gibson, "Reclaiming the Epistemological 'Other,'" 65.

31. Jelin, "Introduction," 3.

32. Gamson, "The Social Psychology of Collective Action"; Friedman and McAdam, "Collective Identity and Activism."

33. McCarthy and Zald, "Resource Mobilization and Social Movements"; Tilly, *From Mobilization to Revolution.*

34. Morris, *Origins of the Civil Rights Movement,* 280, 282.

35. As Gitlin wrote, "Identity politics presents itself as . . . the most compelling remedy for anonymity in an otherwise impersonal world." Gitlin, "From Universality to Difference," 153.

36. Melucci, *Nomads of the Present.*

37. See Randall, *Sandino's Daughters;* Molyneux, "Women's Role"; Deighton et al., *Sweet Ramparts;* Ramirez-Horton, "The Role of Women"; "Women in Nicaragua: A Revolution within a Revolution," in *Envío* 3, no. 25, July 1983; and Stephens, "Women in Nicaragua."

38. According to Martha Morgan, some Nicaraguan feminists argued that, "despite some early feminist pursuits, as the counterrevolutionary war intensified, AMNLAE put the defense of the revolution and its general goals ahead of women's specific problems and devoted too much of its time to mobilizing the Mothers of Heroes and Martyrs, consequently perpetuating stereotypical views of women's role." Morgan, "Founding Mothers," 14. See also Stephens, "Women in Nicaragua."

39. For example, in a 1989 interview with Dora María Téllez, Carmen Herrera and Trish O'Kane asked, "Why has [the FSLN] privileged the Mothers of Heroes and Martyrs? Why isn't AMNLAE a progressive movement?" Téllez responded, "The Mothers of Heroes and Martyrs in this country have not been simply uteruses that give birth to heroes. The majority of families have the mother as the head of the household. We are not speaking of a movement of passive mothers that dedicate themselves to crying, much less sitting around in despair. They go into the streets, actively, proposing an idea, contributing to the transformation process." Herrera and O'Kane, "*Hagamos politica,*" 36.

40. Most notably, Randall, *Gathering Rage,* and the Sandinista women interviewed in Randall, *Sandino's Daughters Revisited.*

41. Chodorow, *The Reproduction of Mothering*; Gilligan, *In a Different Voice*; Ruddick, *Maternal Thinking*; Belenky et al., *Women's Ways of Knowing*.

42. See Scheper-Hughes, *Death without Weeping*; and Stack, "The Culture of Gender."

43. Scheper-Hughes, *Death without Weeping*, 341.

44. Ibid., 402.

45. Ibid., 408.

46. Fisher, *Mothers of the Disappeared*, 60.

47. Scheper-Hughes, *Death without Weeping*, 401; Rhode, "The Politics of Paradigms," 353.

48. Somers and Gibson, "Reclaiming the Epistemological 'Other,'" 40.

49. Kerber asks, "If women can be counted on to care for others, how are we to deal with self-interest, selfishness and meanness of spirit which women surely display as much as do men?" Kerber, "Some Cautionary Words," 106.

50. Rhode, "The Politics of Paradigms," 344.

51. Alonso, *Peace as a Women's Issue*, 11.

52. Kaplan, "Female Consciousness," 547.

53. Ibid.

54. MacLeod, "Hegemonic Relations."

55. Melucci, *Nomads of the Present*, 38.

56. Verba and Nie, *Participation in America*, 3.

"We Want a Free Country for Our Children"

1. Nicaraguan Interior Minister Tomás Borge, "Women and the Nicaraguan Revolution," 1982 speech celebrating the fifth anniversary of AMPRONAC/AMNLAE. Reprinted in English by Publicaciones del Departamento de Relaciones Publicas, Ministerio del Interior, Managua, Nicaragua.

2. See Elshtain, *Women and War*; Elshtain and Tobias, *Women, Militarism and War*; Cooke and Woollacott, *Gendering War Talk*; MacDonald, Holden, and Ardener, *Images of Women in Peace and War*; Lorentzen and Turpin, *The Women & War Reader*.

3. Molyneux, "Mobilization without Emancipation?"; see also Collinson, *Women and Revolution*. Feminists can be mothers, of course. My point is that maternal identity was the dominant identity through which women were portrayed.

4. Randall, *Sandino's Daughters*, 166.

5. *Barricada*, 18 September 1980.

6. Enriquez, "We Women Learned," 258.

7. *Barricada*, 28 September 1980.

8. Deighton et al., *Sweet Ramparts*, 39.

9. *Barricada*, 27 September 1980.

10. Randall, *Gathering Rage*, 45.

11. AMPRONAC, "*La Mujer Nicaraguense*."

12. Ibid.

13. *Barricada*, 27 September 1980; Enriquez, "We Women Learned," 258.

14. *La Prensa*, 8 March 1978.

15. Randall, *Sandino's Daughters*, 70–71.

16. *La Prensa*, 25 January 1978, 1.

17. Randall, *Sandino's Daughters*, 6–7.

18. *La Prensa*, 3 February 1978, 2.

19. Ibid., 5.

20. AMPRONAC, *"La Mujer Nicaraguense."*

21. Alan Riding, "Violence in Nicaragua Stirs Women to Activism," *New York Times*, 3 June 1978, 16.

22. Randall, *Sandino's Daughters*, 8.

23. "Letter from the Committee of Chinandegan Ladies," *La Prensa*, 8 February 1978, 2.

24. Ibid., 28 May 1978.

25. AMPRONAC, *"La Mujer Nicaraguense."*

26. Ibid.

27. Randall, *Sandino's Daughters*, 13–14.

28. Ibid., 15.

29. AMPRONAC, *"La Mujer Nicaraguense."*

30. Alan Riding, "Violence in Nicaragua Stirs Women to Activism," *New York Times*, 3 June 1978, 16.

31. Randall, *Sandino's Daughters*, 16.

32. Ibid., 34.

33. *La Prensa*, 8 March 1978, 1.

34. Ibid., 5 August 1978.

35. Ibid., 12 August 1978.

36. Ibid., 8 February 1978, 2.

37. In the cities that experienced severe bombings—Estelí, Chinandega, and León—AMPRONAC members became scattered, having fled the city, been imprisoned or killed, or gone underground. Up to the overthrow of Somoza, Managua remained the center of AMPRONAC activity. AMPRONAC, *"La Mujer Nicaraguense."*

38. *La Prensa*, 18 February 1979.

39. Ibid., 27 May 1979.

40. Ibid., 26 February 1979.

41. Ibid., 8 March 1979.

42. Ibid., 24 April 1979.

43. Randall, *Sandino's Daughters Revisited*, 26. Carlos Vilas disputes these figures, arguing that the Nicaraguan Institute for Social Security and Welfare (INSSBI) data shows women to have comprised 6.6 percent of the forces. More so than direct combat, he argues that women participated primarily in support tasks. Vilas, *The Sandinista Revolution*, 108–9.

44. Editorial by Elida de Solorzano, *La Prensa*, 12 October 1980.

45. Ibid.

46. *La Prensa* was shut down by the Sandinista government from June 1986 through September 1987.

47. *La Prensa*, 12 October 1980.

48. Ibid., 19 June 1980.

49. Ibid., 3 December 1980.

50. *Barricada*, 28 May 1981.

51. Stephens, "Women in Nicaragua," 7.

52. Gloria Carrion, interview by Randall, *Sandino's Daughters*, 35.

53. Ibid., 37.

54. *Barricada Internacional*, 9 October 1986.

55. National Report, MINSA, March 1989, and Ministry of Education, 1989. Statistics appeared in Montis, Olivera, and Meassick, "A Panorama of Women in Nicaragua."

56. *Barricada Internacional*, 2 September 1989.

57. Randall, *Sandino's Daughters Revisited*, 27.

58. Ibid., 26. It also went against the 1979 Statutes of Rights and Guarantees, which outlawed discrimination against women. Collinson, *Women and Revolution in Nicaragua*, 158.

59. See, for example, *Barricada*, 17 June 1981, 25 June 1981, and 14 August 1981.

60. Randall, *Gathering Rage*, 46.

61. Stephen Kinzer, "Conscription for Young Nicaraguans," *New York Times*, 31 August 1983, A3.

62. Randall, *Sandino's Daughters Revisited*, 26.

63. Lynda Boose, Lynn Higgins, Marianne Hirsch, Al LaValley, and Brenda Silver, proposal for institute on gender and war at Dartmouth College, 1990, quoted by Cooke and Woollacott, "Introduction," ix.

64. See Elshtain, *Women and War*; Elshtain and Tobias, *Women, Militarism and War*; Cooke and Woollacott, *Gendering War Talk*; and MacDonald, Holden, and Ardener, *Images of Women in Peace and War*.

65. Cooke and Woollacott, "Introduction," ix.

66. Elshtain, *Women and War*, 1987.

67. Bayard de Volo, "Drafting Motherhood."

68. Cooke and Woollacott, "Introduction," xi.

69. Chinchilla, "Revolutionary Popular Feminism in Nicaragua," 380.

70. Gioconda Belli, "The Mother," translated by Electa Arenal and Marsha Gabriela Dreyer, in Women's International Resource Exchange, "Nicaraguan Women and the Revolution."

71. *Barricada*, 22 August 1980.

72. Ibid.

73. *Barricada*, 21 October 1980; *La Prensa*, 19 September 1980.

74. *Somos*, AMNLAE publication, May 1984, 2.

75. Denouncement of a contra ambush by Mothers of Heroes and Martyrs, 15 January 1990, unpublished.

76. Deighton et. al., *Sweet Ramparts*, 40.

77. *La Prensa*, 18 February 1979.

78. Borge speech in Managua on 8 March 1980, translated and printed by WIRE.

79. Molyneux, "Mobilization without Emancipation?"

80. *Barricada*, 25 June 1981.

81. Ibid., 15 August 1982.

82. Ibid., 1 July 1981, 1.

83. Molyneux, "Mobilization without Emancipation?" See also Enloe, *Does Khaki Become You?*, 166–67.

84. *Barricada*, 12 March 1984, 6.

85. Molyneux, "Mobilization without Emancipation?," 228.

86. FSLN, "The Historic Program of the FSLN," 147.

87. *Barricada*, 25 May 1981.

88. Ibid., 10 July 1983.

89. Ibid., 1 June 1984.

90. Ibid., photograph, 13 July 1981.

91. Ibid., 16 July 1981.

92. Ibid., 16 May 1983.

93. Ibid., 13 July 1981.

94. Ibid., 9 March 1981.

95. Ibid., 20 May 1981.

96. Ibid., 5 March 1983.

97. Ibid., 6 March 1983.

98. Ibid., 25 April 1984; *Barricada Internacional*, October 1987.

99. *Barricada*, 25 April 1984.

100. *Nuevo Diario*, 28 April 1984.

101. *Barricada*, 23 May 1981.

102. Ibid., 22 April 1981.

103. Leticia Herrera, quoted in *Barricada*, 14 May 1981.

104. *Envio*, June 1991, 34.

105. Interview with Esmeralda Davila, Social Secretary of AMNLAE, in *Somos 25*, Agosto 1985.

Movement as Symbol

1. Matagalpa is in Region VI, which according to the Nicaraguan Human Rights Center (CENIDH) had the highest number of deaths related to re-armed groups: 874 between 1990 and 1994 (compared to the next highest of 264 in Region I and 213 in Region V). The fieldwork for this dissertation was conducted during the peak period of violence, which ran from September 1991 through December 1993.

2. Melucci, *Nomads of the Present,* 31.

3. Ibid., 26.

4. Ibid., 35.

5. This theme of political indebtedness to their children, a reversal of the birth process in which their children engendered political consciousness in their mothers, was also expressed by the Argentine mothers of the disappeared, Las Madres de Plaza de Mayo. As they began to understand their children's concern for social change, they took on their children's demands. As one Madre put it, "Every day when we wake up, we think of the day of work that our children call us to, those children that are in the square, who are in each and every one of us, those children which gave birth to us and to this awareness and to this work that we do" (Hebe Bonafini, interviewed by Fisher, *Out of the Shadows,* 135).

6. Lancaster, *Thanks to God,* 91.

7. Cohen, "Strategy or Identity," 688.

8. Ruddick, *Maternal Thinking;* Scheper-Hughes, *Death without Weeping.*

9. Chuchryk, "Feminist Anti-Authoritarian Politics," 140–41.

10. Analytical linkages between mothers of the disappeared in such countries as Argentina, Chile, and El Salvador and the Mothers of Heroes and Martyrs of Nicaragua should be drawn with caution. Although the former were organized in direct opposition to the state, the Mothers of Heroes and Martyrs were organized by the state.

11. Ibid.; see also Bayard de Volo, "Heroes, Martyrs, and Mothers," 44.

12. Ruddick, *Maternal Thinking,* 40–41. Ruddick is careful to note that while it is usually women who mother, both men and women may engage in maternal work.

13. Ibid., 132.

14. Ibid., 157.

15. Ibid., 156.

16. Ibid., 228.

17. Olive Schreiner, *Women and Labor* (1911; reprint, London: Virago Press, 1978), 172, quoted in Ruddick, *Maternal Thinking,* 186. Ruddick then writes, "Their knowledge derives from the work of mothering, which though it can be shared equally with men, has been historically female. It also derives, at least in part, from an experience or appreciation of female birthing labor on which all subsequent mothering depends." Scheper-Hughes demonstrates that this valuing of human life is not essential to women or inevitably present in mothers (Scheper-Hughes, *Death without Weeping*).

18. *Barricada* Sunday supplement, "Las Chispas" by Carlos Ortíz, 21 June 1992.

19. This discourse, in which mothers suffer more upon the death of a child and value human life more than others, supports antiwar movements and complicates the collective identity of a group such as the Mothers of Heroes and Martyrs that officially promoted the draft and the Sandinista war effort.

20. Some mothers of the fallen played key roles in the creation of the Mothers of Heroes and Martyrs.

21. The title "Mother of the Heroes and Martyrs" is applied to any woman who lost

a child in the service of the Sandinista revolution. They need not be formally organized with the Mothers' Committee. The Mothers also often refer to themselves as *Las Mamas*.

22. This has occurred throughout Latin America. As Alvarez attests, "In contemporary Latin America, political regimes, parties, and organized sectors of civil society have reacted to today's women's movements . . . by harnessing women's political activity into 'auxiliary' women's organizations, co-opting women's movement organizations and/or appropriating their political discourses, acquiescing to limited demands through public policy making, or suppressing women's movement demands altogether." Alvarez, *Engendering Democracy*, 20.

23. Hoyt, *The Many Faces*, 48.

24. Ibid., 6.

25. The FSLN has often projected itself as the "parent" of its mass-organization "children." A typical description by FSLN leaders of mass organizations: When these children are very young, they need to be coddled, led by the hand, yet as they grow up, they need greater independence.

26. "Information Sheet about the Movement of Mothers of Heroes and Martyrs," by the Mothers of Heroes and Martyrs of Matagalpa, 1984 (exact date unknown).

27. All middle-class, articulate, and loyal Sandinistas.

28. According to several Mothers interviewed in nearby Estelí, this was also the practice in that city.

29. Elizabeth Jelin reports a trend in such moves toward autonomy for women's groups elsewhere in Latin America: "There has been a development of women's movements from popular sectors seeking to take control of their own destiny, whether within the women's organizations promoted by the Church or political parties, or in those in which women are subordinate and in a minority (such as the unions)." In Jelin, "Citizenship and Identity," 186.

30. Written copy of speech by Esperanza Cruz de Cabrera for the 28 May 1991 national Mothers of Heroes and Martyrs celebration in Matagalpa.

31. "Introduction and History of the Mothers of Heroes and Martyrs," an unpublished report by the Mothers of Matagalpa, written in 1991.

32. Mothers of Heroes and Martyrs of Matagalpa, open letter to Christian groups, 3 August 1990.

The Priorities of War

1. *Barricada Internacional*, 2 September 1989.

2. Ibid., 2 September 1989; Collinson, *Women and Revolution in Nicaragua*, 142.

3. "Women in Nicaragua: The Revolution on Hold," *Envio* 10 (June 1991), 35.

4. Declaration issued by the AMNLAE branch "Arlen Siu" of Casa Nicaragua, New York, 27 March 1982.

5. Randall, *Sandino's Daughters Revisited*, 28–29. According to Randall, throughout the Sandinista era feminism was thought of as "something foreign" or "an imported fad."

6. *Somos* 25, August 1985, 25; *Somos* 26, 1985, 29; *Somos* 28, 1986, 31.

7. Martha Toruño, "El Problema Familiar: ¿Insoluble?," *Somos* 27, 1985, 6–7.

8. *Somos* 26, 1985, 11.

9. *Barricada Internacional*, 26 June 1986.

10. See Sofia Montenegro, interviewed by Mariuca Lomba, "Futuro, en Femenino."

11. Editorial, *Somos* 31, 1987, 2; Collinson, *Women and Revolution*, 145.

12. Montis, Olivera, and Meassick, "A Panorama of Women in Nicaragua," 22; *Barricada Internacional*, 26 March 1987.

13. *Barricada Internacional*, 26 February 1987; see also *Barricada Internacional*, April 1987; Collinson, *Women and Revolution*, 146.

14. Lea Guido, interview in *Barricada Internacional*, March 1988.

15. *Barricada Internacional*, 25 March 1988.

16. Ibid., April 1991.

17. Ibid., 2 September 1989.

18. Metoyer, *Women and the State*, 27.

19. *Barricada Internacional*, April 1991.

20. Polakoff and La Ramée, "Grass-Roots Organizations," 191.

21. *Barricada*, 30 May 1987, 4.

22. Randall, *Sandino's Daughters Revisited*, 27.

23. *Barricada*, 26 February 1987.

24. Murguialday, *Nicaragua, revolucion y feminism*, 138.

25. Collinson, *Women and Revolution*, 148.

26. Polakoff and La Ramée, "Grass-Roots Organizations," 192.

27. Ibid., 191–92.

28. An unnamed "top Nicaraguan diplomat" quoted by Juan O. Tamayo, "Mothers Fight to Stop Sandinistas from Recruiting Sons," *Miami Herald*, 2 August 1984, 10A.

29. Stephen Kinzer, "Military Draft in Nicaragua Is Meeting Wide Resistance," *New York Times*, 26 June 1984, 1.

30. Juan O. Tamayo, "Mothers Fight to Stop Sandinistas from Recruiting Sons," *Miami Herald*, 2 August 1984, 10A.

31. Kinzer, "Military Draft."

32. Ibid.

33. Ibid.

34. Juan O. Tamayo, "Mothers Fight to Stop Sandinistas from Recruiting Sons," *Miami Herald*, 2 August 1984, 10A.

35. Ibid.

36. Leiken, "Nicaragua's Untold Stories," 28.

37. Stephen Kinzer, "Town Battles Military Draft in Nicaragua," *New York Times*, 2 January 1985, 9; Dennis Volman, "Nicaragua to Enlarge Draft as Contra War Gets Hotter," *Christian Science Monitor*, 14 February 1985, 11.

38. Stephen Kinzer, "Small Political Blocs Seek Changes: Nicaragua's Opposition Groups Brace For Tighter Restrictions on Dissent," *New York Times*, 1 October 1983, A17.

39. *La Prensa*, 1 September 1983, 1.

40. Dodson and O'Shaughnessy, *Nicaragua's Other Revolution*.

41. Kinzer, "Town Battles Military Draft."

42. Ibid.

43. Juan O. Tamayo, "Mothers Fight to Stop Sandinistas from Recruiting Sons," *Miami Herald*, 2 August 1984, 10A; Richard Boudreaux, "Working with Mothers; Nicaragua Tames Draft Resistance," *Los Angeles Times*, 13 May 1987, 1.

44. Kinzer, "Military Draft."

45. Ibid.

46. Richard Boudreaux, "Working with Mothers; Nicaragua Tames Draft Resistance," *Los Angeles Times*, 13 May 1987, 1.

47. Juan O. Tamayo, "Mothers Fight to Stop Sandinistas from Recruiting Sons," *Miami Herald*, 2 August 1984, 10A.

48. Richard Boudreaux, "Working with Mothers; Nicaragua Tames Draft Resistance," *Los Angeles Times*, 13 May 1987, 1.

49. Ibid.

50. Capt. Julio Solorzano of Apoyo al Combatiente, quoted by June Carolyn Erlick, *Miami Herald*, 19 February 1987, 10A.

51. Audeli Montoya, quoted by Richard Boudreaux, "Working with Mothers; Nicaragua Tames Draft Resistance," *Los Angeles Times*, 13 May 1987, 1.

52. Ibid.

53. Major Victor Moreno, quoted by Richard Boudreaux, "Working with Mothers; Nicaragua Tames Draft Resistance," *Los Angeles Times*, 13 May 1987, 1.

54. Boudreaux, "Working with Mothers; Nicaragua Tames Draft Resistance," *Los Angeles Times*, 13 May 1987, 1.

55. 1986 document entitled "Work Plan of the Mothers of Heroes and Martyrs of Matagalpa, Nicaragua."

56. Letter addressed to the Mothers of Heroes and Martyrs of Matagalpa from the FSLN Regional Committee, 5 January 1989.

57. *Barricada*, 30 May 1983.

58. Interview with Esmeralda Davila, Social Secretary of AMNLAE, in *Somos* 25, August 1985, 5.

59. *Barricada Internacional*, 9 October 1986.

60. Drawing upon Plutarch, Elshtain presents an excellent comparative analysis of Spartan Motherhood. Elshtain, *Women and War*.

61. See Randall, *Sandino's Daughters Revisited*, 9.

62. "We Will Bear Children," by Gioconda Belli, in *Ser Madre en Nicaragua*, by Sola and Pau Trayner, 178–79 (translation mine).

63. *Barricada*, 16 March 1987.

64. Ibid., 8 March 1982.

65. Ibid., 1 June 1984.

66. Ibid., 30 June 1988.

67. Randall, *Gathering Rage*, 46.

68. AMNLAE article reprinted by WIRE from ISIS International Bulletin #14, Carouge, Switzerland.

69. Elshtain, *Women and War*, 99–101, 191–93.

70. *Barricada*, 22 June 1983.

71. Ibid., 28 May 1981.

72. Ibid., 31 May 1983.

73. President Abraham Lincoln wrote to a mother who had reportedly lost five sons in the U.S. Civil War, "I pray that our heavenly Father may . . . leave you only the cherished memory of the loved and lost, and the solemn pride that must be yours to have laid so costly a sacrifice upon the altar of freedom." Elshtain, *Women and War*, 106. The World War II film *Saving Private Ryan* (1998) used Lincoln's letter as the impetus behind the need to save Ryan for his mother. As Elshtain demonstrates, maternal war discourse stretches across national boundaries and through time. Note the similarities between U.S. Civil War and Nicaraguan contra war maternal discourse. U.S. Confederate "Spartan Mothers": "I have three sons and my husband in the army. . . . They are all I have, but if I had more, I would freely give them to my country." Also, "The blood of the slain sons called for additional sons to battle for the vindication of those who had fallen." Elshtain, *Women and War*, 100.

74. Whitcomb, "The Committee of Mothers of Heroes and Martyrs."

75. *Barricada*, 24 November 1984.

76. Ibid., 14 June 1988.

77. Ibid., 30 May 1988.

78. Ibid., 22 June 1983.

79. Ibid., 16 July 1986.

80. Ibid., 2 March 1983.

81. *The Militant*, 19 November 1987, quoted in Molyneux, "The Politics of Abortion," 123.

82. *La Prensa*, 30 March 1979.

83. *Barricada*, 5 April 1983.

84. Ibid., 1 August 1988.

85. Arnaldo Zenteno, Managua, date unknown. A mimeograph of this sermon was handed out at the Mothers of Heroes and Martyrs annual celebration on 28 May 1992.

86. *Barricada*, 30 May 1986.

87. Randall reflected, "When we look at recent Nicaraguan revolutionary history in the light of gender . . . we can see that those female combatants who were able to most completely assume a style of analysis and conduct considered to be 'male' rose to the highest levels of power permitted them within a structure controlled by the men. Doris Tijerino and Dora María Téllez are examples of this phenomenon." Randall, *Sandino's Daughters Revisited*, 24. As Téllez later became more critical of orthodox Sandinismo, she was attacked within the FSLN as a lesbian. This is common in many societies — women rise through military ranks by assuming "male" characteristics, yet they live with

the threat of being outed or accused of lesbianism by those threatened by women in positions of power. See Enloe, *The Morning After*, 93, 172.

88. *Barricada*, 30 May 1989.

89. "Women in Nicaragua: The Revolution on Hold," 34; Molyneux, "Mobilization without Emancipation?"

90. Chuchryk, "Women in the Revolution," 147.

91. Letter to Cardinal Obando from the office files of the Mothers of Heroes and Martyrs of Matagalpa.

92. *Barricada*, 18 June 1988.

93. Ibid., 25 November 1988.

94. Ibid., 15 July 1988.

95. Ibid., 12 August 1988.

96. *Barricada*, 11 November 1988; *Barricada*, 6 January 1989.

97. *CAHI Update* 6, no. 38 (25 November 1987).

98. Richard Boudreaux, "Women Working for Political Prisoners Harassed," *Los Angeles Times*, 16 April 1987, 10.

99. I received NED and U.S. State Department files on M22 through the Freedom of Information Act. This yielded M22 propaganda, U.S. State Department publications, interoffice memos, financial statements, and approximately one hundred State Department communications with its embassy in Nicaragua. This was supplemented by information culled from local and foreign newspapers and several interviews I conducted with people who had worked closely with the organization.

100. *Latin American Dispatch*, U.S. State Department, May 1987; U.S. State Department, document 1988MANAGU0667. *Barricada*, 13 September 1988, claimed that M22 was actually initiated by the United States, when in December 1986 U.S. embassy official Janet Crist contacted Sotelo and Erick Ramírez of the PSC to form the mothers' movement.

101. The 1987 funding proposal for M22 submitted to the NED.

102. Collinson, *Women and Revolution*, 166; see also U.S. State Department, document 1987MANAGU08879.

103. The NED is a private organization that receives most of its funding from the U.S. Congress.

104. U.S. State Department, document 1988MANAGU00950.

105. Ibid.

106. Ibid.

107. *Barricada*, 24 May 1988, Ibid., 25 May 1988; U.S. State Department, document 1988MANAGU03824.

108. U.S. State Department, document 1988MANAGU03824.

109. Collinson, *Women and Revolution*, 166.

110. *Barricada*, 23 October 1987.

111. Press Release by the Mothers of Heroes and Martyrs of Matagalpa, October 1987, partially published in *Barricada*, 27 October 1987.

112. *Barricada,* 23 October 1987. Lea Guido, interviewed by *Barricada Internacional,* March 1988, insisted: "Here women have been the main defenders of human rights, and we won't be manipulated by puppet groups that support the war that is mutilating our children." She added, "The message of the right wing not only manipulates the mothers' feelings but also reinforces the traditional role of women in society. By contrast, we present alternatives that promote change."

113. NED Grant Agreement, 28 September 1987.

114. See, for example, U.S. State Department, documents 1988MANAGU08582.

115. U.S. State Department, document 1988STATE384265.

116. Brief statement put out by M22 in celebration of their first anniversary, 22 January 1988.

117. See, for example, U.S. State Department, documents 1988MANAGU04372, 1988MANAGU01518, and 1988STATE084923.

118. Richard Boudreaux, "Women Working for Political Prisoners Harassed," *Los Angeles Times,* 16 April 1987.

119. *Latin American Dispatch,* May 1987.

120. *La Prensa,* 24 June 1988; U.S. State Department, document 1988MANAGU-04748.

121. U.S. State Department, document 1988MANAGU01150.

122. Copy of original letter published in M22 informational pamphlet in honor of their first anniversary, 22 January 1988.

123. According to the U.S. embassy, "One of the women said that Dr. Enrique Sotelo had created problems within the movement and had then abandoned it. Another stated that Erick Ramírez . . . was also exploiting the movement." The U.S. embassy concurred: "Ramírez has little interest in the group other than to use it to his political advantage" (U.S. State Department, document 1988MANAGU04420). In May 1988, NED removed Sotelo from administering M22's funds out of concern that Sotelo was using the funds for his own personal and political purposes (U.S. State Department, documents 1987MANAGU07781, 1988MANAGU03481, 1988MANAGU08352). Sotelo then called for a national assembly of M22 to replace the existing directorate with his own supporters (U.S. State Department, document 1988MANAGU03481). He also complained to the U.S. embassy that "he was being unfairly treated by the movement." At this point, the U.S. embassy predicted that "it is likely that [M22] will continue to be manipulated by local politicians for parochial ends."

124. U.S. State Department, documents 1988MANAGU04420, 1988MANAGU-08352.

125. U.S. State Department, documents 1988MANAGU06671, 1988MANAGU-08352.

126. U.S. State Department, document 1988MANAGU06317.

127. *Barricada,* 13 September 1988; U.S. State Department, document 1988-MANAGU06671.

128. U.S. State Department, document 1988MANAGU06317.

129. U.S. State Department, document 1988MANAGU08352.

130. U.S. State Department, document 1989MANAGU02970.

131. Internal NED documents. See also United States General Accounting Office, "Promoting Democracy: National Endowment for Democracy's Management of Grants Needs Improvement," GAO/NSIAD-91-162.

132. *La Prensa*, 29 May 1989.

133. Ibid., 30 May 1989.

134. With the Central American Peace Accords, *La Prensa* reopened without censorship on 1 October 1987. Violeta Chamorro, as publisher of *La Prensa*, told a U.S. delegation headed by Congressman Donald Lukens in May 1988 that the Sandinista government had recently warned the media of laws prohibiting publishing news on the draft or the poor state of the economy; Chamorro promised to resist such censorship (U.S. State Department, document 1988MANAGU03573).

135. *La Prensa*, 4 February 1988.

136. Ibid., 12 February 1988.

137. Ibid., 25 April 1989.

138. Ibid., 30 January 1988. This letter was signed by thirty mothers.

139. Ibid., 9 March 1988.

The Latent and the Visible

1. Williams, "On Being the Object of Property," 207.

2. The amount of the pensions varied, depending upon whether the fallen soldier also had a wife and/or children, how many children a mother had lost, and irregular adjustments for inflation.

3. Mothers of Heroes and Martyrs of Matagalpa, unpublished report, 1990. The committee claimed that its status as a "productive committee with social projects" in which profits were reinvested made it unique among Nicaraguan mothers' organizations.

4. See Corcoran-Nantes, "Women and Popular Urban Social Movements," 249; Rodriguez, "Barrio Women"; Safa, "Women's Social Movements," 354.

5. Report dated August 1987, from Mothers' Committee office files.

6. Communiqué by the Mothers of Heroes and Martyrs of Matagalpa addressed to the people of Nicaragua, October 1987.

7. By working poor I mean that at least one member of the household had employment in the formal economy, working, for example, as a bricklayer, a driver, or a secretary. While the work was steady, the wages were too low and/or stretched too thin among the extended family to provide a simple brick home with a tiled floor or a steady meat diet. In the 1990s, such items as basic medicine and schoolbooks were a significant burden for these families. I designate as middle class those households with a sufficient income to own a brick house with tiled (rather than dirt) floors, a television and some electric kitchen appliances, and a regular meat diet. Notably, most of the respondents I classified

as working poor and middle class referred to themselves as poor, testifying to both the precariousness of living in a country in constant economic crisis, and these women's belief, supported by the theology of liberation, in the dignity of being poor and the church's preferential option for the poor. For example, Esperanza Cruz de Cabrera, while leading a relative life of comfort in Nicaragua, described herself as poor because she was originally from a poor family and was a member of the popular church. For her and some other middle-class members, it was a rather conscious religious/political act to describe themselves as poor. I know of no middle-class member of the committee who could not be described as a core member. In other words, middle-class mothers of the fallen were either very active in the committee or completely inactive. The overwhelming majority of the membership was poor women.

8. The thirty-two-year-old Mother lost two infants during the revolution. The average age of those I interviewed was fifty-four. Age was not included on the Mothers' Committee forms.

9. The average is based upon the 313 membership forms. The average number of children among those members I interviewed was eight.

10. A survey released in March 1991 found 48.1 percent of Nicaraguan households headed by women. FIDEG study in Barbara Seitz, "Report on a Trip to Nicaragua," 10.

11. See Lavrin, "Women, the Family, and Social Change," 113–14.

12. Fisher, *Mothers of the Disappeared*, 59; Stephen, "Women in Mexico's Popular Movements," 80–81; Rodriguez, "Barrio Women," 38; Deere, "Cooperative Development," 1046.

13. This threat was clearly stated in women's letters and interviews published in *La Prensa* in the 1980s. In their attempts to get their sons out of jail or the draft, these mothers regularly stressed that their son was their only means of financial support.

14. While over 30 percent of members had lost a male companion in the revolution or war, even more were separated from or had been abandoned by their companions.

15. Of the 313 membership forms, 42 did not provide clear information on member's occupation. The following percentages are based upon 271 responses. Also note that many of the Mothers were war refugees forced to move from their rural homes to the city of Matagalpa and that many of these women had been agricultural workers, either on their own land, a cooperative, or as seasonal workers, until they moved. I suspect that a number of those who described themselves as housewives might also be described as unemployed or unable to work. In other words, given the desperate economic state of their families, they would have liked paid work if work had been available or if they had not been too ill.

16. The following occupations represent 2 percent or less of the Mothers' members: cook (nondomestic), factory worker, teacher, agricultural worker, and hospital worker. During the Sandinista administration, 4 percent of the Mothers had jobs in government agencies or Sandinista-affiliated unions. Most of these jobs have since been lost due to the change in administrations and economic austerity programs.

17. Of those I interviewed (n = 55), 59 percent had no income-generating work, 20 percent worked in committee projects, 10 percent had set up a small business in their house (a neighborhood store, bakery, or corn mill), and 8 percent sold tortillas or prepared food.

18. Committee leaders claimed that wealthier mothers had no interest in the committee.

19. This does not mean that there was no support for such policies. The point, as many Nicaraguan feminists attest, is that these priorities were continually deferred or denied. See Randall, *Sandino's Daughters Revisited*.

20. Gilligan, *In a Different Voice*.

21. Though this word is normally translated as politicians, the Mothers were referring not just to those who run for office but to all those formally or informally involved in the party structure of the FSLN.

22. Some mothers even recalled specific conversations in which their children stressed the importance of carrying on the struggle. For example, one Mother remembered: "[My son told me] 'Mama, I don't want to die, but if I die one day, cry, but continue fighting. *Seguir adelante*.' And so for this I continue fighting." Another Mother's son told her: "If something happens to me, you all have to go on. You can't quit because this is a struggle that has to continue if I'm alive or dead."

23. Esperanza Cruz de Cabrera, interviewed by Sola and Pau Trayner, *Ser Madre en Nicaragua*, 35–36, translation mine.

24. Gilligan, *In a Different Voice*.

25. Jelin, "Introduction," 5.

26. Melucci, *Nomads of the Present*, 70–71.

27. Escobar, "Culture, Economics, and Politics," 70.

28. Melucci, "The Symbolic Challenge," 801.

29. Melucci, *Nomads of the Present*, 35.

30. An important exception is Stephen, *Women and Social Movements*.

31. See Bayard de Volo, "Heroes, Martyrs, and Mothers."

32. For cases of male companions restricting women's participation in movements, see also Fisher, *Mothers of the Disappeared*, 59; Stephen, "Women in Mexico's Popular Movements," 80–81; Rodriguez, "Barrio Women," 38, 42.

33. Jelin, "Conclusion," 186.

34. *Barricada*, 8 March 1990.

35. Perhaps in response to this last concern, the familiar theme "the army turns boys into men" was circulated by the military. The army magazine *Revista Segovia* claimed that for young men the SMP "is a school of maturation and friendship in the shared experiences, dangers, and limitations found in military life" (*Revista Segovia*, n.d., 13). Doña Esperanza R. echoed this theme: "I felt that it wasn't bad because there they make men out of boys. They learn many things. They value the many dead youth that were in the mountains. And so I never thought bad of it." It is worth noting that her oldest son

died before the fall of Somoza, and her sons who fought in the contra war survived—factors that might lead her to see the draft in a more positive light than mothers whose sons died as draftees.

36. *Revista Segovia*, n.d., 13.

37. Quoted in *Weekly News Update on Nicaragua and the Americas*, published originally in *La Tribuna*—a Nicaraguan daily and then by ED-LP 12/17/93 from Notimex. See also Castro, "Electoral Results." Notably, the FSLN lost badly in the city of Matagalpa: the FSLN won 36.9 percent of the total votes and UNO 53.4 percent.

38. In focus groups coordinated by Estela Heredia after the war, Vanessa Castro reports that those interviewed stressed that the compulsory aspect of the draft "caused terrible grief to their mothers: it had no antecedents in Nicaragua" (Castro, "Electoral Results"). As David Slater observed: "An antagonism can emerge when a collective subject that has been constructed in a specific way finds its subjectivity being undermined or negated by other practices" (Slater, "Power and Social Movements," 18).

From a War of Bullets to a War of the Stomach

1. UNO won with 54.7 percent to the FSLN's 40.8 percent of the national vote.

2. According to *La Tribuna*, a November 1994 CID-Gallup Poll found that among the 1,264 polled (with men and women equally represented), the suspension of the draft was the principal achievement of Violeta Chamorro's government. *La Tribuna*, 9 December 1994, 1, 5A.

3. Interview with Isais Parrales, 15 June 1992.

4. See, for example, "Women in Nicaragua," and interviews of Gioconda Belli and Aminta Granera in Randall, *Sandino's Daughters Revisited*, 184, 202.

5. Morgan, "Founding Mothers," 106–7.

6. Franco, "The Long March of Feminism."

7. Envio, "Women in Nicaragua," 35.

8. Chinchilla, "Revolutionary Popular Feminism," 391–92.

9. Oquist, "The Sociopolitical Dynamics," 20.

10. Another preelection study found that 59 percent of those women who had voted for the FSLN in 1984 intended to do so again, 4 percent said they would vote for the opposition, and 38 percent were undecided. In accounting for the unexpected FSLN loss, analysts concluded that the undecided groups voted overwhelmingly for UNO. See Cenzontle, *Nicaragua: El poder*, 31. Franco, "The Long March of Feminism."

11. Metoyer, *Women and the State*, 48.

12. *La Prensa*, 30 May 1989.

13. See Kampwirth, "The Mother of the Nicaraguans"; O'Kane, "The New World Order."

14. *La Prensa*, 4 September 1989.

15. *Barricada Internacional*, 20 January 1990.

16. *La Prensa*, 1 February 1990.

17. Such cartoons were published in *La Prensa*, primarily in November 1989.

18. *Barricada Internacional*, 20 January 1990.

19. Ibid.

20. One study found that both campaigns, in courting women's votes, overwhelmingly relied on traditional, domestic images of women. Olivera, Montis, and Meassick, *Nicaragua: El poder.*

21. *Barricada Internacional*, August 1991.

22. *Barricada Internacional*, 20 January 1990.

23. Political advertisements featured in *Barricada* in mid-February 1990.

24. This ad was placed on the back page of *Barricada*, 5 December 1989.

25. Political advertisement featured in *Barricada* several times in mid-February 1990.

26. *Barricada*, 16 December 1989, 33.

27. Belli, interviewed by Randall, *Sandino's Daughters Revisited*, 178–79.

28. Ibid., 183–84.

29. Téllez, interviewed by Randall, *Sandino's Daughters Revisited*, 249.

30. Ibid.

31. Ibid., 250.

32. Ibid.

33. Metoyer, *Women and the State*, 45, 47.

34. Ibid., 55–68.

35. *Barricada Internacional*, April 1991.

36. Metoyer, *Women and the State*, 56, 65.

37. Wessel, "Reproductive Rights in Nicaragua," 544.

38. *Barricada Internacional*, April 1991.

39. The penal code was originally examined by the assembly with the intention of broadening the definitions of sexual crimes and lengthening prison sentences. The entire Sandinista legislative bloc voted against Article 205, which was passed 43–39. Chamorro signed the legislation.

40. *Barricada*, 8 March 1990.

41. Wessel, "Reproductive Rights in Nicaragua," 548.

42. *Barricada Internacional*, April 1991.

43. Ibid.

44. Ibid.

45. *Barricada*, 30 May 1989.

46. Molyneux, "Mobilization Without Emancipation?," 228.

47. Field notes, 9 March 1993.

48. See Quandt, *The FSLN in Nicaragua*, 29–35.

49. Interview with Isais Parrales, political secretary of the FSLN, department of Estelí, 15 March 1992. He likened the pre- and postelection position of the FSLN to the relationship between mother and child. At first, the mother holds the child's hand and guides her. Eventually, the mother lets go and the child walks on her own.

50. United Nations Economic Commission for Latin America and the Caribbean, "Nicaragua." The FSLN had begun its own austerity programs in 1988, which eliminated 20,000 public sector jobs in 1988–89.

51. Safa, "Women's Social Movements," 354–55.

52. Jaquette, "Introduction," 6.

53. Announcement by the Mothers of Heroes and Martyrs of Matagalpa, 4 July 1990.

54. Open letter from the Mothers of Heroes and Martyrs of Matagalpa, 10 July 1990.

55. Open letter from the Mothers of Heroes and Martyrs of Matagalpa and CRAC workers to the Nicaraguan people, 29 January 1991.

56. Central America 2000 and MIR polling firms, June 1995, as reported by Donna Vukelich in the *Nicaraguan News Service*, 4–11 June 1995, 3:24. The question was framed in largely economic terms. An increase in suicides was also noted.

57. Instituto de Estudios Nicaraguenses, "La gobernabilidad y la democracia local en Nicaragua: Investigacion sobre la opinion publica nacional," (Managua) January 1994, 28.

58. "Impressions from Nicaragua: Conversations with the Mothers of Heroes and Martyrs," *CAHI Update* 5, 8 September 1986.

59. Proposal addressed to President Chamorro from INAVG, 23 October 1991.

60. Mothers of Matagalpa project summary, 25 February 1991.

61. This family was given title to the eleven-*manzana* plot through the Sandinista agrarian reform begun in 1984 (a *manzana* is 1.7 acres). The previous owner was one of the many well-to-do who fled the country under Sandinista rule and returned after the elections to reclaim their landholdings backed by Somoza-era land titles.

62. Because in Nicaragua there is very little demand for such facilities as a motorcycle racetrack, the mayor's action was viewed by the Mothers and the NGO supporting the housing project, the Quixote Center's Quest for Peace, as harassment meant to undermine the Mothers' internationally recognized community projects.

63. February 1994 speech by Esperanza Cruz de Cabrera for a Quest for Peace audience.

64. Field notes, 4 December 1992.

65. Speech by Esperanza Cruz de Cabrera at the national Mothers of Heroes and Martyrs celebration in Matagalpa, 28 May 1992.

66. Letter to President Chamorro, 22 January 1991, from the Mothers of Matagalpa office files.

67. *Barricada Internacional*, 19 January 1991, 35; March 1991, 14.

68. February 1994 speech by Esperanza Cruz de Cabrera for a Quest for Peace audience.

69. Oquist, "The Sociopolitical Dynamics." See also Lancaster, *Life Is Hard*, 291.

70. Field notes, 28 May 1992.

71. *Barricada*, 30 May 1992.

72. Mother's Day speech by Esperanza Cruz de Cabrera, 1992.

Testing the Limits of Maternal Identity

1. Melucci, *Nomads of the Present*, 28–29; Jelin, "Introduction," 4.

2. Martin, "Motherhood and Power," 480. For an example of the "push" metaphor, Sonia Alvarez writes that the economic and social policies of Brazil's military rulers undermined the survival strategies of poor families. "This threat to the domestic political economy of the popular classes, I shall argue, propelled some women to seek collective and individual solutions to their families' immediate survival needs." Alvarez, *Engendering Democracy*, 44.

3. Gramsci, *Selections*, 181–82; Femia, "Hegemony and Consciousness," 30–31.

4. Marx and Engels, "The German Ideology," 174.

5. Whittier, "Political Generations," 760.

6. Olson, *The Logic of Collective Action*.

7. Cohen, "Strategy or Identity," 687. See also Pizzorno, "Political Exchange."

8. Doug McAdam argues that value commitments, responsibility to others, and a sense of group solidarity can also elicit individual sacrifice for broadly enjoyed collective goods. McAdam, *Political Process*, 45.

9. Representations of President Chamorro echoed the contradiction. On the one hand she was a passive, grieving widow and mother figure poised to nurture a suffering war-torn nation. On the other hand, her neoliberal policies significantly decreased government support so that individuals might pull themselves up by the bootstraps.

10. Printed version of a speech by Esperanza Cruz de Cabrera at national Mothers of Heroes and Martyrs celebration in Matagalpa, May 1991.

11. The Nicaraguan Resistance (RN, or "contras") was a loose combination of ex-National Guardsmen and disgruntled peasants and small farmers.

12. Identity based upon dominant groups—for example, white power groups—are more easily recognizable as exclusionary. See Cohen, "Strategy or Identity," 694. For a good example of how analysis of exclusion can inform research on collective identity, see Joshua Gamson, "Messages of Exclusion"; Lilia Rodriguez, writing on barrio women's movements in Quito, Ecuador, pointed out that although the new social movement literature on identity tends to ignore power relations: "Popular organizations are not exempt from conflicts over power. Power conflicts occur both within groups and between them and outsiders. Differences between new and old members, young and mature women, owners and renters may promote conflict. . . . It is within these power relations that new identities emerge." Rodriguez, "Barrio Women," 40–41.

13. See Chodorow, *The Reproduction of Mothering*; Gilligan, *In a Different Voice*; and Ruddick, *Maternal Thinking*.

14. Field notes of 13 February 1993.

15. Somers and Gibson, "Reclaiming the Epistemological 'Other,'" 71–72.

16. See Feijoo, "The Challenge of Constructing Civilian Peace," 72; see also Jelin, "Introduction," 8, and "Citizenship and Identity," 186.

17. Feijoo, "The Challenge of Constructing Civilian Peace," 72–73.

18. Ibid., 73.

19. Sills, *The Volunteers*.

20. Gramsci, *An Antonio Gramsci Reader*, 243–44.

Voice, Agency, and Identity

1. Scheper-Hughes, *Death without Weeping*, 533.

2. Rodriguez, "Barrio Women," 45.

3. Molyneux, "Mobilization without Emancipation?," 228.

4. For an excellent discussion on the lack of research on power relations among the resisters, see Ortner, "Resistance and the Problem of Ethnographic Refusal."

5. Sewell, "A Theory of Structure."

6. Ibid., 20.

7. Ibid., 18.

8. Melucci, "The Symbolic Challenge."

9. Belenky et al., *Women's Ways of Knowing*, 18.

10. Levine, *Popular Voices*, 4.

11. *Barricada*, 25 April 1984.

12. They were less able to capitalize on their position as Mothers of Heroes and Martyrs once the war was over and the FSLN was no longer in power. Like the troubles the Argentine mothers of the disappeared (*Las Madres de Plaza de Mayo*) had in the transition from military rule to democracy, the Mothers of Matagalpa were no longer as effective a symbolic force in terms of member's position as *Madres Sufridas* and *Las Continuadoras* after 1990. See Feijoo, "The Challenge of Constructing Civilian Peace."

13. Safa, "Women's Social Movements," 361–62.

14. Ibid., 363.

15. See Molyneux, "Mobilization without Emancipation?" Strategic gender interests are arrived at as women question socially defined women's roles, and tend to be designated as the "real feminist" interests. Practical gender interests are based upon an examination of women's concrete positioning in society—interests that differ across class, race, ethnicity, religion, and time. Women act upon practical gender interests generally in response to an immediate perceived need, as opposed to a long-term strategy of emancipation. Accordingly, they do not set out to challenge the sexual division of labor or traditional ideals of womanhood; rather, their activism is borne out of and aims to protect women's position in the sexual division of labor.

16. Weedon, *Feminist Practice*, 4.

17. The Mothers were also the sites of other subject positions based upon nationality, class, gender, and race, making it impossible to reduce their identity to one solely based on maternal grief. See Mouffe, "Hegemony and New Political Subjects," 90; Slater, "Power and Social Movements," 15.

18. Feijoo, "The Challenge of Constructing Civilian Peace," 87; Fisher, *Out of the Shadows*, 135.

19. Melucci, "The Symbolic Challenge," 800.

20. Speech by Esperanza Cruz de Cabrera, 28 May 1992, Matagalpa, Nicaragua.

21. For a similar finding on the varied impact of activism for women, see Schild, "Recasting 'Popular' Movements," 71.

22. Report dated August 1987, from Mothers' Committee office files.

23. Field notes, 7 July 1992.

24. Martin, "Motherhood and Power," 470–71. See also Warren and Bourque, "Gender, Power, and Communication."

25. Melucci, "The Symbolic Challenge," 801.

26. Martin, "Motherhood and Power," 470–71.

27. Melucci, "The Symbolic Challenge."

28. Feminist consciousness-raising sessions and Bible discussion groups practicing liberation theology are two examples of voice and the political learning process discussed here.

29. Scott, *Weapons of the Weak*, 36.

Conclusion

1. Elshtain, *Women and War*; Elshtain and Tobias, *Women, Militarism and War*; Enloe, *The Morning After*; Zeiger, "She Didn't Raise Her Boy to Be a Slacker;" Bayard de Volo, "Drafting Motherhood."

2. Elshtain, *Women and War*; Bayard de Volo, "Drafting Motherhood."

3. *Envio* 10, no. 119, June 1991, 34.

4. In contrast to Craske, for example, who suggests that maternal collective action can lead to political paralysis rather than empowerment: "As the political situation in Argentina has changed, the Mothers [of Plaza de Mayo] have found it difficult to adapt, since they see their demands as non-negotiable and themselves as above politics. Without the ability to negotiate and compromise, the political process is dead before it begins. It is unclear to what extent this kind of participation leads to empowerment, since the sense of efficacy is lost if the demands cannot be won." Craske, *Women and Politics*, 198.

5. Kaplan, "Female Consciousness."

6. Ibid.

7. However, this never offers full protection, as can be seen in the disappearances of Mothers of the disappeared in Argentina and El Salvador as well as the Nicaraguan National Guard attacks on these protesting women.

8. See Stephen, "Women in Mexico's Popular Movements."

9. Melucci, "The Symbolic Challenge."

10. See Stephen, "Women in Mexico's Popular Movements," 90.

11. See ibid.; Jelin, "Introduction"; Schild, "Recasting 'Popular' Movements"; Rodriguez, "Barrio Women"; Martin, "Motherhood and Power."

12. Jaquette, "Conclusions," 193.

13. Alvarez, *Engendering Democracy*; Waylen, "Women and Democratization"; Friedman, "The Paradoxes of Gendered Political Opportunity"; Baldez, "La política partidista."

14. Prevost, "The Status of the Sandinista Revolutionary Project," 36.

15. Ibid., 38.

16. In the November 2000 municipal elections, the FSLN candidate Herty Lewites won the powerful office of mayor of Managua, demonstrating the continued strength of the FSLN.

17. Juan Carlos Sarmiento, "200 madres eligen directiva," *Barricada*, 20 July 1995, 2B.

18. Ricardo J. Cuadra Garcia, "Serias denuncias contra 'renovadora' matagalpina," *Barricada*, 15 August 1995, 7.

19. Ricardo J. Cuadra Garcia, "Madres respaldan a doña Esperanza Cabrera," *Barricada*, 18 August 1995, 9. Cabrera supporters stressed that many of those accusing her of distributing donations to her friends and denying the neediest Mothers were the same Mothers who gained the most material aid from the committee. Indeed, a number of Cabrera's detractors lived in the houses built through the committee housing project. Throughout my fieldwork, the committee leadership was relatively public about its finances. For example, they had the financial reports copied in large print on banner-sized paper and displayed along an entire wall in the committee office. By the mid-1990s they had hired an accountant to maintain the finances and were still posting financial records on the office walls in 1998 and 1999.

20. See Feijoo, "The Challenge of Constructing Civilian Peace," 72; Jelin, "Introduction," 8.

21. Feijoo, "The Challenge of Constructing Civilian Peace," 73. See also, Craske, *Women and Politics*, 112–3.

22. *Envio* 17, June 1998, 8–9.

23. Ibid., 5.

24. Ibid.

25. The new electoral norms created under the Electoral Law reforms that apply to the municipal elections in November 2000 include the following changes, all of which promote a two-party system and discourage electoral alliances: (1) all parties must present candidates in 80 percent of the country's 150 municipalities; (2) each party must collect 75,000 signatures in forty-five days; (3) two parties forming an alliance must present 150,000 signatures, three parties forming an alliance must present 225,000 signatures, and so on; (4) a party must gain 4 percent of the vote to keep its legal status, an alliance of two parties must win 8 percent, and so on. See Dora María Téllez, "A New Option for the Left," *Envio* 19:224, March 2000, 12–13.

26. *Envio* 17, June 1998, 7; Adolfo Pastrán Arancibia, *El Nuevo Diario*, 20 December 1999.

27. *Envio* 17, March 1998, 9.

BIBLIOGRAPHY

Books and Articles

Alonso, Harriet Hyman. *Peace as a Women's Issue: A History of the U.S. Movement for World Peace and Women's Rights*. New York: Syracuse Univ. Press, 1993.

Alvarez, Sonia E. *Engendering Democracy in Brazil: Women's Movements in Transition Politics*. Princeton: Princeton Univ. Press, 1990.

Alvarez, Sonia E., Evelina Dagnino, and Arturo Escobar, eds. *Cultures of Politics, Politics of Cultures: Re-Visioning Latin American Social Movements*. Boulder, Colo.: Westview Press, 1998.

———. "Introduction: The Cultural and the Political in Latin American Social Movements." In *Cultures of Politics, Politics of Cultures: Re-Visioning Latin American Social Movements*, ed. Sonia E. Alvarez, Evelina Dagnino, and Arturo Escobar. Boulder, Colo.: Westview Press, 1998.

Amnesty International. "Extrajudicial Executions in El Salvador: Report of an Amnesty International Mission to Examine Post-Mortem and Investigative Procedures in Political Killings." New York: Amnesty International Publications, 1–6 July 1983.

AMNLAE. "Women's Participation in the New Nicaragua." In *Nicaragua under Siege*, ed. Marlene Dixon and Suzanne Jonas. San Francisco: Synthesis Publications, 1984.

AMPRONAC. "La Mujer Nicaraguense: Su Lucha Por una Patria Libre (1977–1979)." Reprinted by Women's International Resource Exchange, n.d.

Anderson, Leslie. "Post-Materialism From a Peasant Perspective: Political Motivation in Costa Rica and Nicaragua." *Comparative Political Studies* 23, no. 1 (April 1990).

Angel, Adriana, and Fiona MacIntosh. *The Tiger's Milk: Women of Nicaragua*. New York: Seaver Books/Henry Holt, 1987.

Artz, B. Lee. "Social Power and the Inflation of Discourse: The Failure of Popular Hegemony in Nicaragua." *Latin American Perspectives* 24, no. 1 (January 1997).

The Association of Salvadoran Women. "Participation of Latin American Women in Social and Political Organizations: Reflections of Salvadoran Women." *Monthly Review* 34 (June 1982).

Baldez, Lisa. 1999. "La política partidista y los limites del feminismo de estado en Chile." In *El Modelo Chileno: Democracia y Desarrollo en los Noventa*, ed. Paul Drake and Ivan Jaksic. Santiago: LOM, 1999.

Bayard de Volo, Lorraine. "Drafting Motherhood: Maternal Imagery and Organizations in the United States and Nicaragua." In *The Women and War Reader*, ed. Lois Lorentzen and Jennifer Turpin. New York: New York Univ. Press, 1998.

———. "Heroes, Martyrs, and Mothers: Maternal Identity Politics in Revolutionary Nicaragua." Ph.D. dissertation, Univ. of Michigan, 1996.

Belenky, Mary Field, Blythe McVicker Clinchy, Nancy Rule Goldberger, and Jill Mattuck Tarule. *Women's Ways of Knowing: The Development of Self, Voice, and Mind.* New York: Basic Books, 1986.

Bouvard, Marguerite Guzman. *Revolutionizing Motherhood: The Mothers of the Plaza de Mayo.* Wilmington, Del.: Scholarly Resources, 1994.

Carrillo, Theresa. "Women and Independent Unionism in the Garment Industry." In *Popular Movements and Political Change in Mexico*, ed. Joe Foweraker and Ann L. Craig. Boulder, Colo.: Lynne Rienner, 1990.

Castro, Vanessa. "Electoral Results in the Rural Sector." In *The 1990 Elections in Nicaragua and their Aftermath*, ed. Vanessa Castro and Gary Prevost. Lanham, Md.: Rowman & Littlefield, 1992.

Chinchilla, Norma Stoltz. "Revolutionary Popular Feminism in Nicaragua: Articulating Class, Gender and National Sovereignty." *Gender and Society* 4 (September 1990).

———. "Women's Movements in the Americas: Feminism's Second Wave." *NACLA Report on the Americas* 27 (July/August 1993).

Chodorow, Nancy. *The Reproduction of Mothering: Psychoanalysis and the Sociology of Gender.* Berkeley: Univ. of California Press, 1979.

Chuchryk, Patricia M. "Feminist Anti-Authoritarian Politics: The Role of Women's Organizations in the Chilean Transition to Democracy." In *The Women's Movement in Latin America: Feminism and the Transition to Democracy*, ed. Jane Jaquette. Boston: Unwin Hyman, 1989.

———. "Subversive Mothers: The Women's Opposition to the Military Regime in Chile." In *Women, the State, and Development*, ed. Sue Ellen M. Charlton, Jana Everett, and Kathleen Staudt. New York: State Univ. of New York Press, 1989.

———. "Women in the Revolution." In *Revolution and Counterrevolution in Nicaragua*, ed. Thomas W. Walker. Boulder, Colo.: Westview Press, 1991.

Cohen, Jean L. "Strategy or Identity: New Theoretical Paradigm and Contemporary Social Movements." *Social Research* 52 (Winter 1985).

Collinson, Helen. *Women and Revolution in Nicaragua.* London: Zed Press, 1990.

Cooke, Miriam, and Angela Woollacott. "Introduction." In *Gendering War Talk*, ed. Miriam Cooke and Angela Woollacott. Princeton: Princeton Univ. Press, 1993.

Corcoran-Nantes, Yvonne. "Women and Popular Urban Social Movements in Sao Paulo, Brazil." *Bulletin of Latin American Research* 9 (1990).

Craske, Nikki. *Women and Politics in Latin America.* Cambridge: Polity Press, 1999.

Deere, Carmen Diana. "Cooperative Development and Women's Participation in the Nicaraguan Agrarian Reform." *American Journal of Agricultural Economics* 65 (December 1983).

Deighton, Jane, Rossana Horsley, Sarah Stewart, and Cathy Cain. *Sweet Ramparts.* London: War on Want/Nicaragua Solidarity Campaign, 1983.

Dodson, Michael, and Laura Nuzzi O'Shaughnessy. *Nicaragua's Other Revolution: Religious Faith and Political Struggle.* Chapel Hill: Univ. of North Carolina Press, 1990.

Edmisten, Patricia Taylor. *Nicaragua Divided: La Prensa and the Chamorro Legacy.* Pensacola: Univ. of West Florida Press, 1990.

Elshtain, Jean Bethke. *Women and War.* New York: Basic Books, 1987.

Elshtain, Jean Bethke, and Sheila Tobias, eds. *Women, Militarism and War.* Lanham, Md.: Rowman & Littlefield, 1990.

Enloe, Cynthia. *Does Khaki Become You?: The Militarization of Women's Lives.* London: Unwin Hyman, 1988.

———. *The Morning After: Sexual Politics at the End of the Cold War.* Berkeley: Univ. of California Press, 1993.

Enriquez, Magda. "We Women Learned What We Were Capable of Doing." In *Nicaragua: The Sandinista People's Revolution*, ed. Bruce Marcus. New York: Pathfinder Press, 1985.

Escobar, Arturo. "Culture, Economics, and Politics in Latin American Social Movements Theory and Research." In *The Making of Social Movements in Latin America*, ed. Arturo Escobar and Sonia E. Alvarez. Boulder, Colo.: Westview Press, 1992.

Escobar, Arturo, and Sonia E. Alvarez. "Introduction: Theory and Protest in Latin America Today." In *The Making of Social Movements in Latin America*, ed. Arturo Escobar and Sonia E. Alvarez. Boulder, Colo.: Westview Press, 1992.

Feijoo, María del Carmen. "The Challenge of Constructing Civilian Peace: Women and Democracy in Argentina." In *The Women's Movement in Latin America: Feminism and the Transition to Democracy*, ed. Jane Jaquette. Boston: Unwin Hyman, 1989.

Femia, Joseph. "Hegemony and Consciousness in the Thought of Antonio Gramsci." *Political Studies* 23, no. 1 (1975).

Fisher, Jo. *Mothers of the Disappeared.* Boston: South End Press, 1989.

———. *Out of the Shadows: Women, Resistance and Politics in South America.* London: Latin American Bureau, 1993.

Franco, Jean. "The Long March of Feminism." *NACLA Report on the Americas* 31, no. 4 (January/February 1998).

Friedman, Debra, and Doug McAdam. "Collective Identity and Activism: Networks, Choices, and the Life of a Social Movement." In *Frontiers in Social Movement Theory*, ed. Aldon D. Morris and Carol McClurg Mueller. New Haven: Yale Univ. Press, 1992.

Friedman, Elisabeth J. "The Paradoxes of Gendered Political Opportunity in the Venezuelan Transition to Democracy." *Latin American Research Review* 33, no. 3 (Fall 1998).

Frente Sandinista de Liberacion Nacional (FSLN). "The Historic Program of the FSLN." In *The Nicaraguan Reader: Documents of a Revolution under Fire*, ed. Peter Rosset and John Vandermeer. New York: Grove Press, 1983.

Gamson, Joshua. "Messages of Exclusion: Gender, Movements, and Symbolic Boundaries." *Gender & Society* 11, no. 2 (April 1997).

Gamson, William A. "The Social Psychology of Collective Action." In *Frontiers in Social Movement Theory*, ed. Aldon D. Morris and Carol McClurg Mueller. New Haven: Yale Univ. Press, 1992.

Garcia, Ana Isabel, and Enrique Gomariz. *Mujeres Centroamericanas: Ante La Crisis, La Guerra Y El Proceso de Paz*. San José, Costa Rica: FLACSO, 1989.

Gaventa, John. *Power and Powerlessness: Quiescence and Rebellion in an Appalachian Valley*. Urbana: Univ. of Illinois Press, 1980.

Gilligan, Carol. *In a Different Voice: Psychological Theory and Women's Development*. Cambridge: Harvard Univ. Press, 1982.

Gioseffi, Daniela, ed. *Women on War: Essential Voices for the Nuclear Age from a Brilliant International Assembly*. New York: Touchstone, 1988.

Gitlin, Todd. "From Universality to Difference: Notes on the Fragmentation of the Idea of the Left." In *Social Theory and the Politics of Identity*, ed. Craig Calhoun. Cambridge, Mass.: Blackwell, 1994.

Gould, Jeffrey L. *To Lead as Equals: Rural Protest and Political Consciousness in Chinandega, Nicaragua, 1912–1979*. Chapel Hill: Univ. of North Carolina Press, 1990.

Gramsci, Antonio. *An Antonio Gramsci Reader: Selected Writings, 1916–1935*, ed. David Forgacs. New York: Schocken Books, 1988.

———. *Selections from the Prison Notebooks*. Edited and translated by Quintin Hoare and Geoffrey Nowell Smith. New York: International Publishers, 1971.

Hellman, Judith Adler. "The Study of New Social Movements in Latin America and the Question of Autonomy." In *The Making of Social Movements in Latin America*, ed. Arturo Escobar and Sonia E. Alvarez. Boulder, Colo.: Westview Press, 1992.

Herrera, Carmen, and Trish O'Kane. "*Hagamos politica, trascendamos los grupos de mujeres.*" *Pensamiento Propio* 8 (March 1989).

Hoyt, Katherine. *The Many Faces of Sandinista Democracy*. Athens: Ohio Univ. Press, 1997.

Instituto de Estudios Nicaraguenses. "La gobernabilidad y la democracia local en Nicaragua: Investigacion sobre la opinion publica nacional." Managua: January 1994.

Jaquette, Jane S. "Introduction." In *The Women's Movement in Latin America: Feminism and the Transition to Democracy*, ed. Jane S. Jaquette. Boston: Unwin Hyman, 1989.

———. "Conclusions." In *The Women's Movement in Latin America: Feminism and the Transition to Democracy*, ed. Jane S. Jaquette. Boston: Unwin Hyman, 1989.

Jelin, Elizabeth. "Citizenship and Identity." In *Women and Social Change in Latin America*, ed. Elizabeth Jelin. Translated by J. Ann Zammitt and Marilyn Thomson. Atlantic Highlands, N.J.: Zed Books, 1990.

———. "Introduction." In *Women and Social Change in Latin America*, ed. Elizabeth Jelin, trans. J. Ann Zammitt and Marilyn Thomson. Atlantic Highlands, N.J.: Zed Books, 1990.

Johnson, Barbara. *The Critical Difference: Essays in the Contemporary Rhetoric of Reading*. Baltimore: Johns Hopkins Univ. Press, 1985.

Jonasdottir, Anna. "On the Concept of Interest, Women's Interests, and the Limitations of Interest Theory." In *The Political Interests of Gender*, ed. Kathleen B. Jones and Anna G. Jonasdottir. London: Sage, 1988.

Jones, Adam. "Beyond the Barricades: The Sandinista Press and Political Transition in Nicaragua." *New Political Science* 23 (Fall 1992).

Kampwirth, Karen. "The Mother of the Nicaraguans: Doña Violeta and the UNO's Gender Agenda." *Latin American Perspectives* 23, no. 1 (Winter 1996).

Kaplan, Temma. "Female Consciousness and Collective Action: The Case of Barcelona, 1912–1918." *Signs* 7 (Spring 1982).

Kerber, Linda K. "Some Cautionary Words for Historians." In *An Ethic of Care: Feminist and Interdisciplinary Perspectives*, ed. Mary Jeanne Larrabee. New York: Routledge, 1993.

Kinzer, Stephen. *Blood of Brothers*. New York: G. P. Putnam's Sons, 1991.

Lancaster, Roger N. *Life Is Hard: Machismo, Danger, and the Intimacy of Power in Nicaragua*. Berkeley: Univ. of California Press, 1992.

———. *Thanks to God and the Revolution: Popular Religion and Class Consciousness in the New Nicaragua*. New York: Columbia Univ. Press, 1988.

Lavrin, Asuncion. "Women, the Family, and Social Change in Latin America." *World Affairs* 150, no. 2 (Fall 1987).

Leiken, Robert. "Nicaragua's Untold Stories." In *Nicaragua: Unfinished Revolution*, ed. Peter Rosset and John Vandermeer. New York: Grove Press, 1986.

Levine, Daniel H. *Popular Voices in Latin American Catholicism*. Princeton: Princeton Univ. Press, 1992.

Logan, Kathleen. "Women's Participation in Urban Protest." In *Popular Movements and Political Change in Mexico*, ed. Joe Foweraker and Ann L. Craig. Boulder, Colo.: Lynne Rienner, 1990.

Lomba, Mariuca. "*Futuro, en Femenino*." In *Pensamiento Propio* 7 (August 1990): 38–40.

Lorentzen, Lois Ann, and Jennifer Turpin, eds. *The Women & War Reader*. New York: New York Univ. Press, 1998.

McAdam, Doug. *Political Process and the Development of Black Insurgency, 1930–1970.* Chicago: Univ. of Chicago Press, 1982.

McCarthy, John D., and Mayer Zald. "Resource Mobilization and Social Movements: A Partial Theory." *American Journal of Sociology* 82 (1977).

———. *The Trend of Social Movements in America: Professionalization and Resource Mobilization.* Morristown, N.J.: General Learning Press, 1973.

MacDonald, Sharon, Pat Holden, and Shirley Ardener, eds. *Images of Women in Peace and War.* Madison: Univ. of Wisconsin Press, 1987.

MacLeod, Arlene. "Hegemonic Relations and Gender Resistance: The New Veiling as Accommodating Protest in Cairo." In *Signs* 17, no. 31 (Spring 1992).

Martin, Joann. "Motherhood and Power: The Production of a Women's Culture of Politics in a Mexican Community." *American Ethnologist* 17 (August 1990).

Marx, Karl, and Friedrich Engels. "The German Ideology." In *The Marx and Engels Reader,* ed. Robert C. Tucker. 2d ed. New York: W. W. Norton, 1978.

Melucci, Alberto. *Nomads of the Present: Social Movements and Individual Needs in Contemporary Society.* Philadelphia: Temple Univ. Press, 1989.

———. "The Symbolic Challenge of Contemporary Movements." *Social Research* 52 (Winter 1985): 789–816.

Metoyer, Cynthia Chavez. *Women and the State in Post-Sandinista Nicaragua.* Boulder, Colo.: Lynne Rienner, 2000.

Molyneux, Maxine. "Mobilization without Emancipation? Women's Interests, the State, and Revolution in Nicaragua." *Feminist Studies* 11 (Summer 1985).

———. "The Politics of Abortion in Nicaragua: Revolutionary Pragmatism—or Feminism in the Realm of Necessity?" *Feminist Review* 29 (1989).

———. "Women's Role in the Nicaraguan Revolutionary Process: The Early Years." In *Promissory Notes: Women in the Transition to Socialism,* ed. Sonia Kruks, Rayna Rapp, and Marilyn B. Young. New York: Monthly Review Press, 1989.

Montis, Malena de, Mercedes Olivera, and Mark A. Meassick. "A Panorama of Women in Nicaragua." *Cenzontle* (December 1989). Translated and published by Women's International Resource Exchange, New York, n.d.

Morgan, Martha I. "Founding Mothers: Women's Voices and Stories in the 1987 Nicaraguan Constitution." *Boston Law Review* 70, no. 1 (January 1990).

Morris, Aldon D. *The Origins of the Civil Rights Movement: Black Communities Organizing for Change.* New York: Free Press, 1986.

Mouffe, Chantal. "Hegemony and New Political Subjects: Toward a New Concept of Democracy." In *Marxism and the Interpretation of Culture,* ed. Cary Nelson and Lawrence Grossberg. Urbana: Univ. of Illinois Press, 1988.

Murguialday, Clara. *Nicaragua, revolucion y feminismo (1977–89).* Madrid: Editorial Revolucion, 1990.

Nash, June. "The Reassertion of Indigenous Identity: Mayan Responses to State Intervention in Chiapas." *Latin American Research Review* 30, no. 3 (1995).

Neuhouser, Kevin. "'Worse Than Men': Gendered Mobilization in an Urban Brazilian Squatter Settlement, 1971–91." *Gender and Society* 9 (February 1995).

O'Kane, Trish. "The New World Order." *NACLA Report on the Americas*, 24, no. 1 (June 1990).

Olivera, Mercedes, Malena de Montis, Mark A. Meassick. *Mujeres: Panorámica de su participación en Nicaragua*. Managua: Cenzontle Colección "Realidades," June 1990.

———. *Nicaragua: El poder de las mujeres*. Managua: Cenzontle, 1992.

Olson, Mancur. *The Logic of Collective Action*. Cambridge: Harvard Univ. Press, 1965.

Oquist, Paul. "The Sociopolitical Dynamics of the 1990 Nicaraguan Elections." In *The 1990 Elections in Nicaragua and Their Aftermath*, ed. Vanessa Castro and Gary Prevost. Lanham, Md.: Rowman & Littlefield, 1992.

Ortner, Sherry B. "Resistance and the Problem of Ethnographic Refusal." *Comparative Studies of Society and History* 37, no. 1 (January 1995).

Pizzorno, Alessandro. "Political Exchange and Collective Identity in Industrial Conflict." In *The Resurgence of Class Conflict in Western Europe since 1968*, ed. Colin Crouch and A. Pizzorno. London: Macmillan, 1978.

Polakoff, Erica, and Pierre La Ramée. "Grass-Roots Organizations." In *Nicaragua without Illusions*, ed. Thomas W. Walker. Wilmington, Del.: Scholarly Resources Books, 1997.

Prevost, Gary. "The Status of the Sandinista Revolutionary Project." In *The Undermining of the Sandinista Revolution*, ed. Gary Prevost and Harry E. Vanden. New York: St. Martin's Press, 1999.

Quandt, Midge. *The FSLN in Nicaragua: Conflict and Consensus*. Washington, D.C.: Nicaragua Network Education Fund, 1994.

Ramirez-Horton, Susan E. "The Role of Women in the Nicaraguan Revolution." In *Nicaragua in Revolution*, ed. Thomas W. Walker. New York: Praeger, 1982.

Randall, Margaret. *Gathering Rage: The Failure of Twentieth Century Revolutions to Develop a Feminist Agenda*. New York: Monthly Review Foundation, 1992.

———. *Sandino's Daughters: Testimonies of Nicaraguan Women in Struggle*. Vancouver: New Stars Books, 1981.

———. *Sandino's Daughters Revisited*. New Brunswick, N.J.: Rutgers Univ. Press, 1994.

Randall, Vicky. *Women and Politics*. London: Macmillan, 1982.

Rhode, Deborah L. "The Politics of Paradigms: Gender Difference and Gender Disadvantage." *Feminism & Politics*, ed. Anne Phillips. Oxford: Oxford Univ. Press, 1998.

Rodriguez, Lilia. "Barrio Women: Between the Urban and the Feminist Movement." *Latin American Perspectives* 21 (Summer 1994).

Roseberry, William. "Hegemony and the Language of Contention." In *Everyday Forms of State Formation: Revolution and the Negotiation of Rule in Modern Mexico*, ed. Gilbert M. Joseph and Daniel Nugent. Durham: Duke Univ. Press, 1994.

Ruddick, Sara. *Maternal Thinking: Toward a Politics of Peace*. New York: Ballantine Books, 1989.

Safa, Helen Icken. "Women's Social Movements in Latin America." *Gender and Society* 4 (September 1990).

Scheper-Hughes, Nancy. *Death without Weeping: The Violence of Everyday Life in Brazil*. Berkeley: Univ. of California Press, 1992.

Schild, Veronica. "Recasting 'Popular' Movements: Gender and Political Learning in Neighborhood Organizations in Chile." *Latin American Perspectives* 21 (Summer 1994).

Scott, James C. "Foreword." In *Everyday Forms of State Formation: Revolution and the Negotiation of Rule in Modern Mexico*, ed. Gilbert M. Joseph and Daniel Nugent. Durham: Duke Univ. Press, 1994.

————. *Weapons of the Weak: Everyday Forms of Peasant Resistance*. New Haven: Yale Univ. Press, 1985.

Scott, Joan. "Deconstructing Equality-versus-Difference: Or, the Uses of Poststructuralist Theory for Feminism." In *Conflicts in Feminism*, ed. Marianne Hirsch and Evelyn Fox Keller. New York: Routledge, 1990.

Seitz, Barbara. "Report on a Trip to Nicaragua: Women under Chamorro's Regime." *Against the Current* (January/February 1992).

Sewell, William H. "A Theory of Structure: Duality, Agency, and Transformation." *American Journal of Sociology* 98, no. 1 (July 1992).

Sills, David L. *The Volunteers: Means and Ends in a National Organization*. Glencoe, Ill.: Free Press, 1957.

Slater, David. "Power and Social Movements in the Other Occident: Latin America in an International Context." *Latin American Perspectives* 21 (Summer 1994).

Sola, Roser, and María Pau Trayner. *Ser Madre en Nicaragua: Testimonios de Una Historia No Escrita*. Barcelona: Icaria, 1988.

Somers, Margaret R., and Gloria D. Gibson. "Reclaiming the Epistemological 'Other': Narrative and the Social Constitution of Identity." In *Social Theory and the Politics of Identity*, ed. Craig Calhoun. Cambridge, Mass.: Blackwell, 1994.

Stack, Carol. "The Culture of Gender: Women and Men of Color." In *An Ethic of Care: Feminist and Interdisciplinary Perspectives*, ed. Mary Jeanne Larrabee. New York: Routledge, 1993.

Steinson, Barbara J. "'The Mother Half of Humanity': American Women in the Peace and Preparedness Movements in World War I." In *Women, War and Revolution*, ed. Carol R. Berkin and Clara M. Lovett. New York: Holmes and Meier, 1980.

Stephen, Lynn. "Women in Mexico's Popular Movements: Survival Strategies against Ecological and Economic Impoverishment." *Latin American Perspectives* 19 (Winter 1992).

————. *Women and Social Movements in Latin America: Power from Below*. Austin: Univ. of Texas Press, 1997.

Stephens, Beth. "Women in Nicaragua." *Monthly Review* 40, no. 4 (September 1988).

Stokes, Susan C. *Cultures in Conflict: Social Movements and the State in Peru.* Berkeley: Univ. of California Press, 1995.

Tilly, Charles. *From Mobilization to Revolution.* Reading, Mass.: Addison-Wesley, 1978.

United Nations Economic Commission for Latin America and the Caribbean (ECLAC). "Nicaragua: An Economy in Transition." Mexico City: May 1994.

Valdivia, Angharad N. "The U.S. Intervention in Nicaraguan and Other Latin American Media." In *Revolution and Counterrevolution in Nicaragua,* ed. Thomas W. Walker. Boulder, Colo.: Westview Press, 1991.

Verba, Sidney, and Norman H. Nie. *Participation in America: Political Democracy and Social Equality.* New York: Harper & Row, 1972.

Vilas, Carlos M. *The Sandinista Revolution: National Liberation and Social Transformation in Central America.* New York: Monthly Review Press, 1986.

Warren, Kay Barbara, and Susan C. Bourque. "Gender, Power, and Communication: Women's Responses to Political Muting in the Andes." In *Women Living Change,* ed. Susan Bourque and Donna Robinson Divine. Philadelphia: Temple Univ. Press, 1985.

Waylen, Georgina. "Women and Democratization: Conceptualizing Gender Relations in Transition Politics." *World Politics* 46 (1994): 327–54.

Weedon, Chris. *Feminist Practice and Poststructuralist Theory.* New York: Basil Blackwell, 1987.

Wessel, Lois. "Reproductive Rights in Nicaragua: From the Sandinistas to the Government of Violeta Chamorro." In *Feminist Studies* 17 (Fall 1991).

West, Guida, and Rhoda Lois Blumberg. "Reconstructing Social Protest from a Feminist Perspective." In *Women and Social Protest,* ed. Guida West and Rhoda Lois Blumberg. New York: Oxford Univ. Press, 1990.

Whitcomb, Riley. "The Committee of Mothers of Heroes and Martyrs." *Nicaraguan Perspectives* (Winter 1983).

Whittier, Nancy. "Political Generations, Micro-Cohorts, and the Transformation of Social Movements." *American Sociological Review* 62, no. 5 (October 1997).

Williams, Patricia J. "On Being the Object of Property." *Theorizing Feminisms,* ed. Anne C. Herrmann and Abigail J. Stewart. Boulder, Colo.: Westview Press, 1994.

Women's International Resource Exchange. "Nicaraguan Women and the Revolution." New York: WIRE, 1982.

Zeiger, Susan. "She Didn't Raise Her Boy to Be a Slacker: Motherhood, Conscription, and the Culture of the First World War." *Feminist Studies* 22 (Spring 1996).

Published Reports, Newspapers, and Periodicals

Barricada. Nicaragua.

CAHI Update. Washington, D.C.: Central American Historical Institute.

Cenzontle. Managua.

Envio. Managua. University of Central America.

GAO. U.S. General Accounting Office.

Latin American Dispatch. Washington, D.C.: U.S. State Department.

La Prensa. Managua.

Nicaraguan News Service. Washington, D.C.: Nicaragua Network Education Fund.

Revista Segovia. Managua: *Ejercito Popular Sandinista* publication.

Somos. Managua: AMNLAE publication.

INDEX

Spartan Mothers, 95–99; and contradictory images, 112–13, 146, 151, 216; and
contra mothers, 193–94; Elshtain on,
263n. 60, 264n. 73; and Sandinista
discourse, 101; and U.S. Civil War,
264n. 73
Structural adjustment, 161, 166

Téllez, Dora María, 32, 101, 158, 160,
242, 246; and Mothers of Heroes and
Martyrs, 255n. 39
Testimonies, of Mothers of Matagalpa,
53–58, 71
Tijerino, Doris, 36–37, 101, 163
Trayner, María Pau. *See* Sola, Roser
Triple workload, 240

United Nations, office takeover, 25–26
United Nicaraguan Opposition. *See*
UNO
Universal Motherhood, 39–41, 43, 94–95,
121
UNO, 151, 155–56, 164, 177, 179
U.S. embassy in Managua: and M22,

106–10, 266n. 123; and Mothers of
Matagalpa protests, 72
U.S. State Department, 85, 106–8,
265n. 99

Vargas, Milú, 35, 88, 163
Virgin Mary: and anti-Sandinista dis-
course, 34; and *madres sufridas*, 99–
100; and Mothers of Heroes and
Martyrs, 104, 132, 146, 185; traditional
maternal imagery of, 216. *See also*
Chamorro, Violeta Barrios de
Visible dimension, of collective identity,
115, 126, 127–33, 134–35, 184
Voice, 210, 212–13, 222–29

War, women and, 233
Whittier, Nancy, 189
Women of Masaya, 110
"Women's difference" approach, 14–15,
197, 206

Zenteno, Arnoldo, 100